My Life in Three Acts

My Life in
Three Acts

❊

Helen Hayes

WITH

KATHERINE HATCH

A HELEN AND KURT WOLFF BOOK
HARCOURT BRACE JOVANOVICH, PUBLISHERS
San Diego · New York · London

A leatherbound, signed first edition of this book
has been privately printed by The Easton Press.

Permission to quote from George Bernard Shaw's letter was granted by the
Society of Authors, London, England, on behalf of the Bernard Shaw Estate.
All photos from the Billy Rose Theatre Collection of The New York
Public Library are courtesy of The New York Public Library/Astor,
Lennox and Tilden Foundations.

Library of Congress Cataloging-in-Publication Data
Hayes, Helen, 1900–
My life in three acts/by Helen Hayes with Katherine Hatch. — 1st ed.
p.   cm.
"A Helen and Kurt Wolff book."
ISBN 0-15-163695-8
1. Hayes, Helen, 1900–   . 2. Actors—United States—Biography.
I. Hatch, Katherine. II. Title. III. Title: My life in 3 acts.
PN2287.H35A3   1990
792'.028'092—dc20
[B]   89-15614

Text design by Beth Tondreau Design
Printed in the United States of America
First trade edition

A B C D E

For my son,
James MacArthur

⟫1⟪

It seems only natural to me to see my life, a life in the theatre, in theatrical terms. I visualize it as a protracted three-act play. The first act covers the time when I was guided and strongly influenced first by my mother and then by my husband, the playwright Charles MacArthur. The second opens after Charlie's death, when I realized that I was now on my own and solely responsible for what became of me. Act three concerns the years after I left the stage in a not-too-successful attempt to stay out of the limelight and live quietly at my homes in Nyack, New York, and in Mexico.

I also see my life, to change metaphors, as a kind of mosaic, combining many little varicolored pieces reflecting different worlds, events, people, and places. What does the mosaic represent? I'm not sure. An overall design seems to be missing, a guiding principle or theme that gets me from one act to the next. This is true of a good many theatre people; their careers are not planned according to a straight, predictable course that avoids detours. But what may set me apart from many who have made their mark in my profession is that I never chose to be an actress. The choice was made for me in early childhood.

Before I knew what it was all about, I was pushed on stage at the age of five—in an amateur production. Within a few years I was acting on Broadway and trouping around the country with famous actors and comedians and all sorts of theatre people. It was a very worldly life, but I had no idea how different it was from a child's normal existence.

With no chance to wonder if I had talent or if I would succeed, I became a professional actor and remained one all my life. God knows I have few regrets. I loved working in theatre, loved it with a passion—precisely because I never longed for fame, never had a burning ambition to be up there in the spotlight.

Recently, reading the autobiography of a close friend, the actor Maurice Evans, I couldn't help thinking, "That's not me at all." Maurice had an advantage that I lacked: a strong drive to get ahead. I just floated along, and things somehow fell into my lap.

By nature I was not theatrical, not majestic or awe-inspiring, and no more glamorous than many women who came to watch me perform. Perhaps the absence of glamour contributed to my popularity. It may be that audiences felt comfortable with an actress who seemed cozy, approachable, unlike the flamboyant leading ladies I once knew in the theatre.

Our family background was lower middle-class and quite conventional. We were plain, simple folk living in Washington, D.C., where I was born—I was born October 10, 1900—and as far removed from theatrical life as one could get.

My mother's parents, Ann and Patrick Hayes, had emigrated to America from Ireland during the potato famine in the mid-nineteenth century. They followed the lead of some immigrant relatives and settled in the area of the United States capital. Patrick Hayes managed to get a government post of some sort. His job couldn't have amounted to much, because he could afford only a small house, which became crowded with the children his wife bore, one after another, seven all told.

Grandfather Hayes died long before I was born, so what I knew about him came from stories, which made him seem a singular man. He was said to be inordinately curious, inquisitive about everything that passed before his eyes. A "terrific reader," he read anything he came across, even a scrap of newspaper blowing down the street. His main dream in life was to translate Shakespeare into Gaelic. I never learned if he achieved this ambition, but was told that he'd recite reams of Shakespeare in English, especially when he was in his cups.

His curiosity and love of reading were traits that ran in the family and were passed on to me as well. But his curiosity proved to be his undoing. One morning, on his way to work, my grandfather saw a gang of laborers digging a ditch in the street. He couldn't resist stopping to watch them. A piece of flint, flying, hit him in his eye. Maybe he got the wrong treatment or couldn't afford the right doctor, but he began to lose his sight. This handicap and possibly his drinking cost him his job.

His wife—my beloved "Graddy"—took over the job and kept her household from falling apart. What a tower of strength Graddy was! At seven o'clock every morning she would go to work, then in the evening clean house, wash, iron, and mend clothes, and cook for her large brood.

My grandmother, before she married the Irishman, lived in England, and her speech retained British expressions. For instance, when she left for work in the morning, she would often ask the iceman or the milkman, "Would you please knock up my daughters for me?" Of course she meant, unaware of the American idiom: Knock on the door and wake them up.

Graddy Hayes was a handsome and gallant woman who, like many women of her time, emulated Queen Victoria in dress and deportment. She wore a little black bonnet tied under her left ear, long skirts sweeping the ground, and always gloves. Somehow she kept losing the left glove, so she wore one glove and carried another, and no one could tell they were both right-handed.

3

Graddy was a faithful Catholic but wore her faith lightly, while Grandpa was a fearful Catholic. By "fearful Catholic" I mean that he was fanatical about observing even the most trivial rituals. When money was scarce, Graddy couldn't afford to buy fish, so she'd make a hash or a stew, stretching out leftover boiled beef with vegetables and gravy even on a Friday. Grandpa would sniff at the platter and yell, "Meat! Take it off the table. Don't anyone eat it!"

What a load she had to bear on top of replacing her husband as breadwinner! When some of the children—my mother, my mother's sister Mamie, and a brother—grew old enough to work, they helped support the family. My mother, Catherine Estelle (nicknamed "Essie"), started as a cashier in a drugstore. A high-spirited and imaginative girl, she romanticized her family. Exaggerating her father's virtues and glossing over his faults, she created a legend that was more fantasy than fact. In time I learned, from other relatives, that Patrick Hayes had been a tyrant of a father who drove some of his children to drink or to early marriages in order to escape from home.

After he died, Graddy bought a small farm outside Washington, and the whole family moved there. As a young child I lived on the farm with my parents. So did Aunt Mamie, her husband Fritz Fugett, and their two children. We were an assorted lot of cousins, aunts, and uncles. There was plenty of companionship for playing in the farmyard, tending the vegetable garden, roaming the fields and woods, and sharing huge holiday dinners on Thanksgiving and Christmas, when we exchanged homemade presents, which we children put more zeal than skill into.

My favorite aunt was Mamie, probably because she fussed over me, even though she had her own kids to look after. She used to sew my clothes and dress me up like a bisque doll. But it was Graddy Hayes who ran that household, providing for us, feeding us. She was a fine cook, not of fancy food but wholesome stick-to-

4

the-ribs meals, and she baked like a dream. I still remember her delicious coconut cake made with fresh coconut. When she went to market, she always bought oranges and peppermint sticks for the children. She would cut a hole in an orange, insert a peppermint stick, and then we'd squeeze the orange and suck the juice through the stick. It was one of the best things I ever tasted.

But milk, which children thrive on, didn't agree with me. I developed symptoms that puzzled the doctors. They finally decided I could digest milk only from one particular kind of cow, a Jersey. Graddy got one and kept it on the farm for my sake. But my trouble persisted, and I was declared allergic to all milk.

Graddy Hayes was truly a remarkable woman, the strength of my young life, and the kind of grandmother that has gone out of fashion. Grandmothers nowadays seek eternal youth, compete with their daughters in dress and behavior, use lots of cosmetics, have face-lifts. In Graddy's day women were considered old at fifty, and she was over sixty by the time I was born. Her hands were rough and red from years of housework, her hair gray, her wrinkles honorable signs of survival in a tough world.

Graddy loved the theatre and would scrimp and save in order to buy gallery tickets for plays presented in Washington by touring companies. Among the great actors we saw was Sarah Bernhardt, who performed in French. We didn't know a word of French, but Graddy claimed she could understand most everything because of Bernhardt's broad gestures and intonation. We also went to nickelodeon theatres to see silent movies featuring Maurice Costello, Florence Turner, or Bronco Billy. Back home Graddy would act out a film we'd just seen, regaling the family with her mimicry, a talent she passed on to my mother and probably to me.

There was a time before I was born when Graddy went to Baltimore solely to see Edwin Booth perform in *Hamlet*. Booth was America's preeminent Shakespearean actor of his day, and "his" Hamlet was renowned, but he wouldn't play in Washington because of his brother's assassination of President Lincoln. So agonized and tortured was he by the deed, Edwin Booth couldn't bear to set foot in the city where it had happened, so the Baltimore theatre management ran trains from Washington, and Graddy took one of those.

Mother had two great passions: high society and theatre. She would pore over the Sunday papers, skipping over news of politics and government to the social items and pictures in the rotogravure section. She liked to go to the Willard Hotel to watch the socialites, ladies in elegant gowns and jewels, strolling to take afternoon tea. These excursions fed her fantasy of rising above her station in life to shine among the elite.

Her dream of becoming a great actress was sparked by the visiting troupes. Like Graddy, she'd scrape together the money for a couple of seats in the peanut gallery and take me to see great stars, such as Forbes-Robertson in *Hamlet*. But I, being young, preferred operettas to Shakespeare. Because I was small and agile, I could run up the flights of steps to the galleries faster than anyone, and throw myself across two seats in the first row to save them for Mother and me.

My first remembered theatre experience was Franz Lehar's operetta *The Merry Widow*. I was exalted by it, hypnotized. When the curtain fell on the last act and the audience began to leave, I kept staring at the stage. I didn't budge from my seat. Mother tried to move me, but I wouldn't leave. Finally, a gentleman who saw she was having trouble picked me up bodily and began to carry me out.

I began to scream—this is my mother's story—"I won't leave! I won't leave the theatre!" And of course, I never did.

When we went to see Forbes-Robertson's *Hamlet,* I had trouble understanding it. During the play, I nudged Mother a couple of times and asked her to explain what they were saying. "Helen," she whispered, "I'll tell you afterward."

"I can't enjoy it if I don't know what it's about," I replied, beginning to whimper. The action was leading into Hamlet's soliloquy and I was completely confused. As I began to fuss, a deep, resonant voice from the row behind said quietly, "He is wondering whether he should continue to live or end his life."

I turned around and was face to face with a black man who, from then on, whispered in my ear, helping me through my first *Hamlet.*

Years later, when I was in Washington to perform in *Harriet,* a play in which we had several black cast members, I learned that blacks were no longer allowed in Washington theatres. Remembering with gratitude my childhood experience, I made a big fuss, refusing at first to play there. At the urging of the producer, I relented, but I made it clear to the newspapers that I was playing under protest. It was a disgrace that such a situation existed in our nation's capital, I said.

I urged all actors who were members of Actors Equity to refuse to play in Washington until the theatres were integrated. At this, the manager of the National Theatre threatened to close, saying he would not be responsible for the bloodshed if he allowed blacks in. I persisted in my battle. Friends in Washington were heartsick and begged me to stop making such a row, but I never gave up. Today, of course, this seems like ancient history.

We went to concerts, too. One day, when we came home after hearing the violinist Mischa Elman, Mother bubbled with enthusiasm. She said to Father, "Look at Helen. She's all aglow, her eyes are shining. She just loves music. We'll have to give her violin lessons." Father took a close look at me and said, "It's a fever. I think she's got the measles." And he was right.

Mother managed to save up the money to pay for acting lessons at the Robert Downey School. Through a close friend, who was married to a producer named Fred Burger, she then got a job with his fifth-rate touring company. His wife Bess and my mother appeared in the chorus of a terrible show called *Liberty Belles;* it played one-night stands.

This taste of show business—one can't really call it theatre—whetted her appetite for the next tour. After all, it was experience and, despite the sleaze and hardships, would lead to better things—or so she thought. Father traveled too, as a salesman for a wholesale meat and poultry company. I was left in the care of Graddy and Aunt Mamie. Between tours my mother would alight at home like a glamorous visitor. She would entertain us with funny anecdotes and takeoffs of the troupe's actors and other characters whom she met on the road.

How desolate I felt, at the age of three or four, when my mother went away, and how thrilled, when she came home again.

And to think that, many years later, I could treat my own children the same way. Whenever I went on tour, I'd leave them with their father or a governess or a nursemaid. I remember going down the front steps of our house one day, with my daughter Mary holding on to my hand. "Mommy, I want to go everywhere you go," she said. This came from the heart of a little girl who made so few demands. I still get tremors when I think of it.

Graddy knew how to dispel my blues when Mother went away. She would tell me hair-raising stories. Now that we hear complaints about all the violence on television that children are exposed to, I remember Graddy's tales; they were just as scary, but I lapped them up. I would sit on the floor at Graddy's knee—like a storybook picture of a child sitting at the knee of dear old Grandma—and listen raptly to her spine-chilling yarns. One that stuck like a burr in my memory was about a bride who died at the altar. The mourning bridegroom was about to lower her coffin into the grave when, with a great push, she opened the coffin and sat up. She hadn't been dead at all, but only in a trance or coma.

Graddy had tales more gruesome, about people who got buried

alive. When their graves were later dug up, their bodies were found to be all contorted in the desperate struggle to get out. While Graddy related these weird tales, she would embroider a sampler or a cushion cover, and I would sort out the raw silk threads for her. A strange combination: this gentle old-world craft and the violent story-telling.

My grandmother was the first person I ever lost. When she died at the age of seventy-eight, I thought my world had come to an end. I remember, as if it were yesterday, her pale still figure in the casket. I remember praying that she would waken, dreading that she might be buried alive like the characters in her stories. Decades later, I still couldn't accept her death, couldn't believe I'd never see that good soul again.

Her last years weren't as happy or peaceful as they should have been after a long hard life. When she sold her farm, Graddy no longer had a home of her own, but lived with one or another of her daughters. If she had a quarrel with Mother, she would go to Aunt Mamie's house. I'd watch her sadly from a window as she walked away from our door and headed for a streetcar to Mamie's place. She'd stay there for a while, until a quarrel would send her back to Essie's. They weren't really quarrels, as Graddy was too gentle to fight with anyone, but she deplored her children's bad habits. It was one bad habit, really, which she thought they had inherited from their father: a taste for alcohol, the Irish curse.

As I grew older, I realized what everyone else knew, that my parents were a decidedly mismatched couple. My advent didn't ease their differences, only aggravated them. My father, Francis Van Arnum Brown, had fallen in love with Catherine Hayes, an attractive, lively girl who could be a delightful companion. He married her despite his mother's opposition. Grandma Brown felt that Frank, one of five sons, married beneath him; the bride's family were poor Irish immigrants, while the Browns, whose forebears came to America before the Revolution, were solidly middle-class. The Hayeses, to Grandma Brown, were "scamp" Irish, too wild and unstable.

It soon became apparent that the young couple had little in common. My father, an affable man, was content with what life had to offer him. But Mother was dissatisfied: he lacked the ambition to rise in the world, to take her into an orbit higher than that of a pork-and-poultry salesman. His job suited him, because he was gregarious and liked mingling with people on his selling rounds.

He was a domestic soul, a homebody, while my mother longed to escape from boring household routine. She didn't want a child, not yet; evidently I was an accident. Father was delighted with his little daughter, but it took Mother time to get used to motherhood. After the raffish tours with *Liberty Belles* ended, she settled down, more or less, and became a caring parent.

Set on introducing me to culture, she took me to plays and concerts and museums. On such occasions she was transported out of her drab everyday existence into higher realms of beauty and creativity. Thus she gave me a start, later furthered by other mentors, toward an appreciation of the arts.

My father indulged in simpler pleasures, which satisfied the boyish streak he'd never outgrown. He took me to Glen Echo Amusement Park to ride the Ferris wheel or to hear the U.S. Marine Band conducted by John Philip Sousa, who played his rousing marches at the bandstand near the Washington Monument. Father was a great baseball fan, so on a Sunday we'd go and watch the Washington Senators. Their pitcher, Walter Johnson, was Father's idol.

At the ballpark my quiet, easygoing father was transformed into a vociferous fan, shouting praise or opprobrium at the home team. I'd sit there munching Cracker Jacks, not really understanding Father's commentary but mesmerized by the drama and

10

excitement both on the field and in the bleachers. At the dinner table that night Father would replay the game for my benefit. Mother, who could be a voluble talker when a subject interested her, kept silent, having no use for baseball.

My schooling began at the Holy Cross Academy at the age of five. Even though Mother, defying her strict and pious father, had left the Church, she still believed that a parochial school was a safe haven for a child. I was so drawn to the nuns that I dreamed of becoming one myself, and spent a lot of time praying on my knees. Apart from these devotions and schoolwork, there were sometimes theatricals, staged by the sisters. In *A Midsummer Night's Dream* I played Peaseblossom, my first role.

My education was interrupted again and again after I became a professional actress. While working in New York or on the road, I did lessons on my own. Back home I attended school regularly, or rather a series of schools.

After Holy Cross I went on to the Sacred Heart Academy, where I had a happy time among the nuns and my school chums. Some of my classmates became close friends for life: Margie Buchanan, whose daughter is married to Donald Regan, and Dorothy Guider, whose father, Frank Hogan, and son-in-law, Edward Bennett Williams, were great attorneys. I see both Margie and Dorothy as often as we can get together.

I was always a favorite of my teachers, not very bright in schoolwork, but they liked me. I think that personality is what buoyed me through my whole career. That, and my small stature. Whatever quality it was I had, people have always been protective of me.

My very best neighborhood friend, Virginia Fagan, followed me to Sacred Heart. She was ten days younger than I, but every time we boarded the streetcar for the ride to school, the motorman would take her nickel but let me ride free because I was "younger." It nearly broke up the friendship, but that's the way everyone was with me, wanting to do me favors and be protective.

As an adolescent I insisted on attending a coed public school. After the all-girl Catholic schools, I was eager to be around boys. So I enrolled at the John Eaton School in Cleveland Park. It was a select school; some government officials sent their children there. My first beau was Jonathan Daniels, son of Josephus Daniels, secretary of the navy in President Wilson's administration.

An eighth-grade teacher, a Miss Burke, made a lasting impression on me. One day, we giggled in class, and Miss Burke reprimanded a girl sitting at the desk in front of me. But I was the culprit. With great reluctance, I stood up and confessed. Miss Burke kept me after school. Instead of scolding she used a smarter tactic. "When you came here," she said, "you became one of my favorite pupils. You were never pushy and you never made trouble." Then she said, "I've been watching you. You've changed. What's wrong?"

I told her I didn't know, but of course I did. I was showing off for the boys. Miss Burke wasn't aware of it, but she was responsible for a turning point in my life. Then and there I stopped trying to impress people, to get attention at any cost. She brought me to my senses and settled me down.

After grammar school I went on to Central High, where I encountered another dedicated teacher, Martha Clark. She wore what was practically a uniform in those days: a floor-length circular skirt, a shirtwaist with a stiff collar and front, and a black patent-leather belt. Miss Clark went beyond the call of duty by taking me to the theatre when she got tickets for a new show.

Eventually, when I no longer felt the need to be popular with boys, I returned to Sacred Heart Academy. One of my teachers, Sister Mary Eileen, became a lifelong friend. After she retired, she used to come with another nun to see me at the theatre. They would have dinner out and then sit in the back, trying to be

12

inconspicuous in their habits. It's not surprising that Roman Catholics can be theatre buffs, for there is a lot of drama in our church.

As a student I was not outstanding, but always tried to learn and pay attention. I respected my teachers. Usually, I obeyed the rules, but one day at Sacred Heart I got to class late. "I would reprimand you," said Sister Mary Eileen, "but you greet me with such a bright smile, I think, 'Here's little Mary Sunshine,' and I can't scold you." That smile wasn't affected to curry favor, it came naturally. Maybe my sunny disposition was inherited from my father.

Mother, anxious to give me every advantage even if it strained her budget, had me enrolled in Miss Minnie Hawke's School of Dance, where the children of Washington's upper crust learned the rudiments of terpsichore.

The genteel Miss Minnie and her sister Miss May held a recital every year at the Belasco Theatre to display their pupils' skill and raise money for charity. As a little tot I first appeared clad in a green silk dress with sequin shamrocks sewn on by Aunt Mamie. I was supposed to do an Irish reel, but stage fright sent me running off the stage.

At the next recital I was decked out in a Dutch girl's costume, another Mamie creation, and sang something about the Zuyder Zee. Mother had coached me to sing with feeling, even pretending to sob a bit. That act evoked laughter and applause, though my singing was no better than my dancing.

The following season I did a solo as a Gibson girl bathing beauty, wearing a low-cut black suit, with my hair swept up in a pompadour. I warbled a song from *The Ziegfeld Follies*:

> *But, why do they call me a Gibson girl?*
> *Gibson girl! Gibson girl.*
> *What is the matter with Mr. Ibsen?*
> *Mr. Ibsen! Why Dana Gibson?*

Wear a blank expression
and a monumental curl,
And walk with a bend in your back,
then they'll call you a Gibson girl.

Again tutored by Mother, I assumed a world-weary air, which struck the audience as funny.

It happened that Miss Minnie had a slight acquaintance with Lew Fields, a producer and star of musical comedies, who was playing in his own show at the Belasco at that time. He dropped by our recital one afternoon and must have been amused by my act, for he sent a note to the manager, saying that if my parents wanted a stage career for me, he would like to see them about it in his office in New York.

Though Father took parental pride in this tribute, he wasn't really interested. But Mother was delighted. To her it seemed that destiny in the person of Lew Fields had come and tapped me on the shoulder. But she wisely decided that at the age of six I was too young to brave New York.

14

⇒·2·⇐

Nowadays young actors usually start out in regional theatres or
the straw-hat circuit or off-Broadway. In my day neophytes could
gain experience in one of the many stock companies around the
country.

In Washington a company called The Columbia Players was
organized by Fred Burger, the same producer who had sent
Mother on tour with *Liberty Belles*. Now he presented better
plays; but with small means and mostly local talent, they weren't
exactly professional productions. Still, they provided a showcase
for would-be actors.

When Fred Burger planned to stage *The Prince Chap*, which
needed a child actress, he asked Mother to let me play the role.
As extra bait he offered her a part, too, and she agreed. I remember playing a boy in an uncomfortable corduroy suit with a stiff
collar and tie, but on the plus side, I appeared with my mother,
just as years later my daughter, Mary, made her debut acting with
me in summer stock.

The Columbia Players staged several plays in which I performed during their summer seasons. Among them were *The*

Prince and the Pauper and *Little Lord Fauntleroy.* I didn't get into skirts until later.

During the run of *Fauntleroy* there was a mishap, one of those unexpected things that give actors nightmares. In one scene Fauntleroy has to pull a red bandanna from his pocket and hand it to his grandfather. It is absolutely essential; everything that follows depends on that bandanna. But one night I reached for it and it wasn't there.

What to do? I had to come up with something fast. "Well, I must have left it in my room," I improvised. "I'll go and fetch it." Marching offstage, I grabbed the bandanna from the prop man and marched back again. The poor actor playing my grandfather had in the meantime stood there, paralyzed and unable to think of anything to say to cover my absence. I don't know what he thought afterwards, but my mother praised me for being resourceful, and decided I was now ready for Broadway.

My father was bewildered by my mother's love of the theatre and her ambition for me. But he was a good-natured man and indulged her whims. I suppose he thought this was just a whim, and we'd soon come home with nothing gained but a look at New York. So he gave us enough money to spend a few weeks there.

Although we had the invitation from Mr. Fields, we didn't start with him. My mother, having visions of my becoming the next Modjeska or Mrs. Fiske, turned up her nose at musical comedy. But when we were unable to see the producers of important plays, such as Charles Frohman, she lowered her sights and took me to Mr. Fields' office.

We were greeted by a secretary who said Mr. Fields was in conference with Miss Lotta Faust. Miss Faust was a famous beauty and musical comedy star who was known for having "the most beautiful back in the world." In those days, a specific part of the anatomy of each of the famous beauties was singled out, like the legs of Mistinguette, the eyes of Anna Held, and the back of Lotta Faust.

16

We could hear Mr. Fields and the glamorous Miss Faust laughing, and my mother became increasingly ill at ease. She was dressed in a homemade blue serge suit, a severe white shirtwaist, and, as usual, her pince-nez glasses clipped to her nose. She leaned over and whispered, "I don't dare speak to him after he's been with Lotta Faust." As it happened, she barely had the chance.

Pretty soon, they came out of the inner sanctum and passed by us without a glance. Mr. Fields took Lotta to the elevator and returned. As he approached where Mother and I sat, Mother jumped out of her chair and thrust a photograph of me as the Gibson Girl under his nose. To this day, I can see his glowering expression as he stared at her. "Do you remember this child?" Mother asked.

Only then did he glance down. Yes, he remembered. He invited us into his private office and asked us to sit down. As luck would have it, he was planning to produce a Victor Herbert musical, *Old Dutch*, and he needed children for the cast. He offered me a contract and Mother accepted. My salary was to be fifty dollars a week, a handsome sum, and rehearsals started in six weeks.

As Mr. Fields raised his pen to sign the contract, he inquired of my mother, "What is the little girl's name?"

"Helen Hayes Brown."

"That's too long for a theatre marquee. We'll call her 'Helen Hayes.'"

I was eight years old. We went home to Washington to wait until rehearsals began. That was probably the longest six weeks my mother ever lived through. She kept worrying that Mr. Fields might change his mind. Though Father was pleased, he couldn't quite understand why we were so excited. I knew he felt left out, but when we left for New York again, he sent us off with a generous gift of money to tide us over until my salary started.

I made my New York theatre debut on November 22, 1909,

playing Little Mimi in *Old Dutch* at the Herald Square Theatre. What an opening night it was! All of the flowers that had been sent to the cast were arrayed along the walls of the lobby, placed in fragrant tiers almost to the ceiling. People in the orchestra seats wore formal dress, and two of the most glamorous personalities of the day were in their boxes, Diamond Jim Brady, sparkling all over with the stones that gave him his nickname, and Lillian Russell, dressed in a gown that showed her generous bosom and the diamonds thereon. It was like a fairyland, and Mother and I watched from the secrecy of the box office until we had to scamper backstage for the opening curtain.

From that very first performance, I was hooked on the theatre. Everything was intriguing: the costumes, the scenery and lights, the festively dressed people out front. The actors and crew were my playmates, and the backstage area was my special, magical playground. It was all make-believe, but I didn't pine for an ordinary existence as other child actors did. Of course I'd already had some experience in stock, but it was nothing like a Broadway production.

An obedient child, I was used to doing what I was told. It was part of my nature, too, to perform any task to the utmost of my ability. Now, seeing how much I had to learn, I set to work—and was blessed with excellent teachers.

Of course Mother was always on hand to guide and lend moral support. She was anything but a typical stage mother. Brownie, as everyone called her, was warm, friendly and ebullient, and she never forgot that I was, after all, still a child. She might pass on tips that she picked up backstage, but was careful not to intrude in rehearsals or get in the way of my mentors.

The first was Lew Fields, who could be said to have "discovered" me. He had been one-half of the famous Weber and Fields comedy team, but the pair didn't get along well. After they broke up, Fields began to produce a series of musical burlesques which introduced Marie Dressler and other stars of the period. He was known to have an eye for talent. So it was considered a privilege to be singled out by Mr. Fields.

The score of *Old Dutch* was by Victor Herbert, and the cast included John Bunny, a popular comedian, and Vernon Castle, who was soon to be famous as a ballroom dancer. Vernon was tall, slender, graceful, and handsome. All the girls in the show fell in love with him, including me. It was my first crush, and Vernon unwittingly encouraged it by giving me gifts and writing affectionate little notes. He insisted that Fields write a special part for me for his next show, *The Summer Widowers*. But Vernon was in his twenties and I was nine, so my passion went unrequited. But it was a real, consuming passion. I was violently jealous of any lady whom Vernon so much as smiled at.

This created problems, because in the cast of *The Summer Widowers* was a young woman named Irene Foote, soon to become Mrs. Vernon Castle. As bad luck would have it, Irene and I were assigned to the same dressing room. I'm afraid I made backstage life pretty unpleasant for Irene. Years later, in her autobiography, she wrote: "When I arrived to share Helen's dressing room, it was like the snake entering the Garden of Eden."

Mr. Fields was very protective of me, and he didn't want me exposed to backstage bad habits. He posted a sign on the call board that forbade swearing in the dressing rooms, but that was about the only real concession made to my youth. Usually, things didn't get that rowdy at a Fields show; he wouldn't stand for loose behavior.

All of his precautions were noisily undone one day by the chorines whose dressing room happened to be on the same floor as Irene's and mine. A noisy fracas erupted and the air was blue with language. I ran out of our dressing room, ever curious, in time to see one of the girls being pushed out of their dressing room. "Goddammit! You turn around three times and come back in!" her tormenter, another chorus girl, yelled.

The girl in the hallway was crying as she turned around three times, all the while screaming back, "Fuck you! Fuck you!"

This gave me two backstage lessons at once: in colorful language and an important actors' superstition. The girl who was the object of wrath had begun to whistle in the dressing room, unaware of or forgetting that stage tradition says the person nearest a backstage whistler will be the next one fired. The only way to remove the spell is to leave the room, turn around three times, and return.

By the time the stage manager ran up three flights of stairs to the chorines' dressing room, silence reigned and nobody would confess. I thought it was all most exciting.

One time I shared a dressing room with one of the great show girls of all time, Billie Coupier. She was a ravishing girl with a tall, shapely figure, magnolia skin, and blonde hair. Billie had a protector, a gentleman of great wealth. She always arrived at the theatre in a big shiny limousine driven by a liveried chauffeur. Between a matinee and evening performance she would send out to an expensive restaurant across the street for chicken à la king and champagne, which she shared with Mother and me in her dressing room. I was then ten years old. I hoped that when I grew up, though I could never be as beautiful as Billie, I too would be able to afford champagne and chicken à la king anytime.

From Mr. Fields I learned that there were three key words for success in the theatre: discipline, discipline, discipline. Mother added bits of practical advice offered by cast members, such as: "Let the writers write, the directors direct, and you stick to what you know best. That's acting." Another proverb passed along from an old vaudevillian was: "Always leave them wanting more."

My career with Lew Fields ended when I was twelve, the start of that awkward age when an actress is too old for a child's role and not mature enough to be an ingenue. So we returned to Washington and I went back to school on a regular basis. While we were away, I'd missed my father terribly and had insisted that we pay him a visit whenever we had any free time, if only for a few days.

We were both happy to be reunited. Thinking Mother and I were home for good, Father bought a small new house on Eighteenth Street near Rock Creek Park. After we got settled and resumed our family life, the years spent in the Fields shows seemed an exciting but distant interlude.

But for Mother the readjustment was difficult. Washington seemed a provincial town—back in 1912 it wasn't the bustling, sophisticated city it is today. She missed the tempo, activity, and glamour of New York. Above all, she missed the theatre, which had got into her blood and was like an incurable fever.

Mother tried to fend off boredom by keeping busy, with flurries of cleaning and cooking, playing bridge, visiting friends and relatives. She made a heroic effort, but all the while she felt trapped and longed desperately to break free.

Though I kept acting occasionally in summer stock, that seemed a comedown to Brownie. She was frustrated by my lack of progress, and her frustration started her drinking again. Oddly enough, during our years in New York she had controlled what Graddy called her "bad habit." She was so involved and enchanted by the theatre world and so busy furthering my career, she didn't seem to think about taking a drink. Besides, she wouldn't dare chance incurring the disapproval of the stars and directors and crew members she respected.

At home, feeling somehow stuck and unhappy, she occasionally overindulged. Father was incredibly patient with her, gently leading her upstairs, having her lean on him. His voice would break as he murmured, "Oh, Essie. Oh, Essie."

21

I was ashamed of my mother's weakness and felt wretched because of it and my inability to help her. Some nights, I cried myself to sleep. The next day, she'd be contrite and apologetic, although I sometimes found it hard to sympathize or forgive her for causing Father such a bad time. I was too young to understand what ailed her or that the drinking spells were a kind of sickness.

For years, I couldn't admit that my mother was an alcoholic. Our family kept the problem hushed up, as families did in those days. But in time, the roles of Mother and myself were reversed: I became the mother, taking care of her, undressing her and putting her to bed. The first time that happened, I had just turned twelve, during a tour with John Drew. Everyone in the company was crazy about Brownie; had I dared complain or seek help, they would have drummed me out of the theatre.

It was a difficult life, but perhaps coping with Mother strengthened me. Perhaps it was something like being in the Marines, in boot camp: once you went through it, you were ready for anything. Griping and self-pity got you nowhere.

At the start, Mother's devotion couldn't be faulted. When she transferred her ambition to me, I was her vicarious career, and she nurtured it admirably. But as I grew older, Mother became so dependent that I never could do enough for her. Maybe I was too submissive, too quick to feel, as she felt, that I owed her for all that she had done for me.

People assume that I am a strong person. We all have to develop strength, backbone, to survive, but in my case that was a slow process. I still feel compelled to look after others, though I don't like this compulsion and sometimes anger builds up in me.

A cousin of mine, a doctor with a lot of insight, has studied the influence of alcoholic parents on their children. He found that when those children become adults, they carry with them a feeling of inferiority. Not that they're ashamed, but they feel they are put on this earth to serve, not to take. Maybe that explains my attitude.

About two years after we came home, I received an offer to return to Broadway. To Mother it seemed a miracle, an answer to her desperate prayers. She perked up at once and got so busy preparing for our departure that she stopped drinking. To Father and me that itself seemed a miracle.

But how long would it last? Father was worried about letting us go, fearing I was too young to look after Mother if she fell off the wagon. With the optimism of youth I told him that we'd be all right, that it would do her good to get away—not from him, but from the household routine that so depressed her. The theatre world that she loved would keep her happy and on her good behavior, as it had in the past.

Father still had his doubts—he thought I needed a chaperon—but knew he could do nothing to stop us. Mother was straining at the bit. He made me promise to let him know if we needed any help. When he took us to the train and kissed us good-bye, I thought I saw a glimmer of relief in his eyes.

He was a remarkably forbearing and generous man. Though his home life was being destroyed by Mother's burning desire to make me a star, he never showed resentment. He kept sending us money, even after I started earning a good salary, so that we could live even more comfortably.

Although he took pleasure in my ultimate success, the theatre didn't mean much to him. What made him proud was a radio show I did in the 1940s, dubbed the "Helen Hayes Theatre of the Air." By then I had helped him buy a house on Chesapeake Bay in Maryland, and he and his pals would get together in the evenings when I was on the air. They would sit around and listen to the show: that was something he could share with them. The stage hardly existed for them, but the radio was part of their daily lives.

When I had children of my own, I used to take them to visit their grandfather. He doted on them, and they responded in kind. By that time he and Mother had lived apart for years. It was an amicable separation; they had not wanted a divorce, had never thought of remarrying.

Sometimes I wondered if I was responsible for their separation. Could I have kept them together? But I doubted that. Even if I hadn't come on the scene, Mother would never have been satisfied with the placid, uneventful life Father offered her. She wasn't meant to be a homebody and would have found another outlet for her energies—if not in the theatre, in some other field. Of course Mother didn't drag me kicking and screaming into the theatre. I loved it too and wanted to succeed.

My return to Broadway was under the most auspicious circumstances. This time I was cast in a serious play, not a musical, and it was staged by Charles Frohman, the most prestigious producer of that era. His stable of stars included Ethel Barrymore and Maude Adams. James M. Barrie allowed his plays to be presented in America only by Frohman. Members of the so-called 400 of New York society always showed up at a Frohman first night.

The play was *The Prodigal Husband,* and it starred John Drew, who was the uncle of Ethel, Lionel, and John Barrymore and a distant uncle of Drew Barrymore. Mr. Drew was a great matinee idol—handsome, debonair, the epitome of Edwardian elegance. But he wasn't a first-rate actor; he always played himself. Yet his magnetism kept audiences spellbound.

My mother was intimidated by Mr. Drew. "Don't speak to him!" she told me. "Don't break his train of thought. Wait until he speaks to you before you say anything to him."

This warning left me terrified on the first day of rehearsal. I obediently held my tongue until Mr. Drew, about a foot taller than I, smiled down kindly. "How do you like your part?" he asked.

"I think I'm going to like it very much," I managed to say. He seemed pleased, not so much by this response as its tone. Most child actresses were too stagy, but he thought I sounded natural and unspoiled. He began to call me "Childey."

In the middle of our New York run, the actress who played my role grown up left the play and a Swedish actress, then finishing a run elsewhere, was to take the part. Since I appeared only in the first act, the director told Mother to take me to see this actress, Martha Hedman, so I could pick up her accent and the character would be consistent.

One night, as we were leaving the theatre to go catch her performance, Mr. Drew called, "Good night, Childey," as he always did, and advised me to "get a good night's sleep."

"No," I replied, "I'm going to hear the Swedish actress so I can imitate her accent."

Mr. Drew was furious. "What? Nothing can be gained from that!" He yelled for the company manager and told him, "You tell everybody that the new actress is going to imitate little Helen's accent. That's that!"

The Prodigal Husband was well-produced but it was a weak play, a slight romantic comedy translated from the French. Even John Drew's presence couldn't save it, and it closed after a short run. He had liked the play, despite Mr. Frohman's lack of enthusiasm. In order to help recoup the New York losses, he consented to tour in the show. The management thought John Drew's name was sure to attract audiences on the road.

Mother and I went along on that tour, which was mostly one-night stands. During our train rides, Mr. Drew took the trouble to give me French lessons, and he led me through museums and art galleries during stopovers. He thought my education shouldn't be neglected while I was away from school.

But when it came to finding shelter for us, Mr. Drew was not so solicitous. At a railroad station some bigwig or other would meet him in an automobile and drive him home or to a hotel, where a suite was reserved for him. Well, star treatment was his due. The rest of the cast had to shift for themselves. Nobody arranged lodging for us in advance, and sometimes we had to rough it.

Our worst experience occurred when we reached a town during a snowstorm. No taxis were available, so some of us hired a sleigh to haul us around. We nearly froze to death before we got settled. The only hotel in town was full, and rooming houses kept turning us away, no doubt because actors were considered bad risks. Finally, Mother and I and two other actresses were sent to a saloon which had two dreary upstairs rooms for rent. Gratefully, we took them.

Instead of a bathroom, we had a chamber pot under the bed and a pitcher of water and a basin on the washstand. Mother quickly dumped the water into the basin and sent the pitcher downstairs to the saloon to be filled with beer. She ordered up sarsaparilla for me, and we all had a merry old time. Relief to be out of the storm gave our impromptu party a special warmth.

When the tour ended, Mr. Drew gave me a farewell present, a beautifully illustrated biography of Joan of Arc. This book remains among my treasured mementos.

Years later, when I was married to Charlie and we had a daughter, John Barrymore came to visit us. He was enchanted by our Mary and said she looked like a Boutet de Monvel drawing. "You know Boutet de Monvel, of course," he said.

I went to a bookshelf and pulled out *Jeanne d'Arc*, which had illustrations by Boutet de Monvel. I showed Jack the inscription, which read, "To Helen from John Drew."

After the *Prodigal* tour was over, Mother and I landed again on Father's doorstep. As usual, he was glad to have us back. Mother didn't have much time to give way to boredom because I soon got another offer: the leading role in a touring company of *Pollyanna*. I hated the play, and our schedule of one-night stopovers was grueling—unheated trains without sleeping cars—but it was challenging, for we never knew how the audience would respond.

One day we arrived in Miles City, Montana, where we were greeted by the theatre manager, who was wearing a ten-gallon hat and high-heeled cowboy boots. "I hope the show's good," he said. "We're sold out to a bunch of cowhands just in from a roundup and a big payoff. If they don't like it, they might start shooting through the ceiling."

We hoped he was joking, but before the performance I peeped out at the audience and saw the toughest-looking crew imaginable. They had their hats on, and many of them were chewing tobacco. I was terrified. What possible appeal could a goody two-shoes like Pollyanna have for them?

I dreaded the end of the second act, when Pollyanna is carried on, both her legs broken in an accident, and she wails, "I'm so glad, glad, *glad* it happened! For you have to lose your legs to really love them!" As I said this, I waited for the shooting to start. Instead, a strange, loud noise could be heard in the auditorium. It wasn't gunfire, it was sobbing. Those tough guys were openly weeping and blowing their noses like trumpets.

After several months of playing Pollyanna, I began to get poor reviews. In an effort to sustain that boring role I had become shrill.

"You must learn not to hunch your shoulders or do anything that shows you're tense," advised a veteran actress in the company. "If you have to tighten up something, tighten up your toes. No one can see them."

27

I took her advice so much to heart that I've since spent a good part of my life with my toes curled in my shoes. Perhaps this has helped me look so relaxed on the outside, even when I suffered the worst butterflies.

In those early days I got a lot of help from experienced troupers. They could be generous and supportive to small fry. If they saw a little talent, they tried to nurture it, to pass along the tradition handed down to them. I don't remember anybody being unkind to me. My career from earliest childhood was like a bright shiny bucket in a bucket line—I was passed along from hand to hand with everyone helping.

After my first break with Lew Fields, he wrote roles into plays for me for years. I must have had a noticeable talent, like Shirley Temple's, for one of the harshest critics in New York said one time that the best performance of the season was that of "little Helen Hayes in *The Summer Widowers.*" I didn't continue dancing lessons, because Miss Minnie Hawke said I was hopeless at that, so I just went on stage without them. It wasn't until much later that I had lessons, to provide me with a technical base for what I was doing when the youthful ebullience was no longer enough.

It's highly unlikely that every single person I worked with was enthralled by me, but I simply don't remember any mean tricks played on me—which is how actors punish someone when they think he is getting too full of himself.

Only once, when I was grown, did someone try to get me. A great romantic leading man, Hamilton Revell, was very devoted to me, and he and I were in a play that was a disaster, *Loney Lee.* George Tyler had produced it among a whole string of terrible little plays he was putting me in at the time.

Hamilton Revell was so stricken at the failure of this play, which had a star role for me, that he offered to back it financially and take it to Broadway, so I could be seen in it. It was a gallant gesture, but even as he was making it, he was upstaging me in every scene we had together.

My mischief finally took over one night and I thought, "I'm going to go one step upstage before he does." I did. Then he stepped up, and I stepped up, leaving him downstage with his back to the audience. We finally upstaged each other until we were both at the backdrop.

Upstaging was the old actors' trick; they couldn't help themselves. But I can't remember any other tricks against me.

≫·3·≪

When the *Pollyanna* tour ended at last, George Tyler, who produced the show, asked me to join his roster of actors. This was an opportunity, since Mr. Tyler had a lot of clout in the theatre. He wasn't as illustrious as Charles Frohman, but he had played an important part in the careers of many stage stars.

My first Tyler production in New York was Booth Tarkington's *Penrod*, in the fall of 1918. I played Margaret Schofield, a seventeen-year-old ingenue, close to my own age. There was a pre-Broadway tryout in Atlantic City, where we first met the author. Mr. Tarkington was so stagestruck that he came to the theatre even when he wasn't needed for consultations or rewrites.

I don't know how widely read Tarkington is today, but his work used to be very popular. His novels *The Magnificent Ambersons* and *Alice Adams* both won Pulitzer prizes. He based the play on two of his humorous books, *Penrod* and *Penrod and Sam*.

Penrod and his friend Sam are prankish boys, both about ten years old, living in a small town in Indiana. They have a couple of pals, little black boys named Herman and Vermin. The four meet in an alley behind Penrod's house to plan their escapades.

The actors were all bright, but the boy who played Vermin was especially good, and devilish. In one scene Herman and Vermin are supposed to come through a hedge to join Penrod and Sam in some adventure they are about to launch. Herman comes first and Vermin follows. But one night Vermin made his entrance backwards; his little behind squirmed through the hedge, and then he slowly turned around to reveal his face all plastered with white flour. The audience howled, and the other three boys on stage were simply undone; they rolled around in stitches. The little rascal stopped the show, exactly what he wanted.

Mr. Tarkington was crazy about Vermin and didn't care if he ruined the script. "To hell with the play," said the author. He would go out on the boardwalk and follow Herman and Vermin to watch their antics. He heard them say to people, "We're in a show at the Apollo Theatre. It's called *Penrod.* We're actors!" And the passersby would gape with astonishment, which sent Mr. Tarkington back to the theatre doubled over with laughter.

Booth Tarkington was a likable, unusual man. He used to drink a lot but got control of his habit before it destroyed his health and his writing career. What reformed him, he once told me, was an experience he had had in Paris, where he lived for years. One morning, some street cleaners found him in a drunken stupor, lying beside a statue of Joan of Arc. Taken to a police station, he was charged with defaming the statue, one of the treasures of Paris. He was expelled from the city he loved, a great humiliation.

One night—this was before he reformed—he went out with his good friends George Ade and Irvin S. Cobb. All three were noted humorists and serious drinkers. Already quite drunk, they decided to go back to Tarkington's house while they could still walk. On their way, holding each other up, they came upon a figure lying in the gutter, in worse shape than they were. Coming closer, they turned him over, tipsily pitying the poor fellow. One of them said, "He looks like Edgar Allan Poe," a renowned

31

author and drunk of an earlier era. Another exclaimed, "Why, it *is* Edgar Allan Poe!" Whereupon they picked the man up and carried him to Tarkington's house, where they propped him up in a living room chair.

The three agreed that they had to do something "worthy of Edgar Allan Poe." So they decided to tell him their best yarns, and sat up the rest of the night doing this. Then they took him back to the same spot where they had found him and laid him down in the gutter. The poor man never knew what a remarkable experience he had missed while comatose.

When Prohibition came, the Volstead Act, I was against it. Not only did it lead to an increase in crime, but it killed off practically a whole generation of gifted American writers—because these writers, by their very nature, rebelled against being told what they couldn't do. In their defiance they overindulged, and some drank themselves to death.

Penrod was a successful play, but, ironically, that success created a problem for me. Soon after it opened, I was offered a more desirable role in James M. Barrie's *Dear Brutus* by the Frohman company. I wanted desperately to do it, but Mr. Tyler refused to release me. Then came a national catastrophe that worked to my advantage. A great flu epidemic swept across the country after World War I, claiming many lives and closing a lot of Broadway shows, especially those appealing to family audiences. Parents were afraid to take their children to crowded places where contagion was likely. *Penrod* closed and I was free to appear with William Gillette in *Dear Brutus*.

Gillette is probably best remembered as the theatre's first Sherlock Holmes. He was a superb actor, very understated, very modern, almost naturalistic. Even though he was an acclaimed star, he wasn't arrogant or egotistical. He never patronized me, but was always kind, protective, and encouraging.

A well-known British director, B. Iden Payne, was guiding our production. One day, early in rehearsals, he spoke to me about my accent which, he said, he couldn't place. Mr. Gillette rushed in. "She has a slight trace of a Southern accent," he said, "and I will work with her to eliminate it." Payne gave me a book of Shakespeare's sonnets which I religiously read aloud every morning and evening, crossing my t's and sounding my g's, and many evenings, Mr. Gillette and I would meet in Mr. Frohman's office to rehearse our scene. I had only one scene, but it was the highlight of the play and performed entirely with Mr. Gillette. I was determined to do it perfectly.

Dear Brutus was a great success and earned glowing reviews for all. Even the acerbic Dorothy Parker, writing a review in *Vanity Fair,* was uncharacteristically kind to me. As I waltzed into Mr. Gillette's dressing room, I exclaimed, "Weren't the reviews wonderful?!" He raised a warning finger and said, "Never read your reviews. If they praise your work, they will only serve to make you self-conscious. If they criticize you, which most of them usually do, they can cause you real harm. Let your director read reviews. If he thinks something should be changed, he will tell you." Of course he was right, and it's a lesson I tried to master, with varying degrees of success, until I did films. In a film, nothing anyone said could affect my performance; it was canned for good.

After *Dear Brutus* closed, I returned to Mr. Tyler, who kept me steadily employed for the next few years. He was a benevolent despot who dictated what roles his actors would play and how they should comport themselves offstage. He wouldn't let me go to a nightclub. He wouldn't let me go near a dance floor. He said, "The public does not care to pay two and a half dollars to see you on stage if they can go to a nightclub and see you." I was kept in a gilded box. He also considered it his province to advise us what to wear, what to read, and whom to model ourselves after. Fortunately, Mr. Tyler had good taste.

An actress he advised me to study was Mrs. Fiske, a great comedienne of the day. I was then in a show playing Wednesday matinees, and her play was giving matinees on Thursday, so every Thursday afternoon I went to see Mrs. Fiske in a frivolous piece called *Mary, Mary, Quite Contrary.* I couldn't get enough of it. I followed every move she made, every nuance of her performance, and that's when I learned there is no such thing as spontaneous comedy. Great comedy acting is a technical wonder. The wonder is that the technique is so concealed, everything seems spur-of-the-moment.

At each performance, a moment came when Mrs. Fiske brushed a crumb from a tea table as she spoke a particularly witty line. The first time I saw it, it looked impromptu, a delicate gesture. It appeared just as impromptu when I watched it the twentieth time.

Laurette Taylor was another actress Mr. Tyler sent me to observe. I needed no urging, for Laurette was a star of the first magnitude. She was beyond technique and had the gift of intimacy on the stage. Whatever she was doing seemed utterly spontaneous, as if it had just occurred to her. She was so at home on the stage, so absorbed in the story, you hardly noticed her performance until you realized how effective it was. I always especially loved her exits. There's a temptation among actors to make an exit a momentous happening in order to bring a round of applause. Laurette simply walked out of the room.

My association with Booth Tarkington continued when I appeared in another play of his, titled *Clarence.* It was a smash hit and benefited all of us in the cast, especially Alfred Lunt, who rose to stardom in his first leading role. Mr. Tarkington was thrilled by this stage success, perhaps more so than by the best-selling books he continued to turn out.

Alfred Lunt and Lynn Fontanne were among the future stars

under contract to Mr. Tyler; at that time, they were not yet married nor did they perform together. In *Clarence*, all of the female characters on stage were in love with Clarence; offstage, all of the actresses—Mary Boland, Elsie Mackaye, and myself—were a bit in love with Alfred, too. Sadly for us, he had eyes only for Lynn, who used to meet him at the theatre after every performance. Years later, Lynn told me she could feel our envious stares stabbing her like daggers in the back.

Tarkington later undertook to write a play for me. He called it *The Wren;* the title was derived from a saying about the wren fighting for her own against the owl, quite an uneven match. That was the theme of the play. Leslie Howard was brought over from England for his first American appearance in this production. Unhappily, *The Wren* was a terrible play, and it flopped. Franklin P. Adams (who signed his column "F.P.A.") gave me a notice saying, "Helen Hayes was suffering from fallen archness."

It was clear to all of us in the cast, during rehearsals, that *The Wren* wasn't going to make it, that no amount of effort or rewrites could save it. The wren, as hard as it fought, lost.

While playing in *Clarence,* I learned the hard way that Mr. Gillette had been right to warn me not to read reviews. I had been praised for a certain line; it provoked laughter that stopped the show on opening night. But after a few weeks it wasn't arousing even a titter. What went wrong? I was stumped and embarrassed.

Mary Boland, who had been John Drew's favorite leading lady, came to the rescue. "You're anticipating the laugh," she said. "Stop trying to be funny. Just stay in character and then you'll get the response you want." It sounded easy, but it took a while to regain the spontaneity of opening night. Finally, the laugh came as before.

As I'd never had any acting lessons, I began to wonder if some professional training might be necessary. My mother was against it; she feared I would become too "actressy." I could rely on her, she said, to point out when I was pushing my lines, overacting, or doing the wrong thing. So far she'd been perceptive and helpful; she didn't let me get lazy or too puffed up.

Mr. Tyler decided, while *Clarence* was still playing, to produce a new drama by Eugene O'Neill, whose first success, *Beyond the Horizon,* was then on Broadway. His new play, *The Straw,* was based on an incident in his own life. As a young man he'd spent a year in a tuberculosis sanatorium, where he fell in love with a young girl who later died. In the play she expires with Camille-like melodramatics.

The Straw doesn't rank high even among O'Neill's earliest plays, but Mr. Tyler thought it might work with the right actress. He had me in mind, though I didn't have much in common with the heroine except Irish ancestry.

"Who is Helen Hayes?" O'Neill demanded. Tyler took him to see *Clarence,* and O'Neill wasn't at all impressed. He thought I wasn't old enough in stage or life experience for the part. "The role is so tremendous," he declared, "that only one of the best dramatic actresses, someone of proven ability, should be allowed to attempt it."

Tyler thought that was pretty conceited. He pointed out that the playwright's middle name was Gladstone and that his initials were E.G.O.

O'Neill was unrelenting in his refusal to consider me. I hate to have setbacks or failures of any kind nagging at my memory, so many years later, when I had the "Helen Hayes Theatre of the Air" on radio, I asked if I could do *The Straw.* Permission was granted. We had two live performances, one at eight o'clock for East Coast listeners, and the second at eleven o'clock for the West Coast. After our eight o'clock show, I received a telegram from O'Neill: "It is seldom that a playwright has the privilege of

36

hearing his character realized exactly as he had imagined it. Tonight, you have given me that."

O'Neill's disdain didn't shake Mr. Tyler's faith in me. He believed I was ready for stardom, or maybe circumstances arose that made him willing to take a chance.

He took that chance in 1920, when I was twenty (the century and I are the same age). The play was *Bab,* and it opened at the Park Theatre on Columbus Circle, which had a great big sign running across the front.

Bab was based on a story by Mary Roberts Rinehart. Mr. Tyler wanted the marquee to announce: BAB BY EDWARD CHILDS CARPENTER, FROM THE BOOK BY MARY ROBERTS RINEHART. But there was no way to fit all that lettering on any sign, however large. Finally, he pared it down to HELEN HAYES IN BAB. So that's how I got to be a star—my name was the right size.

I was thrilled to see my name up there, but Mother became livid with rage. Yes, that's what she wanted for us, but not just yet, she explained. Tyler intimidated her, as had Drew and Gillette, but she was prepared for a showdown.

Marching into Tyler's office, she argued that I was too young for the responsibility of stardom. Either my name came off that sign or I'd leave the show. While Mother worked up quite a lather, Mr. Tyler remained silent. There would be no alteration in the sign, he finally said. Contractually neither Mother nor I had anything to say about the matter.

By opening night I began to think Mother was right: that big sign looked too presumptuous. Making my first entrance, I was so scared that my voice became shrill and I never did get it pitched correctly; and I was so tense that I pounded lines and fell back on cute mannerisms.

The critics trounced me, deservedly so. Still, it was a painful disappointment. Both Mother and I now realized that despite some years on the stage, I was still an amateur. I didn't know how to sustain a role, how to make it seem fresh for each performance like Laurette Taylor and Mrs. Fiske. And I still had that trace of a Southern accent. So far I'd managed to get by, but youth and cuteness weren't going to keep me afloat forever.

We turned to a couple of good friends, Ina Claire and Ruth Chatterton, both fine actresses, for advice. They looked on me as a sort of favorite child, and now they offered to refine what they considered an instinctive but unpolished talent.

Ina sent me to her vocal coach, Frances Robinson-Duff, who had worked with Mary Garden, the soprano acclaimed as one of the best singing actresses in opera. Robinson-Duff later coached Katharine Hepburn and Clark Gable. She used the Delsarte method, named for a noted French elocutionist and based on the proper use of the diaphragm and breath control.

Although some aspects of Delsarte's method struck me as funny, especially diaphragm placement to express love and hate, it did work on the whole. I learned what many actors overlook: how to project your voice and enunciate clearly, how to breathe without strain; and I no longer had to worry about being heard or gasping before reaching the end of a sentence.

Ruth Chatterton recommended a course in body movement taught by Florence Fleming Noyes. It was a rigorous course, but I kept at it for a couple of years. One day, we were doing interpretive dancing, very impressionistic, and our instructor asked us to pretend we were an animal and to move as it moved. Among my classmates were some fat ladies trying to reduce. We were all lying on the floor when our teacher said, "Now imagine you are sea lions. Roll around, roll around like sea lions."

Well, I never saw a sea lion, but I flailed around like the rest of the class. One hefty woman rolled right on top of me. When I realized nothing was broken and I wasn't squashed flat forever, I decided it was time to quit before I did get hurt. I had learned enough about body movement and never would be an interpre-

38

tive dancer, anyway. But that class did teach me something valuable: the importance of good posture.

Mr. Tyler continued to take an interest in me, despite the bad reviews for *Bab*. He was like a surrogate father to the players he had singled out for special attention. But he was a strict taskmaster too. Nothing escaped his notice, and young actors like myself stood in dread of him. He could flay you with a few sharp words. No back talk was allowed. You toed the line—or else. He was regarded as a deity, for he had presented to the public such eminences as Eleanora Duse, Sarah Bernhardt, Laurette Taylor, and George Arliss. His roster included, besides Alfred Lunt, Lynn Fontanne, and myself, Jeanne Eagels and other young actors on the rise.

George Tyler once told me that if I were only four inches taller, I could reach the heights, too. It wasn't a disparaging remark but just a statement of fact. Being short bothered me, but I didn't let that stand in my way. Nothing could be done about my height, but my bearing and acting ability could be improved. In that body-movement class I had learned how to stand tall, so that on stage I appeared somewhat taller than my five feet.

Robinson-Duff's coaching also did some good. I lost no time applying her instructions to the role of Bab, and by the end of the run I was giving the performance I should have given on opening night.

≽· 4 ·≼

To the Ladies, by George S. Kaufman and Marc Connelly, came along after a couple of flops had left Mother and me low in money and morale. We weren't destitute, as Father still helped out, but I felt it was high time to free him from this burden and be self-supporting.

When I had begun to earn a better salary, we'd moved into a nice duplex on East Nineteenth Street, converted from the Astor family's former carriage house. It was a decided improvement over the one-room flat in a Lexington Avenue walk-up that Mother and I had once shared. But to continue paying the rent I had to get a new job pretty soon. At first, it was touch and go whether I'd land in *To the Ladies.*

The playwrights came to our apartment to talk it over with Brownie and me. The heroine, they explained, had to play the piano; this was crucial to the plot. "Do you play the piano?" George Kaufman asked.

"Of course," I replied. Mother stared at me but held her tongue. She knew that if my life depended on it, I couldn't find middle C on the keyboard.

"One other thing," Mr. Kaufman continued. "Our heroine is a Southern belle, and she sings a couple of Negro spirituals. Can you manage that?"

"Oh, yes. I've been singing spirituals all my life," I answered. Mother now looked at me with real alarm. They couldn't ask me to play the piano because we didn't have one. But what if they suggested a song or two? I didn't know any spirituals, and my voice wasn't great. But I assumed they weren't looking for a concert soprano. Evidently they were taken in by my act. Mr. Kaufman and Mr. Connelly didn't put me to the test and soon departed.

Mother and I immediately put on hats and coats and rushed out to buy a piano. The cheapest one at Wurlitzer's was seven hundred and fifty dollars, with a one-third down payment. Mother eventually persuaded the clerk to accept fifty dollars as a first installment. While writing out the check, she kept her thumb over the balance figure, which was less than a hundred and fifty dollars. We would need money, too, for someone to teach me how to play the piano we now owned.

To solve the problem of singing I got the black woman who worked part-time as our cook to teach me Negro spirituals. The cook spent most of her time singing for the next few weeks, while Mother prepared the meals.

Mr. Tyler, who produced *To the Ladies,* helped convince the playwrights that, whatever my musical deficiencies might be, I was suitable for the part of Elsie Beebee. At first, George Kaufman was aloof and dour, but eventually he was won over.

One day, I told him about an experience I had on the way to rehearsal. The driver of the cab I was in rammed into the back of another cab. "And both drivers hurled the most terrible *epitaphs* at each other." Kaufman's long glum face cracked a smile and then he broke into laughter.

Sophisticates like Kaufman got me flustered; attempting to

41

keep in step with them, I would stumble into malapropisms. Kaufman found this diverting, and perhaps, too, it gave him an opportunity to show off his wit.

To the Ladies became a hit, running well over a year; it got me over the slump following *Bab* and provided a steady income. One of the best rewards from that play was a lasting friendship with Jean Dixon, who appeared as the second female lead. She lived with Mother and me for a while and also influenced my acting.

Jean was to have a long and distinguished career in theatre and films, usually as the leading lady's wisecracking confidante. I suppose she played that role for me offstage as well. She was like an older, wiser sister whose comic view of the world kept us in good humor.

Her father had been one of Mr. Tyler's close friends. When he died, Jean and her mother went to live in Paris, where Jean studied at Sarah Bernhardt's acting school. She was such an apt student that she won a place in the school's touring company, which eventually came to the States.

When we went on tour with *To the Ladies,* we did a lot of reading, especially on train rides between stopovers. One of the books we tackled in French was Rostand's *L'Aiglon,* which had been a great success for Bernhardt. Jean was then reminded of the tricks she'd picked up from Mme Bernhardt and passed them along.

One trick had to do with French playwrights' propensity for writing long speeches—from Racine and Corneille to Giraudoux and Anouilh. They let a character go on and on for paragraphs at a time. Sarah Bernhardt had a method for handling this problem: the actor had to find the key word in a sentence and let it come out strong and clear. Bernhardt would rattle along for a while, then punch the telling word or phrase. This gave the audience the impression that they had absorbed everything, and it kept them from getting restless or bored. It also helped the actor, who, if he enunciated every word, would be hoarse by the end of the first act.

Bernhardt's technique can be applied to English drama as well, but with some modifications, depending on the play. What American actors need most of all is clearer enunciation. Too many of them garble their speeches, so that you can't understand them even if you sit in a front row, not to mention the strain on people in the upper balcony.

But as long as critics continue to accept slovenly diction as "realistic," actors won't bother to improve. Perhaps that's why so many TV specials and movies emphasize spectacular visual effects. They're like silent movies just beginning to learn to talk in monosyllables.

Not long ago, my friend Lillian Gish and I discussed this problem. At the time we were both watching a TV miniseries about Peter the Great. We were excited, at first, because so many actors we knew and admired were in the cast. After the third installment I asked Lillian what she thought. "I've stopped watching," she replied. "It was just a lot of actors dressed up for a costume party." Exactly what I thought. Here were actors who had made Shakespeare's words ring like golden bells mumbling their way through what was essentially no more than a series of *tableaux vivants.* It is hard to know where to place the blame: on actors who don't consider their dialogue worth delivering well, or on writers who don't bother writing literate dialogue when so few actors make an effort to speak well.

In any event, Jean Dixon added the final ingredient to what I call my salad-dressing style of acting: from her I got a dash of Bernhardt. Earlier there was a touch of vaudeville from Mr. Fields, a bit of understatement from Mr. Gillette, and the basic technique learned in my speech and body-movement classes. All thrown together haphazardly. But for me, at least, it seemed to come out all right.

I was the youngest star ever to come to Broadway, and while

43

I mingled somewhat with the young set, most of the time I sat on the sidelines, guarded to the point of smothering by my mother and George Tyler. It was, perhaps, the most wistful time of my life.

There would be more tragic times, but up to then, this was the most unhappy, unfulfilled—the years between my late teens and mid-twenties—until Charlie came along like the prince in *The Sleeping Beauty* to deliver me from the spell.

You cannot imagine the yearning that went on in my poor heart. The world was a constant Mardi Gras of laughing and loving and drinking and dancing, all carefree madness. We had made the world safe for democracy and everyone was having a celebration, fueled by the Volstead Act, which made drinking a wild adventure. Many young actresses were emulating the much-beloved and glorious Ellen Terry and having children out of wedlock. They seemed to think you had to experience everything in life to be equipped for playing serious roles, so everybody was getting pregnant. My closest friend was having an affair with a British actor, and when that fell apart, she married another British actor, but had her child by an American actor. This spirit of giddy freedom permeated our lives like an irresistible whiff of danger.

While I was pining for love and a fellow of my own, my life at night after the theatre would be a bridge game with Mother, Mrs. Chatterton, Ruth's mother, and Ruth or another of Mother's friends. That would be it, playing bridge. The rest of the time, I worked and took care of Mother. Any possibility of changing my routine was vetoed by Mr. Tyler, who didn't want me to be seen in public.

There were times at the theatre when one or another of the young actors would make a pass, but invariably they reconsidered, deciding I was too "sweet." I was cursed with innocence.

Culturally, Mr. Tyler thought I was a desert, and he was

44

probably right. Mother's kind of literature was *Redbook* and *Cosmopolitan* and popular stories of passion. He made me read his favorite writers—O. Henry, William Allen White—and he insisted that my mother and I tour Europe with him.

We got to Paris, and it was so bright and gay, I began having a good time in spite of my lack of freedom. One night, we went to a restaurant in the Bois de Boulogne with friends of Tyler's and, of course, with Mother, who never left my side. Mr. Tyler hated her, couldn't stand her, so there I sat between these two glowering older people at a table of middle-aged strangers while the band played and the dance floor began to fill with couples my own age.

"That's a disgusting exhibition," Mr. Tyler said. Staring at me, he added, "You are never, *never* to dance in public."

I thought my heart would break.

A few nights later, I had another spell of lovesickness. We were staying in a small inn near a romantic chateau south of Paris. After dinner, I was sent up to my bedroom while Mr. Tyler, who was being friendly for a change, joined Mother for a nightcap.

I had gone to bed when I heard a little band begin to play a familiar love song. Moonlight streamed through my window, and I put the pillow over my head and cried myself to sleep. There was so much yearning in me, not for a life in the theatre but for life itself and romance.

In Florence, we stayed in the Grand Hotel on the River Arno, and our rooms were on the riverside. I went out one day without Mother—I think she was tired of going through galleries—and on my return, I passed Mr. Tyler's room on the way to ours.

"Helen," he called. I hadn't noticed that his door was ajar and he was sitting on a chaise by the window, watching me.

I answered something, probably "Yes, sir." I stopped and waited.

The next thing I knew, he embraced me and gave me the first

45

passionate kiss of my life. It scared the wits out of me. I scrambled away and ran down the hall as fast as I could. I was so shaken and frightened by what I was yearning for, it's a wonder I ever got around to accepting it. We never mentioned the incident. I didn't tell my mother, and he didn't try it again.

To the Ladies, which opened in 1922, was my last show for Mr. Tyler. Under his management I'd fared well, despite his despotic ways. He had nurtured my career and even commissioned plays for me. He staged his productions lavishly, though some actors complained that he was stingy when it came to paying their salaries.

Still, I would have remained loyal to him if he hadn't taken such an intransigent stand against Actors Equity, the fledgling actors' union. At the very mention of Equity, Tyler foamed at the mouth. My friends, all Equity members, urged me to join. Eventually I decided that it was my duty to support my fellow actors and not management.

When I informed Mr. Tyler, he said that if I signed with Equity I would never act for him again. My mother was apprehensive, but I went ahead and did what I thought right. And Mr. Tyler did what he thought right: I never appeared in a Tyler production again.

After that, I found work readily enough, but for the next three years my plays weren't much good. One of these was *Quarantine,* which, said a critic, was where it should have been kept to protect the public.

A string of busts, even if one gets good personal notices, doesn't exactly enhance an actor's reputation. My mother was troubled. "What happened to all those cute tricks, Helen?" she would ask. I shuddered, because I had been doing my utmost to shed the girlish mannerisms that she wanted me to hold on to.

As an actress I had matured, but not as a woman. I was still my mother's prodigy. We went everywhere together, and I suppose most producers considered me a mama's girl. Because they thought me too sweet and virginal, I lost parts—lost them occasionally to actresses who looked sweet and innocent but really weren't, as the producers well knew.

One was a friend I'll call April. She came to visit Mother and me at a summer cottage we rented on Long Island. One afternoon we were having tea in the garden, and April sat on a bee. She was in great pain, but refused to let us call the local doctor. He was too young to look at her naked bottom without lascivious thoughts, she protested.

Now everyone knew that April's bottom was not exactly unsighted territory, but we went along with her. We spent hours driving around Long Island looking for a long-bearded physician who could gaze at April's bottom dispassionately.

That year April got a shady-lady role I wanted very much, while I went into *Quarantine.* The heroine was more sophisticated than any I had played before, but still an ingenue. I had reached another awkward age: not yet acceptable as a woman of the world, I was getting a little beyond the age to pass as a flapper much longer. Then something unexpected happened to change all that.

One afternoon I went Christmas shopping, and crossing Fifth Avenue I bumped into Marc Connelly. Mr. Connelly was looking for a gift for his current lady friend and asked me to help him choose something appropriate. I was hesitant, thinking he had something intimate in mind, like lacy lingerie. But no, we went to a bookstore, where he selected a copy of *Alice in Wonderland,* illustrated by John Tenniel. Then he insisted that I accompany him to Neysa McMein's studio on West Fifty-seventh Street, and I reluctantly agreed.

It's hard to believe that I'd ever have to explain who Neysa was. In the '20s and '30s everybody knew her. Neysa was a calico cat of a woman, who had gone to art school; a tawny-haired beauty, she was a regular cover artist for *The Saturday Evening Post* and an illustrator for many leading magazines. If she had put her mind to it, she might have provided competition for Lorelei Lee, heroine of *Gentlemen Prefer Blondes,* but she preferred independence to diamonds.

Between four and seven every evening, everybody turned up at Neysa's—Irving Berlin, George Gershwin, Harpo Marx, Janet Flanner, George Abbott, Jascha Heifetz, among others. Neysa, wearing a pastel-smudged smock, would greet them briefly, then return to her easel and model, who was sometimes wearing little more than Eve in the Garden of Eden. Neysa liked to supply provocation for certain of her male guests.

When Mr. Connelly asked me to come with him to Neysa's, I feared I wouldn't fit in. I was terribly shy, especially with celebrities, maybe because my mother was awe-stricken by famous people. "Don't push yourself forward, don't bother them," she always said. Neysa's guests were all so sophisticated, so clever, so ready with well-honed repartee. I didn't know these people, didn't enjoy drinking. How could I hold my own in such a crowd? I wasn't flashy, and I lacked a colorful past—no flaming affairs or bohemian adventures to make them sit up and exclaim, "How brave! How devilish! How chic!"

At Neysa's studio I picked up a glass of sherry to fit in and retreated to a secluded niche. About twenty minutes later, a good-looking fellow with curly brown hair and sparkling green eyes came over, maybe because he felt sorry for me sitting there all alone. He held out a small paper bag. "Wanna peanut?" he asked. "Thanks," I said. He poured a few in my hand and said, "I wish they were emeralds."

Well, I was bowled over. Right then and there I fell in love with Charles MacArthur, the most beautiful, most amusing, most amazing and dazzling man I had ever met. Charlie had that

48

kind of electrifying effect on people. He was already something of a legend to the crowd that gathered at Neysa's.

Charlie had ridden with the cavalry chasing Pancho Villa through the Mexican desert, had fought in France in World War I, had been a Chicago reporter with all the energy, curiosity, and bravado that go into the making of a good newsman. He left Chicago and conquered New York with the irresistible flash and sparkle of an exploding Roman candle.

Soon he was adopted by one of the most exclusive groups in town, the Algonquin Round Table. This was more than a literary or social gathering. The people who sat around that table in the Algonquin Hotel's Rose Room set the style for New York, dictating what one should read, think, wear, eat, what plays to see, what opinions to have, and so on. The Round Table regulars exuded a world-weary superiority that made ordinary mortals feel inferior, including me. And here I was in love with a favorite of that elite circle.

Charlie took me home that day. We left Neysa's and he hired a horse-drawn cab to drive us down to my apartment at Thirty-sixth and Park Avenue. Somewhere along the route, he suddenly stopped charming me with his stories and tried to kiss me. I fought. I guess it was the George Tyler memory and the shock of this coming from someone I had just met. I was about ready to jump out of the cab when he quieted down and stopped.

When we parted, he said he would come and see me in the play I was rehearsing, *Caesar and Cleopatra.* I told him I hoped he would.

It was a play I had longed to do for years. George Bernard Shaw made Cleopatra a sort of early British flapper, a girl who cared only about flattering her own vanity by seducing generals. It was very anti-romantic because, I'd been told, Shaw wrote the play while on his honeymoon with the Irish heiress, Charlotte Payne-Townsend, whom he hadn't married for love.

The critics didn't approve of my Cleopatra. George Jean Nathan said I was "biologically" unsuited to the role. Another critic wrote: "There must have been someone in the wings saying, 'Be cute, be cute.' " This was a crack at my mother, who was known to be always on hand, guiding me. Personal attacks of that kind are the shabbiest form of criticism. But I began to wonder if perhaps Charlie, too, thought I was too cute; maybe that's why he didn't come around.

I confided in Helen Westley, a superb character actress who played Fatateetah to my Cleopatra. "Helen, if I wanted to see a man that much," she said, "I'd call him." Oh, I couldn't do that. "Why not?" she asked. "I keep calling them until they move."

One Saturday night, Charlie idly wandered into the theatre. I couldn't let him go again. Mother, June Walker, another friend, and I were sharing a house in Syosset, Long Island, that had been lent to me by an admirer while he spent a month in Europe. I had a car, too, and drove back and forth to the theatre every evening. I invited Charlie to come for the weekend, and without a toothbrush or another thought he got in the car with me.

The next night, my life with Charlie began. Everyone else had gone to bed and we were together on the outdoor swing. "You know, Helen, I want more than a stolen kiss," he said. "I want all of you." I would have done anything to keep him in my life. That was my blessed, beautiful seduction, and to this day, I thank God for it. Thus began what became a long courtship.

My mother was aghast. Charlie was a "satire," she said ominously, meaning "satyr." Friends issued dire warnings, too. Dorothy Parker had almost committed suicide because of Charlie. He had a string of girls, including Beatrice Lillie, who was then in England. Maybe I was just a summer replacement until the star returned. I was warned that he drank too much. Alec Woollcott predicted that I'd never see a happy day after we married.

Neysa McMein, a romantic at heart, was encouraging, though I think even she doubted that I was right for Charlie. She once told me that the only man she had really loved was killed in the First World War. I was so moved by this story that I shed tears.

"It wasn't that sad!" said Neysa. "For God's sake, Helen, we slept together for months before he died."

Everyone kept reminding me that Charlie still had a wife, though they had been separated for years, and that I was a Catholic. Marrying Charlie meant excommunication, so to me it is still astonishing that I never hesitated, that from the start I was prepared to rebel against Mother *and* Mother Church and anybody else who tried to come between us.

We tried to hide from Mother, thinking we were clever. Charlie had a flat, an elegant place full of modern art that had been lent to him by Mary Harriman Rumsey, Averell Harriman's sister, and we would go there some nights after he picked me up at the theatre. There we would have our trysts, have our love, and then we'd eat delicatessen sandwiches and I'd totter home at two o'clock in the morning. That was the way it went.

All this time, Mother was in a state, in a stew, because I just sailed away. I didn't fight her or make any kind of dramatic break. I simply left when I wanted to, and that meant with Charlie. She did everything in her power to subdue me. When I would come home from the theatre, sometimes she wouldn't be there. It turned out she went to Grand Central Station and sat there and then returned to our apartment, slipping in about five in the morning. She did this to frighten me; I wouldn't know where she was, but she would tell me later.

It was a rocky road, our romance, but it had its merry times. Looking back, I can't see that people have really slipped much in their moral behavior since then. In fact, it's amazing how little things have changed.

An event I learned to look forward to with Charlie was Otto

Kahn's annual "cultural weekend" at his magnificent Long Island estate. Kahn was a colorful financier and patron of the arts who capped the summer season with a gathering of twenty or thirty artists, chosen for him by Alec Woollcott. We always had a lively time.

The first time I went was before we were married. My bedroom was on the other side of a bath and dressing room from Charlie's; everyone had a private bedroom, unless they chose not to. Among the guests was Michael Arlen, the Armenian author who had realized great success with *The Green Hat;* he was the great writer of the moment in New York.

In the middle of the night, I was awakened by a scratching on my hall door, which was locked. I didn't say anything and the scratching continued. Thinking it might be Charlie, I crept to the door. "Who is it?"

"It's Michael Arlen. I want to come in."

I wasn't sharp with him, but I sent him away.

The next morning downstairs, he said, "I only wanted to make you happy."

I thanked him and told him I was with "my friend, Charlie," and that we were going to be married.

"Oh," he said sadly. "Here's another Armenian massacre."

That was life among the supposedly high-class artistic crowd, but it was no different from vaudeville, where chorus girls on the road slept with the company comedians in order to save on hotel bills.

Charlie had his own scruples about our marriage: he couldn't bear to take a wife better known than he was. Charlie aimed to be a playwright. Soon after we met, he wrote with Edward Sheldon, his close friend and relative by marriage, a play called *Lulu Belle,* a modern-day version of *Carmen.* Produced by David Belasco, it became a hit, but most of the credit went to Belasco and to Sheldon, who was already established as a popular playwright. So this didn't bolster Charlie's self-esteem.

With Ben Hecht, his friend from Chicago newspaper days, he started writing a play that he hoped would make him worthy of me, though in my eyes he was already more than worthy. The play was *The Front Page,* and it was based on Charlie and Ben's memories of Walter Howey, the legendary Hearst editor. Howey was the model for Walter Burns, one of the play's two leading characters. Charlie wooed me with Howey stories. I imagined Howey was the most fascinating man on earth. Charlie really idolized him, and that wasn't at all typical of Charlie, who didn't idolize people, as a rule.

Years later, I finally met Walter Howey. Charlie and I had dinner with him at the '21' Club. He hardly said a word the whole evening after "Hello." I think Charlie even ordered dinner for him. It seemed incredible, but apparently he was awed by me. That this witty, acerbic editor should be stricken dumb in the presence of a stage actress seemed downright silly.

The fact that I was more recognizable to the public than Charlie would always be a problem for us. He couldn't accept the reality that actors are seen and heard but playwrights, though they make actors possible, are heard but unseen.

While Charlie and Ben worked on *The Front Page,* I was rehearsing *Coquette,* a play about a Southern belle with a father whose incestuous feelings result in tragedy for both. Charlie didn't like the play, with good reason. It was very unfocused as we went into rehearsal, and trying to salvage it became a nightmare.

Coquette was produced by Jed Harris, whose name was to Broadway what Robespierre's was to the French Revolution. Jed reigned through terror and tantrums. He would suddenly show up and rip apart everything that the actors and director had struggled all day to put together. Everything had to be reduced to chaos before Jed could become creative. But he was responsible for some of the best productions of the late 1920s.

This boy genius had four hits running simultaneously on

Broadway before he was thirty. But to those who knew him, he could be an awful nuisance. Once he got into your life, you couldn't shake him off. To Charlie and me he became a terrible trial, because he was determined to split us up. One night, when Charlie came to the theatre to pick me up, Jed was lurking in the dark alley and took a swing at him. Charlie dodged the punch. But he wasn't always so ready to avoid a fight, as I learned later, unhappily. That night, however, he just rushed me away.

Charlie hadn't been able to get a divorce, because his wife, who had been the first to sue for divorce, changed her mind and then blocked his own suit. Finally Charlie and I, two young people deeply smitten and terribly frustrated, became lovers.

During *Coquette's* tryout the cast went on rehearsing in Philadelphia. We rehearsed endlessly, until all of us were dead on our feet. Finally, we had a free weekend. Instead of going back home to New York, I agreed to meet Charlie in Atlantic City. Whereupon Jed Harris called another rehearsal. I protested, saying I'd already arranged to go to Atlantic City for a much-needed rest, that I had a hotel reservation and intended to go and relax.

Jed was far too clever and cynical to be taken in. A great womanizer himself, he assumed Charlie would be meeting me there. He called my mother and purred: "I think you ought to know that Helen is going to Atlantic City and that Charlie, unless I miss my guess, will be with her."

Naturally, Mother was alarmed. She disapproved of any man I cared for, and in Charles MacArthur she saw a serious challenge to her control over me. So she phoned me and asked, "Are you going to Atlantic City?"

"Yes, I am," I said.

"Are you going alone?" she asked. I didn't answer, not wanting to lie to her. "Are you going with Charlie?" she demanded.

"Yes," I admitted.

"I disapprove!" she burst out.

"I know you do, and I'm sorry I was forced to tell you. But that's the way it is."

After a slight pause Mother said, "Would you like me to come along?"

"No," I said.

With that she hung up, leaving no doubt about what she thought of me.

I never talked about my relationship with Charlie. Not that there was any reason to conceal it or to feel ashamed or guilty, but to give fuel to gossip was distasteful and unnecessary. Eventually, our union was legalized, and I never loved another man.

While I was appearing in *Coquette,* Jed Harris produced Charlie and Ben's *The Front Page.* So he remained very much in our lives, often calling each of us at home. George Kaufman once said, "Every playwright has to have his Jed Harris." It applied to actors as well.

Charlie and Ben invented a nickname for Jed when he told them he'd never had a nickname and wanted one. They called him "Chick," and he liked that. What he didn't know was that it was short for "chickweed," which rubs your skin raw and is hard to remove.

Charlie had a theory about what made Jed tick. The pattern of Jed's whole life showed a compulsion to tear things down and then build them up again to suit his own purpose. Whether he was involved with a play, a friend, a lover, whatever, he needed to destroy to prove his power; then, if he felt like it, he'd pick up the pieces and put them together his own way.

It's a wonder he didn't ruin *Coquette.* He kept us in turmoil with incessant rewrites, learning new lines overnight, rehearsing till we dropped, switching directors like George Cukor and George Abbott. Yet the play became a hit and proved worthwhile for me, as it extended my range beyond light comedy. But I never wanted to go through another show with Jed Harris.

Eventually he decided to establish a repertory theatre, as many others now and then try to do. Jed had grandiose plans; he would recruit top stars. I've forgotten who the men on his list were, but the women included Pauline Lord, an idol of the critics; Jane Cowl, a shining star who gave a memorable performance in *Romeo and Juliet;* Katharine Hepburn; and myself. He planned to have each of us play a small part one week and a starring role the next, rotating roles that way.

When he approached me, I refused. The mere thought of working with Jed again gave me the willies. But he wouldn't take no for an answer. One night, after a performance, he showed up in my dressing room and kept hounding me. I had to ask him to leave so I could change my clothes and go home. Jed followed me out of the theatre and, when I got into a taxi, he climbed in, too. He continued to argue and harangue, and I kept repeating that I wanted no part in his project.

Just then the taxi stopped in a traffic jam. Suddenly Jed blurted, "You're so stupid, I can't talk to you anymore," opened the door, and leaped out. I couldn't help laughing. The driver must have thought I was hysterical. He turned around and said, "You want me to get out and sock that guy?"

Maybe I should have told him to go ahead, just to see what would have happened. Anyway, Jed had vanished, and I never did see him again.

But he earned my gratitude not only for *Coquette* but for closing the show on the opening night of *The Front Page* so that I could be there. My fate depended on its reception. If it was a hit, Charlie would no longer have an excuse not to ask me to marry him on the day when his divorce became final.

With Charlie and Ben Hecht and his wife Rosa, I sat in the balcony. They all fled to a fire escape shortly after the curtain went up. A few minutes into the first act I knew we were in. Percy Hammond, the *Tribune* critic, was chuckling and pounding his companion on the back. Charlie Chaplin's eyes were rolling. The audience was breaking up with laughter.

I ran to the fire escape and shouted, "It's a hit!" Whereupon Charlie opened his arms and asked, "Will you marry me, Helen?"

≫·5·≪

Our wedding day was joyous and hectic, like a giddy comedy of errors. Charlie and I went down to City Hall to obtain a marriage license, and then we couldn't find anyone to marry us, because it seemed that the rite might be illegal. Charlie's divorce had just been granted, but his ex-wife claimed it was fraudulent and she threatened to file an injunction to block our marriage.

Before I ever met Charlie, she had started and then withdrawn a divorce suit when she learned that he was becoming a successful writer and that he and I were "an item," as columnists reported. For three years she hung on, refusing to set him free. It was an agonizing time for us, as we longed to start our life together. Finally, he won a divorce over her protests. And now that bitter woman threatened to keep us legally apart. I think there was a twenty-four-hour limit before her injunction could take effect, so we had no time to lose.

Charlie called everyone he could think of, but no one was available or willing. We couldn't go to a priest, because Charlie was divorced, so it had to be a civil ceremony, and at that point I didn't care who performed it. Someone in a minister's costume from Central Casting would have been all right with me, I was that anxious to get it over with and become Mrs. Charles MacArthur.

Finally, Charlie's friend Edmund Wilson, the critic and author, got to work and found a judge willing to preside. Edmund told him the ceremony should be kept secret, so the press wouldn't interfere, because we were a well-known couple.

When we got to the judge's office on Forty-second Street, he asked us to sit down and wait. He kept us waiting a long while, and I became more and more nervous, thinking he might be checking up on the legality of the rite he was about to perform.

Finally, the reason for the delay became evident. While we sat cooling our heels, the judge had got word to the press, and he kept us waiting until a bunch of reporters and cameramen poured in. Alec Woollcott, Charlie's best man, laughed; he had a wicked, perverse sense of humor and liked the joke the judge had played on us. But the rest of us—Charlie and I, my mother and Jean Dixon, my witness—were furious. We had to restrain Charlie from getting into a fight with that judge.

The ceremony was over in about ten minutes. I've often wished, since then, that we'd had a second, beautiful wedding, but it probably wouldn't have been as much fun.

We had no time for a celebration afterwards, because I had to perform in *Coquette* that evening. When the show closed several months later, Charlie and I went to Bermuda for a belated honeymoon.

My mother was not pleased by my marriage. She hated the very idea of my marrying—not just Charlie but anyone. I had been her ticket of admission to the magic world of the theatre, and now she feared being shut out. She said to me, "Well, I suppose you'll start having children now." I told her that Charlie and I planned to wait before starting a family. "Oh, I did too," she said.

"I did everything I could not to have children. But you see what happened." Well, she certainly made sure that I was the only child.

But after our prolonged and not-so-secret romance, she might well have killed Charlie if he *hadn't* married me. Mama Brown, as he called her, was the model for the nagging old lady in *The Front Page.* Of course she knew that she was portrayed as Mrs. Grant. She never let on, but she *knew.*

Mother never completely accepted not being at the center of my life. She lived in an apartment of her own now. Charlie and I tried to include her in our doings whenever we could. But of course for her it wasn't the same as being my guide, companion, mentor, and manager.

In time she and Charlie made their peace. Ben Hecht once said that Charlie had a remarkable allure for anyone who came across him, and that was true even for Brownie. They became friends, though in a sense they were always opponents.

All throughout our courtship and even in the early years of our marriage, people kept asking, "What does he see in her?" Well, bless him, Charlie saw the woman in the girl. He brought me out of the shadows and helped me grow both as an actress and as a woman. Charlie came along when I was moving from ingenue to mature roles, and living with a man of his taste and discernment provided me with a real education.

The few times I went against his artistic judgment, I regretted it. He sought perfection in everything he did; that was the only way he could function. He was precise about words, choosing them with great care. In this respect he was the antithesis of Ben Hecht. Words poured out of Ben as from a fountain. Charlie used to try to stem the flow; it was too much, too rich, like a dinner at the Hecht house, with everyone waddling away from the table scarcely able to breathe.

I learned from Charlie constantly. What would he say or do

about this? I'd ask myself. He got me reading better books. He introduced me to many remarkable people, among them Edward Sheldon, his collaborator on *Lulu Belle.*

Ned Sheldon was a gifted writer, but his greatest gift was what he gave to others. He was an invalid, bedridden, nearly blind, atrophied by arthritis. He received an endless flow of visitors in the beautiful Italianate drawing room, its walls paneled in blue brocade, of his New York apartment. He had been a very handsome man, and the pain he suffered gave him an ethereal look.

At one time Ned had shared an apartment with John Barrymore, on whom he had exerted a beneficial influence. Barrymore had been wasting his talent on silly farces, and Ned led him into serious plays, primed him for *Richard III* and *Hamlet.*

Charlie once asked Barrymore why he now visited Ned so rarely. At the time the actor was frittering away his talent in Hollywood. "I love that son of a bitch," he said. "But he's my conscience and I can't face him."

That was Ned's effect on his friends. He led them, guided them with his own infallible instinct toward achieving what he felt was their potential. He was tremendously knowledgeable about the theatre and was an inspiration to all of us.

I got into the habit of having dinner with Ned before my opening nights. He steadied me, gave me inner strength and balance. He knew every play I did and was always ready to discuss it with me. If this or that scene worried me, he would suggest the right way to handle it. He never intruded, but if I needed his help, he was always there to offer advice and encouragement.

Both Charlie and Ned created the mature me, the mature actress. Charlie could give acute tips on a performance without being cutting or hurtful. We complemented each other well most of the time. And we were able to comfort one another when either of us felt low.

I remember one night when we were lying in bed and I held

him in my arms and tried to talk him out of a depressed mood. He was suffering, as he often did, from writer's block. He said he was finished as a writer, while I was at my peak as an actress.

"Look, Charlie," I said, "everything I've done will be forgotten soon after I've left the scene. But what you've contributed to the American theatre will go on forever." Then I quoted from a Shakespeare sonnet: "So long as men can read and eyes can see this . . ." That seemed to cheer him up.

But we had our disagreements, and one was about a play called *Mister Gilhooley,* which Charlie didn't like at all, but I was tempted to do it because the woman's role was unlike any I'd played before. It was an Irish drama about a big, strong fellow who is destroyed by a tart he tries to rescue from the gutter. I was the tart, a bit of blatant miscasting, Charlie thought. And he was right. The play didn't go.

On opening night during the intermission he ran into Marion Davies and a group of her friends. "Hi, Charlie," she said. "Come and have a drink with us. We're quitting this dog." Charlie replied, "Sorry, Marion, I think I'd better stay. My wife's in this dog, you know." Poor Marion was so embarrassed.

Charlie and I also disagreed about *Coquette,* as I've already mentioned. When its New York run ended, I went straight into the touring company of that show and later wondered if Charlie got me pregnant so I'd have to leave the tour before it was over.

The doctors warned me that I might endanger the baby if I went on performing. I was having a hard time, and while we were playing in Los Angeles I was forced to quit one day between a matinee and evening show. I couldn't risk losing the baby I wanted so much.

Jed Harris closed the production without the two weeks' notice required by Actors Equity. So the cast sued for the two weeks' salary they felt he owed them. Jed countersued, claiming the show had been closed by "an act of God," my pregnancy. He thought Equity shouldn't hold him responsible for what God and Charlie had wrought.

The press had a field day over this case. When it came to court, the cast won, I was happy to hear, and Jed had to pay them, which seemed to prove that my daughter Mary wasn't an act-of-God baby after all.

When I left the show, I stayed in Los Angeles, forced to remain in bed, propped up so my feet were always above my head. And I wasn't supposed to have any sort of physical or emotional stress.

Charlie tried to keep news hounds away and to shield me from hearing about what was going on. Even so, he was unable to protect me from all the news. To overcome boredom while immobilized I had to do something, so I read a lot. One day, I came across an article that Charlie had forgotten to snip out of a newspaper. It was by Louella Parsons, and it was cruel.

She wrote that Helen Hayes was a clever woman when it came to publicity; Hayes certainly knew how to make a big fuss about pregnancy and childbearing. Can you imagine? The whole column implied that I had worked out this brouhaha to push myself into the limelight.

Charlie persuaded me that Louella's allegation was too absurd for any intelligent person to believe. He managed to calm me down enough so that no damage befell me or my unborn child.

That nasty article symbolized for me the general attitude of Hollywood. Hollywood can't believe that anyone does anything without an eye on the public, as if every actor wants to read about himself in the papers. It's depressing to think that such an artificial and unbalanced community exerts so much influence on our country.

The "act of God" hullabaloo should have told me that I would never be happy in Hollywood, but I chose to ignore the signals. Charlie was working there when I left *Coquette,* and he was soon offered a term contract by MGM. After the coming of sound, the big studios started looting Broadway of stars, writers, directors, and anyone else with talent who was willing to make the trip west. By the early 1930s, with the Depression at its worst and the number of Broadway shows dwindling year by year, everybody started going Hollywood.

Irving Thalberg, then head of production at MGM, wanted Charlie, and to keep him happy he brought me out there, too. So in 1931 I signed a contract stipulating that I'd spend six months in Hollywood and six months in New York for the next few years. It sounded like an ideal arrangement. And I convinced myself that filmmaking might still be as much fun as it had been back in the 1910s, when I'd first played in a movie.

That came about when I was appearing in a Lew Fields show. One day an actor we knew approached Mother to ask if I'd like to take part in one of the little films made by the Vitagraph Company, located in Brooklyn. He was recruiting talent, and Vitagraph needed a girl of about my age.

At first, Mother wouldn't hear of it; the mere thought of my appearing in a film horrified her. She shared the view of stage actors, who at the time looked upon movies as a worse fate than starvation or walking the streets. But the wages paid for only a couple of days' work began to tempt her. Besides, my name wouldn't be listed in any credits, since actors got no credit in those days.

So Mother decided it would be all right as long as I appeared in disguise. She curled my hair and applied makeup to change the contour of my mouth and eyes. Apparently this makeover worked, as even a fellow stage actor failed to recognize me when we passed in the street.

We trekked out to Brooklyn, and Vitagraph hired me for a film called *Jean and the Calico Doll.* I wasn't playing either of the title characters. Jean was a collie that rescued me when I fell into a ravine by grabbing my doll and racing to my father and leading him to the scene. I spent most of the time offscreen in the ravine. But even if I'd been on screen all the while, I doubt that I would have presented any challenge to Mary Pickford. Maybe I'm being too modest, for Vernon Castle later told me I was better than the collie.

Making the picture seemed a lark. It was all so spontaneous and inventive. Everyone in the small company pitched in, contributing ideas and work. Since there weren't enough extras, two of Vitagraph's leading actors, Maurice Costello and Florence Turner, pulled hats over their eyes and joined in.

One scene was supposed to be set in the garden of a large estate. So we packed lunches and went off to New Jersey, where the director found an ideal site. We went to work and finished shooting hurriedly, before the property's owners unleashed the dogs to chase us away. It was a colorful memory, of actor-vagabonds setting up their stages like poachers setting traps, on land that wasn't theirs.

Shortly after I started working on a film, I met Marlene Dietrich, who stopped by the set one day. She took my hand and spat on it, then said, *"Viel glück haben."*

Here, I thought, was one of those Hollywood bitches out to destroy my career. Seeing my bewilderment, Marlene explained that it was a German good-luck charm, akin to the British tradition of saying "Break a leg" to a fellow actor.

When I got to know Marlene, an exceptional human being, I realized she was incapable of putting a hex on anyone. But her spit on my hand still sums up my feelings about Hollywood at that time.

Charlie had a better time of it than I did. He and Irving Thalberg hit it off and became fast friends. Irving treated him—and all writers—with respect, an unusual attitude when most studio executives tended to put writers at the bottom of the totem pole.

Charlie had an unerring ear for dialogue; he made characters sound true, something not all playwrights can achieve. He also had an uncanny ability to doctor an ailing script, a talent that made him invaluable, because every second movie script seemed to be in distress.

Irving Thalberg, the legendary "boy genius," and his wife Norma Shearer, a top MGM star, personified the good looks, glamour, and success that Hollywood projected in the '30s. It was a time when the studios began to turn out worthwhile pictures, bringing together leading authors such as William Faulkner, Scott Fitzgerald, Somerset Maugham, top-notch screenwriters such as Charlie and Ben, and fine actors such as Ronald Colman, Charles Laughton, and John and Lionel Barrymore.

Irving fell for Charlie—but who could resist dashing, clever Charlie?—and he and Norma took to me, too, and I took to them. All four of us saw a lot of each other and spent weekends and holidays together.

But nobody at MGM knew exactly what to *do* with me. The studio already had most of the female superstars under contract—Garbo, Harlow, Shearer, Crawford, Jeanette MacDonald, Marion Davies. How was a plain Jane like me to stand out in such a glamorous lineup?

Louis B. Mayer, the chief executive of MGM, told me that if only I had Crawford's face, I might be a great movie star. Years earlier, George Tyler had said I could be a great stage star if only I were a few inches taller, and that hadn't held me down. But Mayer's "if only" was intimidating. What you looked like on screen was then so important.

I didn't have Crawford's bone structure or Garbo's mystery. I wasn't sexy like Harlow or naughty like Marion, and I didn't have the figure to carry off clinging white satin like Norma. There were so many things I didn't have or wasn't, that it seemed best for me to quit then and there. But Mr. Mayer had an idea. I would be promoted as "The Great Actress."

What this meant was that I was relegated to weepy melodramas in which I would die more deaths than Sarah Bernhardt or a Wagnerian soprano. In one picture I actually did expire as the *Liebestod* was piped into my hospital room.

My first MGM picture was *The Sin of Madelon Claudet,* based on a Belasco play that had been a hit twenty years before. Charlie was appalled because they had saddled me with such a turkey. It was about a young misguided girl who turns to the streets to support her illegitimate child. But I tried to take a positive view. *Stella Dallas* had been a big hit not so long ago, and this was the same kind of tearjerker.

During the production something happened that should have tipped me off that moviemaking wasn't for me, but I guess I wasn't paying attention. There was a key scene in which a millionaire invites Madelon to dinner at his mansion. The first course is oysters, and Madelon, never having seen an oyster, has to be taught how to eat them.

The millionaire was played by Lewis Stone, a fine actor best remembered today as Mickey Rooney's father in the Andy Hardy series. Stone had trouble remembering his lines, and the director wanted the scene photographed in full shot, then medium, then close-up. We started at 10 A.M. and by noon I was still gulping down oysters, sick to my stomach.

The picture was completed in ten weeks and then previewed at a theatre in a Los Angeles suburb. All the studio executives were there except Irving, who was in Bad Nauheim, Germany, on his annual visit for therapy for his heart trouble.

If he had been there, his heart probably wouldn't have stood the shock. It's hard to say who liked the picture least—the audience that hissed at the end or the trade paper critics who ripped it apart. Or me.

When Irving returned, he asked about my picture and was told it was shelved permanently. He had it screened and decided it was only half-bad. Rewriting and reshooting could salvage it. Irving was brilliant about this sort of doctoring, so no one argued, but Charlie was uneasy when Irving chose him to do the rewriting.

By then, I was making a picture on loan-out to Samuel Goldwyn, an adaptation of Sinclair Lewis's *Arrowsmith;* this time I died after carelessly smoking a cigarette tainted with infectious germs. For a while I worked six days a week on *Arrowsmith* and on Sundays reported to MGM for reshooting on *Madelon.* When Goldwyn heard what was going on, he pronounced that, like God and most mortals, I deserved a rest on Sundays. He must have figured I'd be too tired playing MGM's Madelon to give my all to his *Arrowsmith.*

Ronald Colman was Lewis's hero, and our director was John Ford, as celebrated for the extraordinary number of great films he had turned out as he was notorious for his drinking. Ford's affection for the bottle was then beginning to jeopardize his career, and Goldwyn hired him with the understanding that if he took even one drink while the film was in production, he would be dismissed immediately.

Everything went smoothly at first; John and I got along perfectly. But then I noticed funny things were happening—pages of the script were being tossed out, entire scenes eliminated, all sorts of shortcuts taken—and why? Because he wanted to pare away the days till he could have another drink.

He was very tense, suffering from all the symptoms of alcohol withdrawal. I was sympathetic, but still, what he was doing was irresponsible. I could have complained to Sam Goldwyn, but that would have been tattling, so I decided to confront John himself. Maybe I chose the wrong moment. The next time he made one of his abridgments, I lost my temper and protested.

"If you cut one more word," I said, "Sam Goldwyn is going

to hear about it. He won't let you get away with this. The picture is to be shot the way the writer wrote it. And Goldwyn will make us do the whole scene again, as written."

John Ford was every bit as tough as his favorite actor, John Wayne, and certainly wasn't about to be intimidated by a Broadway snippet like me. "You'll do as I tell you," he growled. "I'm the director of this picture. You're only acting in it."

Everybody had always handled me so gingerly, I was shocked by his comeback. His words hit like a punch in the ribs, taking the wind out of me. My knees were giving out, but somehow I found my way to the chair with my name on it. Studios supply them, I then realized, so actors don't forget who they are when directors like Mr. Ford tell them that they are no more than puppets.

I sat there, trying to recover my poise and my breath, while across the vast sound stage, John started to chew on his handkerchief. That was something he did whenever he was nervous, chomp away on his handkerchief until it looked like a flock of moths had attacked it. After a while, he came over to me and said, "What's the matter, honey? Did I get you mad?"

I wanted to crush him with my dignity. I said, after a good pause, "I am not accustomed to being *speaken* to in that manner."

The entire crew burst into laughter, and what can you do when everyone is laughing at you? You laugh, too. That was the end of the spat. John made no more cuts, and we went back to getting along beautifully.

Meanwhile, I was surreptitiously working at night on *Madelon.* Goldwyn had said no Sunday work, so instead we spent evenings at MGM getting Charlie's rewrites on film. It was grueling for both me and Charlie, who was trying to save a film that might very well determine his wife's future in pictures.

Irving Thalberg's judgment proved to be accurate: the revised

Madelon became a great hit and won me my first Oscar. But after that first disastrous preview I never had the courage to sit through it again. I tried, and went with Charlie to see it at the Capitol Theatre in New York. We moaned so much that a man sitting behind us protested: "Some of us are enjoying this very much. If you don't like it, why don't you leave?" So that's what we did.

Moviemaking did have its compensations, as I discovered on my next film, another loan-out, this time to Paramount for Ernest Hemingway's *A Farewell to Arms*. Never in working in film have I felt as comfortable with a director as with Frank Borzage, who had a wonderful gift for intimacy: he knew how to get inside an actor's heart and mind, and that rapport gives a special glow to his films.

My leading man was Gary Cooper, and like half the women in the world, I was, in the words of the Noël Coward song, "Mad about the boy." It was all very innocent, but Gary and I had this passionate love scene, and it didn't take Stanislavsky or the *Liebestod* to get me into the mood: I played it to the hilt. When the film came out, that scene was praised for its delicate eroticism, but some years later, when it was reissued, it had been cut from the movie by the Hays Office, Hollywood's self-censor.

There was so much that was absurd about Hollywood that Charlie and I began to feel we should move out before the lunatics took over the asylum. I was aware that my stage training didn't transfer well to filmmaking. It was hard to adjust to those endless takes followed by endless waits while the camera and lighting were adjusted. Only a short part of each day was spent acting; the rest was a game of patience. The jigsaw-puzzle aspect of filmmaking irked me too: shooting one scene today and the following scene maybe a week later or two weeks earlier.

Another problem was our family life, increasingly disrupted by our schedule. Our daughter Mary would see one parent or the other or both of us or neither, depending on our commitments.

70

We needed a balanced life and knew it couldn't be found in the movie colony.

Of course no one had dragged us out there. We had joined the great gold rush to California when hard times hit the rest of the nation and Hollywood became a boomtown, grinding out movies to feed people's hunger for escape. Although Charlie and I had done well in the theatre, in films our earnings zoomed. As we became more and more uneasy, we decided there was nothing to do but work out our contracts. I did get six months' reprieve annually, and that was filled with theatre work.

I suppose we shared the general attitude of other émigrés who were curious about moviemaking, intrigued enough to give it a try, and attracted by the Hollywood bonanza. This was true not only of theatre people—playwrights, directors, actors—but of famous novelists such as Faulkner and Fitzgerald. They all thought they'd cash in and then go back to work they preferred, serious work.

Some, not wanting to endanger their reputations as important writers, actors, or artists, quit the movie mill as soon as they could. And some, we thought, took themselves too seriously.

I am reminded of what my old friend Anita Loos, a veteran of screenwriting before she became a best-selling author, once said: "We never thought filmmaking was an art. It was just a job, and we worked hard at it. We earned pots of money, spent it like water, and had lots of fun."

When the Thalbergs took us under their wing, they saw to it that it wasn't all work and no play for us. At their parties we met such luminaries as Clark Gable, Robert Montgomery, and Jeanette MacDonald. Not Greta Garbo, who usually avoided party-going. And not Joan Crawford, who didn't get along with Norma. But Joan and I later met at a party given by Bill Haines.

Bill had been a popular MGM star until he was arrested for sexual misconduct in Pershing Square in L.A. The studio boss,

Louis Mayer, gave him an ultimatum: Either he'd have to mend his ways or quit the studio. Bill chose to quit and later became a leading decorator, decorating the mansions of many stars.

In a large tent in back of his house he gave elegant parties. At one party that I remember, there were about a hundred guests milling around. The tent was festooned with thick garlands of gardenias that were torn down soon after the cocktail hour and draped around the necks of the more raffish stars, like Lilyan Tashman. Her husband, Edmund Lowe, once a Broadway buddy and drinking pal of John Barrymore, followed Lilyan, saying, "I have a new lei. What do you think of it?" Everyone knew he meant "lay." I didn't find it very funny. Thanks to Charlie, I wasn't as prudish as I used to be, but I still didn't like coarse jokes. Eddie Lowe's quip seemed to point up what I found wrong with Hollywood. Things would start out well, like this elegant party of Bill's, but before long they would degenerate into vulgarity.

Hollywood affected people in a special way, affected all our movie friends. Early on, when Norma Shearer and I became chummy, she gave me an inkling of a mind-set that was still new to me. Charlie and I were then staying at the Beverly Hills Hotel. One night the Thalbergs came to pick us up before we all went out to dinner. When they arrived, Norma said, "I'm going to powder my nose." Then she turned to me, asking, "Would you please come along?"

We repaired to the bathroom and, shutting the door behind us, Norma announced, "You know, I'm pregnant again." She looked and sounded very tense. Didn't she want another child? I wondered. Was she worried about her figure, or what? Norma went on, "Irving is going to be furious with me, because he's got my new picture all lined up, and I'll never be able to finish it if I start now."

"What are you going to do?" I asked. The thought of abortion didn't cross my mind or hers. "You'd better tell Irving."

72

"I know I'll have to tell him," said Norma. "But first I must tell Louella Parsons. I promised to let her know the minute I got pregnant—that she would be the first to know."

I didn't know what to say. Maybe all Norma needed at that moment was a chance to confide in someone she trusted. But didn't she trust her own husband?

By that time I knew that everyone lived in deadly fear of incurring the displeasure of Louella Parsons or her arch-rival Hedda Hopper. These two women were tough, mean monarchs, reigning over the movie colony with their viper tongues or typewriters.

Sooner or later Norma must have told Irving, for she had her baby and he seemed happy to have little Katharine join Irving, Jr., in the nursery. Then they went right on making films together.

Irving, too, was such a complete product of the movie world that he couldn't understand why anyone would want to leave. He once called me while I was on tour in *Mary of Scotland,* a few years later. The Theatre Guild had produced the play and asked me to take it on tour during my six-month respite from movies.

After a performance in Pittsburgh I went back to my hotel and straight to bed. I had barely dozed off when the phone rang. Who could be calling that late? I immediately feared hearing bad news about Charlie or our child.

When I picked up the receiver, a familiar voice said, "Helen, this is Irving." My heart stopped. He wouldn't call at this hour unless something had happened to Charlie.

"Are you pregnant?" he asked right off. I was so startled that I couldn't gather my wits for a moment. Irving repeated the question and I answered, "No."

"Charlie is gone," said Irving. "The message he left said that he was seeing Helen. Where is he? Isn't he with you?"

"No. I don't know where he is. I thought he was in California."

"He left yesterday," Irving said. He sounded distressed, as if Charlie's sudden departure, using me as an excuse, had hurt him.

Though I was perturbed, I couldn't help being amused by Irving's assumption that the only reason why Charlie would want to leave him and come to me was that I was pregnant. I had no idea why or where Charlie had gone, but he soon called to explain. He'd taken French leave because he just got fed up with the studio—not with Irving. Before long both of us would quit and move back east. The Thalbergs never understood our defection, but we remained good friends. After Charlie and I bought a house in Nyack, they came to see us when the place wasn't yet furnished. We all sat around on apple crates chatting about old and new times.

⟫·6·⟪

In the old days, when we used to gad about with the Thalbergs, they were our guides in California. When we went abroad, our roles were reversed, and they expected us to take charge. On a vacation trip to the French Riviera we made all the arrangements: for hotel reservations, restaurants, sightseeing excursions. At times Charlie and I felt they were depending on us too much and we might lead them astray. But it worked out fine. We were good companions and traveled well together.

On another holiday we had a surprising experience showing how far-flung and inescapable the movies' influence was. We took a cruise through the Panama Canal and spent a few days in Panama. At our hotel someone told Charlie and Irving that in the red-light district the prostitutes used the names of their favorite movie stars. The brothels displayed signs bearing these well-known names as a lure to customers.

Naturally, the men had to see that titillating sight, and the ladies went along. We drove in a hired car through the heat and dust to the red-light district. The driver knew where "Norma Shearer" worked, and he took us to a ramshackle house; there on the front was a sign with Norma's name in big bold letters.

We all thought it was very funny, except Irving, who found it offensive. He would often get serious about things that no one else thought important. He said he was going to demand that the brothel's owner take that sign down immediately. The madder he got, the more we laughed at him. But Norma, who was so refined on screen and off, seemed flattered by this tribute to her name. I escaped the honor, proving that to the customers of the Panamanian ladies of pleasure I was no drawing card.

When it came to pictures, Irving's judgment was infallible. He picked good properties and spared no expense on buying them, on adapting scripts, on casting, and his productions were lavish.

In 1933 I appeared in a Thalberg movie called *Night Flight,* based on a book by Antoine de Saint-Exupéry, the noted pilot, adventurer, and author. The all-star cast included Clark Gable, Lionel and John Barrymore, Robert Montgomery, and Myrna Loy.

Both Barrymores were splendid actors, but I feared I'd be in trouble with John. There was no telling how we'd navigate through the long scene we had to play together. John had a tempestuous personality and a well-deserved reputation for throwing people off, for unnerving even the most experienced actors. He could turn nasty, I'd heard, for no apparent reason. Determined to give him no cause to blow up at me if I could help it, I memorized my lines until I could say them in my sleep.

John was known to use cue cards because his memory had become unreliable. Perhaps his consumption of alcohol through the years had affected his concentration. There was always someone standing at the side of a set, off-camera, holding up a large poster with his lines printed on it.

When we were about to shoot the scene, we took our places

and the camera began to roll. The scene unfolded without a hitch, as nearly perfect as one could get in a film, and I was greatly relieved.

Our director, Clarence Brown, was astonished. "I can't believe it, John," he said. "You didn't need the idiot cards. What happened?"

"I was working with a real actress," said John. "I didn't want to make a goddamn fool of myself."

That, coming from John Barrymore, America's great actor, remains my favorite notice.

While I was acting, Charlie was writing. In 1932, Thalberg produced *Rasputin and the Empress,* a historical melodrama starring the three Barrymores—Ethel, John, and Lionel. Charlie wrote the screenplay, and when the movie opened, he found himself with a million-dollar headache.

After the film was finished, but before it was released, studio higher-ups watching the rushes decided there wasn't enough of a motive for Prince Yusupov, played by John, to murder Rasputin, the mystical, oversexed advisor to the Russian royal family. There had to be some great provocation for the murder, so they decided to have Rasputin rape the prince's wife, played by a lovely English actress, Diana Wynyard.

Charlie was furious. "But their paths never crossed," he said.

"Doesn't matter," they said. "We need a motive the audience can understand."

They made Charlie write in a scene where the wife goes in to pray with Rasputin and comes out a wreck, hair streaming and head bowed, so that the audience will know that the worst has happened.

Charlie continued to object—he couldn't bear to deviate from the truth like that—but it was no use. The picture opened.

The next thing that happened was the real prince Yusupov

filed a million-dollar lawsuit against MGM, and also against the director and against Charles MacArthur, the writer. The Barrymores were left out; they were just puppets, I guess.

At the time, we were trying to assemble our beautiful house in Nyack, looking for furniture, draperies, while this suit was hanging over our heads. Usually, Charlie and I laughed at the same things, but I happened to joke that I thought even a Russian prince would like a particular color we were using, and Charlie hit the ceiling. It was no laughing matter to him.

The prince did win his suit against MGM; a million dollars was a lot of money in those days, so he decided to drop his suits against Charlie and the director.

Charlie had fewer complications writing for the theatre. He and Ben wrote another successful play, *Twentieth Century,* and the screen version starred our friend John Barrymore and Carole Lombard. Barrymore played a producer named Oscar Jaffe, who was modeled on David Belasco, with whom Charlie had so many adventures when he was doing *Lulu Belle*. On a train trip from Chicago to New York aboard the Twentieth Century Limited, Oscar tries to persuade his ex-wife, an actress played by Carole, to appear in his next play. The film was a merry romp, and the actors kicked up their heels in it.

Ethel Barrymore was an actress of great beauty, dignity, and warmth. Perhaps her finest achievement was the schoolteacher's role in *The Corn Is Green* in 1940.

Every year when income tax time draws near, I think of Ethel and her tax problems. At one time some agents from the Internal Revenue Service called on her and reminded her that she hadn't paid her taxes for several years, or hadn't paid enough. She was many thousands of dollars in arrears. "This is very serious," she was told.

I could picture Ethel sitting in her parlor, looking ever so dignified and unruffled. The tax men tried to explain that unless she paid up now, a lot of additional penalties would be piled on top of the amount she already owed. The total could be astronomical, rising day by day.

Finally, Ethel spoke. "Gentlemen," she said, "I've worked all my life, and I am very tired." The tax men were flabbergasted as she dismissed them with a grande-dame gesture.

Probably Ethel did look tired. She was middle-aged, had been on the stage for years, and that meant a lot of wear and tear. Word of her plight reached the ears of a VIP in Washington, maybe President Roosevelt himself. That person decided Ethel Barrymore was a national treasure and that she deserved better treatment. So a special law was passed, exempting her from income taxes, past, present, and future.

Everyone thought Ethel's theatre career was finished, that she would never earn another penny. But they didn't count on her resilience. After *The Corn Is Green* closed in 1942, someone asked her to come out to Hollywood. She didn't intentionally go looking for work, it just fell in her lap. She played in a movie titled *None But the Lonely Heart* and won the 1946 Oscar for best supporting actress. Having clicked, she became the formidable star again, earning loads of money, without having to pay a cent to Uncle Sam.

When I last saw Ethel, she was living in Gladys Cooper's house, which she took over. Gladys was the Ethel Barrymore of England, a supreme beauty and stage star. She had made a few pictures and bought herself a lovely house in Pacific Palisades. When Ethel was not feeling well, Gladys asked her to stay in her house until she recovered. But Ethel didn't get better and stayed put.

Calling on Ethel proved to be quite an experience. When you walked in the front door, you saw a television set facing you from the living room, turned up loud enough to be heard in the foyer.

The maid took you down a hallway, passing another TV set in a study. At the far end of the hall stood another set. They were all tuned to the same program and loud enough to be heard along the way.

Then you entered Ethel's bedroom—formerly Gladys'. There she was in a lacy bed jacket, sitting up in a bed covered with pink sheets. She looked beautiful, her skin exquisitely pale and a slight blush on her cheeks. She was watching a television set that stood at the foot of her bed, and it was tuned to the same program as the other sets scattered around the house. Whenever Ethel moved about, she didn't miss a frame of whatever show she was watching. This is the way she spent her last years.

Personally, I don't like television. Not only is the quality of the programs generally poor, but the actors murmur and mumble their way unintelligibly through them. The news anchormen don't speak clearly either; they drop whole syllables and consonant sounds. In the theatre, too, good clear diction is rare. When you go to a Broadway play, you pay forty-five or fifty dollars for a seat, and another five dollars for a little gadget that amplifies and clears the speech of actors who otherwise can't be understood or even heard.

One evening, friends took me to see *The Real Thing*, the Tom Stoppard play, starring Jeremy Irons and Glenn Close. We sat in the third row center, but I couldn't understand what was being said on stage. I was stricken, thinking my ears were at fault, though I had had no trouble hearing ordinary speech outside the theatre. Knowing my host had paid forty-five dollars each for three tickets, I couldn't be rude and say anything about the problem.

There was nothing to do but bluff it through. Seeing out of the corner of my eye that people were smiling, I tacked on a smile, too. If they laughed a little, I let out a titter. If the audience laughed heartily, I threw back my head and ha-haed. At the final curtain the audience stood up and applauded, an ovation that is now customary. Maybe my performance deserved a bit of applause too, for I'd worked as hard as anyone on stage to look appreciative.

Afterwards I said to my friends, lying through my teeth, "That was a wonderful evening. It was a fascinating play."

My host and his wife, both much younger than I am, smiled and nodded. Then he said, "I'm going to have to get a copy of the play and read it, because I didn't understand a lot of what the actors said tonight." And his wife nodded.

So they had both put on an act, as I had, pretending with the rest of the audience.

I think the movies and television are to blame for robbing actors of good speech. With high-powered microphones, actors now have to speak softly, and they've lost the ability to project. Afraid that they won't look pretty if they move their mouths or their faces too much, they don't enunciate clearly.

At the time when Charlie and I were working in Hollywood, actors who could speak the language were highly valued. That's why studio moguls, fearing that silent screen stars couldn't adapt to talkies, imported so many actors trained in the theatre. In the 1940s, when Ethel Barrymore was brought back to the screen, not only skillful acting but a beautiful voice and good diction were still highly prized.

After Irving Thalberg's death in 1936, there were signs that this golden era of Hollywood would wane. Charlie and I grieved, for we had loved and esteemed Irving. His untimely death removed a preeminent figure. MGM and the other studios survived for a while, continuing to turn out some good pictures, but then the studio system broke down. In the ensuing free-for-all, standards declined.

Irving's death brought to mind the good times we'd had with him and Norma. There had been bad times too—not Irving's fault but due to rivalry between the studios and the competitive hoopla of promotion people and gossip columnists.

I once got into a ticklish situation because Norma decided that I was her best friend, and so did Joan Crawford. Each of them said so in newspaper interviews. This was not particularly flattering, as no movie actress calls another a best friend whom she considers a rival. They are all fiercely competitive, or were at that time, fighting for the best scripts and roles, the most appealing leading men, the greatest studio attention.

Why Norma and Joan were at odds I wasn't sure, though Joan was quoted as saying, "How can you compete with someone who sleeps with the boss?" But surely they couldn't have been rivals for the same roles.

In any case, I found myself in an awkward situation: teetering on a tightrope between two "best friends." If either one guessed I was seeing the other, she might think I was being disloyal.

After Charlie and I moved back east, the friendship with Joan more or less petered out, though I'd see her now and then. With Norma, whom I was very fond of, the intimacy continued for a while, and she asked me to stay at her house when I visited California.

In later years, whenever a job took me out there, I'd make sure to call Norma. She would sound pleased to hear from me, but I could never get a glimpse of her; she never came near me. What had happened to our old friendship? I wondered. Had I done or said anything to offend her?

Trying to account for her withdrawal, I thought perhaps that Norma didn't want to be seen, as she aged, by one who had known her when she was young and beautiful. Or maybe she'd had a face-lift, as so many stars did, and it turned out badly, which sometimes happens. But all this was supposition, typical Hollywood supposition. I couldn't help thinking that I was lucky, because looking young and glamorous had never concerned me.

Some years after Irving Thalberg's death, I heard that Norma had remarried. Her second husband was a ski instructor named Martin Arrouge, who was a very good husband to her.

The next time I got to Hollywood, I phoned Norma just to say hello and see how she was. Martin answered, saying she was out. "I think I saw Norma going into a drugstore on Sunset Boulevard," I said. "I was in a car in traffic and couldn't stop. I waved and called out her name, but she ducked into the drugstore, and then the traffic moved on."

Norma never called back; instead she sent a letter to the house where I was staying. It was a sweet note saying she wished she could see me, but she had a cold and didn't want to expose me to it.

An acquaintance later explained Norma's attitude. When she had remarried and retired from the screen in 1942, she said that she "wanted to live quietly and privately." It was something she hadn't done for a long time, and it must have taken some getting used to.

Surprisingly, I did see Norma again. In the late 1960s, when I appeared with the APA-Phoenix Repertory Company in Los Angeles, Norma came to our opening night party. She was as warm and charming as ever, and we had a happy reunion.

≫·7·≪

The value attached to objects left behind by deceased celebrities defies understanding. When Joan Crawford's personal effects were auctioned after her death a few years ago, people vied avidly for everything, no matter how trivial. When I read about it, I thought Joan's ghost might be pleased that her name was still good box office and that her things drew such high bids. And I was reminded of the time when Joan showed off her possessions to a friend and me.

In the mid-fifties, we played the Hartford Theatre in Hollywood during a tour with Barrie's *What Every Woman Knows*. The cast included Bethel Leslie, a young protegée of mine who had been a friend of my daughter Mary. Bethel was trying to make her way in the theatre and was also planning to do a screen test for Sam Goldwyn. She thought it would be fun to meet Joan Crawford, so I called Joan and she asked us to lunch.

When the meal was over, Joan offered to show us around her house. After touring the elaborate ground-floor rooms, we went upstairs to her bedroom suite. She opened a door to reveal a walk-in closet about half a block long, with dozens of short dresses ranged along one side and lots of long dresses on the other. There were rows and rows of suits and cloth coats, and dozens of fur coats too. A second closet contained several hundred pairs of shoes.

"Bill Haines did this house for me. He knows every woman's needs," Joan said as she closed the doors.

"Every woman's needs, eh?" Bethel remarked when we left. "I've got two pairs of shoes, one for daytime and one for evening."

The contrast was striking. Though I earned good money, it was nowhere near a movie star's income. I didn't have to count pennies, but I didn't spend wildly either. Bethel and I both lived rather austerely, she out of need, I out of habit.

When Joan Crawford adopted me as her best friend back in the '30s, I couldn't understand why. We were such different types. Perhaps this glamorous fashion plate didn't feel threatened by me at MGM, and maybe she wanted a confidante. Joan was an extraordinary figure in the movie world, and I was fascinated by her.

Most people thought she was as hard as nails, like the characters she portrayed in pictures. But some of us sensed there was a vulnerable, insecure woman behind the tough mask. She had fought hard to escape impoverished beginnings, and I suppose she never stopped struggling to stay on top.

Joan had married and divorced several men. Her early husbands had "class," like Douglas Fairbanks, Jr., and Franchot Tone, who came from a very wealthy family. Living with a dominating woman like Joan couldn't have been easy. She wanted children but couldn't have any, so she adopted several. Joan was not quite rational in her raising of children. You might say she was strict or stern. But cruel is probably the right word.

I got to know her children, Christina and Christopher, who wound up in an institution. One day Joan brought them to a matinee of *What Every Woman Knows.* I always tried to give Joan's youngsters a lift, and it happened to be Christopher's birthday, so I'd had my dressing room festooned with balloons and a big sign saying HAPPY BIRTHDAY, CHRISTOPHER.

Christopher got very excited when they came in, but Joan was furious. She resented my turning his birthday into a celebration. She always resented anything anyone did for those kids.

When my young son Jim came to stay with me, we would go out to lunch with them. Joan would snap, "Christopher!" whenever he tried to speak. He would bow his little head, completely cowed, and then he'd say, "Mommie dearest, may I speak?" Joan's children had to say "Mommie dearest, may I speak?" before she allowed them to utter another word. It would have been futile for me or anyone else to protest. Joan would only get angry and probably vent her rage on the kids.

On one of my Hollywood trips about this time, I ran into Dinah Shore in the hairdressing department of MGM. She beckoned me to come over, then began talking in a whisper. "Helen, everybody knows that you're Joan Crawford's close friend. Can you do something about her treatment of those children? We're all worried to death."

I said, "Look, you people out here see her all the time. Why can't you say something?" and Dinah said, "That's the problem: we're around her all the time, and I don't think we could get away with it, but you come and go, Helen, so you could talk to her and then leave."

Well, I was frightened to do it. We were all afraid of Joan—which is always the biggest problem in this kind of situation, as we've seen with fatal results. No one would speak up.

I have read that people who are abused as children often become abusive parents. Maybe it was Joan's tough childhood that made her exert her power like that over her own children. But understanding the reason did not make their suffering any easier to watch.

86

I happened to be in L.A. on Christina's sixteenth birthday. At sixteen a girl starts going to parties, so I wanted to send her an evening bag as a gift. When I phoned Joan's house, her secretary answered. "Can you tell me how to get a gift to Christina?" I asked. "Is she still away at school or at home on vacation?"

"She's still at school," said the secretary. "It's closed for the summer, but her mother wanted her to stay there so she'd realize how much better off she was at home."

I was shocked. How could Joan condemn the girl to stay in school all alone, perhaps with just a few caretakers around? It must have felt like a prison to Christina. When I insisted on getting the gift to her, the secretary said, "Miss Crawford would rather not have the child receive any gifts." At that point I didn't care if Joan got mad. I managed to worm the school's address out of the factotum and sent the present there, but I never did find out whether Christina received it.

Joan married yet again and settled in New York. One night she gave a party for Ingrid Bergman. She had asked Ingrid for a list of friends to invite, and I was on it. Joan's husband, Alfred Steele, was the head of Pepsi-Cola, and his fellow Pepsi executives were invited too.

Joan's apartment was decorated all in white, even the carpets. You had to change into slippers at the door. It was like entering a mosque, but this was a temple to Mammon, not to Allah. I arrived at about eight o'clock, an hour after the cocktail party was to begin. The place was jammed with Pepsi men and their wives. But no Ingrid, and nobody else I knew either.

Now and then a serving cart sailed through like a comet, moving too fast for anyone to dip into the huge bowl of Beluga caviar—those delicious big gray eggs, with all the trimmings—nestled in a big swan of carved ice.

I was dying of boredom, annoyed that I'd come all the way from Nyack for this nonsense. When I was about to leave, the guest of honor finally showed up. I said hello and good-bye to Ingrid and headed for the door.

On the way out, I ran into Stanley Marcus and his wife. We chatted while waiting for the elevator. Apparently we'd missed each other among the crowd, which had spread through several rooms. From the hallway we looked through the open door and saw the serving cart being pushed around. "Did you have any of that caviar?" I asked. "No," Stanley said. "What do you say we go back in and get a big spoonful right now?"

We stopped the cart in mid-flight. The caviar looked pristine, not an egg out of place. We dug in, spread some on crackers, and munched, then beat a hasty retreat. In the elevator, on the way down, we decided that the cart must have been rented for the evening just for show and that no one was supposed to touch the caviar.

I didn't see much of Joan after that. I was occupied in the theatre, and she was preoccupied with Pepsi-Cola. She became a member of the board after her husband died. Her fame and flair for promotion must have proved useful.

Another good friend from my moviemaking days was Marion Davies—as different from Joan as day from night. Marion was warm, effervescent, and very generous. The MGM workers loved her because she always remembered their names and never forgot their birthdays. Charlie and I loved her.

Marion's longtime companion, the press lord William Randolph Hearst, was determined to make her a movie star after he discovered her as a chorine in *The Ziegfeld Follies*. She got very special treatment at the studio. An elaborately decorated mobile home followed her to whatever stage was set for her filming, and her personal chef cooked lunches in the kitchenette. Mr. Hearst would always take visiting dignitaries to Marion's trailer for lunch.

Other actors went to the commissary or to a restaurant, if time permitted. Some of us would just have a light lunch and a little rest in our dressing rooms before going back to work. I found relaxation during the midday break essential. But Marion had to preside at a table with the likes of George Bernard Shaw or Winston Churchill. Keeping up her end of the conversation couldn't have been easy.

After lunch she had to go back to her acting job. Mr. Hearst wouldn't let her out of that either. I always thought that the requirements made on her by Hearst contributed to Marion's excessive drinking. Sometimes she simply wouldn't stop after the champagne luncheons. She would sip a little champagne, perhaps to relax, and then would go on to brandy or whatever else she could get hold of. Maybe she had started drinking before she got to Hollywood, but her situation there may well have made the problem worse.

She must have had a high tolerance for alcohol, for she was never noticeably drunk during shooting. She was able to keep her wits about her and continue with her career.

Marion was a gifted comedienne and at her best in light romantic comedies. But Mr. Hearst, wanting her to be a great dramatic actress, pushed her into period extravaganzas like *Dorothy Vernon of Haddon Hall*, roles that didn't suit her at all. He poured millions into a production company founded for Marion, but most of the pictures she made under his aegis were failures.

Charlie and I first met Marion through her nephew, Charlie Lederer, a talented writer and a witty, engaging man, a boon companion of my Charlie. Lederer wrote the book for the stage musical *Kismet* and adapted *The Front Page* for a movie called *His Girl Friday*, based on Charlie and Ben's play. In the film Cary Grant played the irascible editor and Rosalind Russell was the reporter. The movie was a romantic comedy that lacked some of the play's bite, but it was entertaining and quite successful.

One night Charlie Lederer gave a party at his Beverly Hills house. He told us that Marion, his adored aunt, was coming, and he seemed proud that she'd be there.

I have to digress a bit before explaining what happened next. There had long been rumors that Marion had had a child, fathered by Hearst. The rumor mill then augmented the offspring to twins, perhaps because that made a better story. Hearst was very much in love with Marion and they were always together, but he couldn't marry her because his wife, who was a Catholic, wouldn't agree to a divorce. Hearst kept Marion in great style, doing all he could to promote her career. He even ordered his newspapers to mention her name at least once in every edition. The rumors about an illegitimate child were widely circulated, but no one knew what had become of the alleged baby—or twins.

A lot of Hollywood big shots showed up at Charlie Lederer's dinner party. But there was no sign of Marion. We were seated at the dinner tables when she finally swept in, followed by Truman Capote, who had made her his movieland–Beverly Hills crush. That wasn't surprising, since Marion had the requisite fame for Capote's taste and was a bubbly, fun-loving companion to boot.

Marion had a tendency to stutter when she got excited, an endearing trait. On this occasion she entered the dining room, looked around, and said, "Oh, h-h-hello, h-hello, everybody." Then, glancing back at Truman Capote behind her, she gave us all a big smile and said, "Oh yes, everybody. I want you to m-m-meet my illegitimate son by C-C-Calvin C-C-Coolidge."

Marion and Hearst had a lavish beach house in Santa Monica. To me it looked like a replica of Mount Vernon. One day we were invited to lunch there with several other guests. Marion hosted alone. Hearst was often away, attending to his newspapers' affairs; he was usually involved in some promotion scheme designed to amaze the readers and outdo the competition.

At that time he was underwriting the Graf Zeppelin, trying to get the first detailed story of its flight from New York to Los Angeles. His wife Millicent had broken a bottle of champagne on the zeppelin before it took off, and Marion was supposed to greet it upon its arrival in Los Angeles.

During lunch, Marion got word that Mrs. Hearst had left New York and was rushing to the family ranch in San Luis Obispo so that she could greet the zeppelin when it reached L.A.

In front of her guests, Marion asked a servant to bring her a telephone. She dialed Hearst's private number and politely told the secretary who answered that she wanted to speak to Mr. Hearst. When he got on the phone, she asked him, "Wh-wh-who gets the Graf Zeppelin? Me or the other p-p-party?" Marion got it. There wasn't anything he wouldn't do for her.

Charlie and I first visited San Simeon, the enormous Hearst estate, with Irving Thalberg and Norma Shearer. Among the other weekend guests were two governors, the renowned Hearst editor Arthur Brisbane, Charlie Chaplin (a regular visitor there), and some other notables from the worlds of film and politics. Film and politics were Hearst's chief interests, besides journalism.

The dining table could seat at least twenty, maybe more. Hearst sat at one end, with me at his right. Marion presided at the other end, with the guests arrayed between them. Conversation was pretty much confined to those seated beside you, for general chat was impossible at such a huge table. I don't remember any tidbits of Mr. Hearst's talk—this was back in the 1930s—but he was a considerate host who let his guests carry the ball.

Charlie and I were quite impressed by the place. So much has been written about San Simeon that a detailed description would be superfluous. Some people considered it a gloomy mausoleum. To us it looked like an awesome castle, with vast grounds and lots of outbuildings, erected by an eighteenth-century monarch reincarnated as a twentieth-century press king.

One of the first marvels I noticed was in the bathroom of our suite. On the wall behind the door was a Murillo madonna. The whole house was chock-full of priceless art. Hearst owned so many pieces that they couldn't all be displayed. On a refectory table downstairs were half a dozen large albums, about two feet square and a foot thick, containing photographs of the artworks stored in warehouses: paintings, sculpture, woodwork, silver. Hearst was one of those monomaniacal collectors, and he had the wherewithal to indulge his mania.

Another visit, years later, was entirely different from that first one. We weren't headed for San Simeon, but Marion insisted that we stop over.

Charlie and I were driving from San Francisco to Los Angeles for the opening of *Victoria Regina.* I had quit the movies and gone back to the theatre. *Victoria* became my biggest hit, and now, after a long Broadway run, we were taking it on a cross-country tour.

I wondered how *Victoria* would be received in L.A. Then, as now, anything that happened beyond the hermetic confines of the film colony, beyond the mental horizons of its inhabitants, for most of them simply didn't exist. If it wasn't part of their little world, they weren't interested—and they still aren't.

It was around this time that Fred Astaire decided to quit the movies. He talked to the boss of RKO, the company he was working for then. "This means the end for you," the boss said. "What are you going to do?"

"I'll get along," said Fred. "I'll go back to the theatre."

The boss scoffed at the idea. "Do you know anyone who has done that?" he asked.

"Yes," Fred replied, "Helen Hayes."

"And look what's happened to her," said the boss.

At the time I was acting in *Victoria Regina,* a national hit, but he knew nothing about it.

Well, I was pretty nervous on the way to the L.A. opening with Charlie. The words "And look what's happened to her" kept running through my mind. I was afraid that the audience might scorn me or arrive so late that the first two or three scenes would be ruined.

On the way down the coast we passed through San Luis Obispo, where San Simeon was. "Let's give Marion a call," Charlie suggested.

"Oh, Charlie, wait a minute," I protested. "You know how nervous I am about the opening, and I have a masseuse coming tonight. Let's not call."

But Charlie thought that since we were so close, we ought to call Marion. If she wasn't there, we'd just leave our regards. We hadn't seen her in a long time. I cared about Marion, and Charlie did too, so I gave in.

We stopped at a drugstore, and Charlie went inside to a phone booth. A few minutes later he came back to the car. "You'd better come and talk to her," he said. "I can't reason with her. She wants us to come and spend the night. She won't listen to me. Maybe you can convince her that we can't stay."

I went to the phone and found he was right: Marion insisted, stammering, "J-j-just come up. P-p-please do." I told her we were due in L.A. and I had a masseuse coming that night. "I have one here," said Marion. "You c-c-can get a m-m-massage right here. You and Charlie s-s-sleep here tonight and go in the morning." I argued, but she wouldn't take no for an answer. We wound up at the ranch.

Marion led us to the same suite we'd stayed in before. "The masseuse will come up later," she said as she was leaving. "You're coming down to dinner, aren't you?" I thought not. I was tired from our drive and couldn't eat anything. "Oh, you must come down to dinner. P-p-please."

She was stammering awfully, nervous as a kitten. I wondered

why until she went over to a window and looked out. "There he goes, the old son of a bitch!" she exclaimed. "He hasn't spoken to me for four days."

I looked out and saw a big figure—Hearst. Iron-gray hair, iron-gray suit, and two gray terriers at his heels. They were walking off into the twilight. "If you c-c-come down to dinner," said Marion, "he'll have to s-s-speak to me."

With nerves already taut and Marion's problem in mind, I went down to dinner with Charlie. We sat at the same long table, Hearst at one end, Marion at the other. But this time there were only two guests besides Charlie and me: Dorothy Dalton, a one-time screen star and a close friend of Marion's, and Lloyd Pantages, a devotee of Marion's whose father owned a string of theatres. What a bleak dinner it was! We had to shout to make ourselves heard across the endless table. Hearst, looking glum, didn't say much. Marion sat quietly, staring longingly at Hearst. She really loved him, and later proved it: when Hearst went broke, she pawned her great jewelry collection to bail him out. We beat a hasty retreat after the meal.

When the masseuse came to my room that night, she told me that she was really not a masseuse but a nurse. "Mr. Hearst hired me to take care of Marion because she's been drinking and he can't stop her." She was a talker, and I wasn't averse to listening.

She said that Marion had somehow got hold of liquor. Everyone suspected that Lloyd Pantages had brought her some. (If so, he wasn't the only one. Friends had told me that guests started sneaking liquor to her after Hearst outlawed alcohol. The fools thought they were doing her a favor.)

"Mr. Hearst detected it," the nurse went on, "and he was enraged. He hasn't talked to Marion for days."

They had been rattling around in that vast house in silence. Marion must have thought that it was a godsend when Charlie and I dropped by. Hearst talked to us, of course, and so ended up talking to Marion. So I suppose our reluctant visit did them some good.

Eventually Marion and Hearst moved from their permanent home, a Beverly Hills mansion, and into a small house that they found more comfortable, where Marion could be closer to him, occupying a bedroom next to his. By then Hearst's health was deteriorating rapidly. When the doctors told Marion that the end was near, she sat up with him night after night. She was exhausted.

One night, a doctor told her that she was near the breaking point. "Marion," he said, "you've got to get some sleep. You can't go on like this. I'm going to give you an injection to make you relax." Marion protested, but the doctor insisted. "I'll give you this injection, and you'll get a good night's sleep. You must do it if you want to be any help to him."

The shot knocked her out. She awoke late the next morning, feeling so groggy that it took her a few moments to come to. When she finally got out of bed and ran into Hearst's room, she was stunned to find him gone. There was no sign of him or of any of his belongings. It was as if he'd risen from his deathbed and walked away. Everything connected with Hearst and Marion had been removed—clothing, photographs, mementos.

She called her nephew Charlie Lederer, who later told us the story. "C-c-come over here," Marion said to him. "I'm in trouble. They've taken him away, and I don't know what to do."

Lederer rushed to the house and found Marion sitting by a window, sadly looking out at the small garden. He was shocked when he heard what had happened. "Marion," he asked, "is there anything I can do?"

"Y-y-yes," said Marion. "You can cancel my subscription to the *Los Angeles Examiner.*"

The *Examiner,* of course, was a Hearst paper.

They later found out that Hearst had died the night before.

The attending nurse had telephoned Hearst's physician and his family, and the corpse and personal belongings had been hastily removed to protect the family's reputation.

Some time after Hearst's death, Marion finally got married, to a Captain Horace G. Brown. I never met the man, but I heard she was happy with him. She deserved happiness.

8

It was a scene out of a Charlie Chaplin movie: the funniest man in the world is banished from the land where he has achieved his greatest success and fame. Finally, after many years, he is brought back to receive the formal recognition due him. This is his vindication, his night-of-nights. The crowd is on its feet, applauding, cheering. But the frail figure is too old to enjoy it.

Even before Charlie Chaplin returned to the United States for the Academy Awards ceremony honoring him, a great revival of his films was under way. I think you can safely say that somewhere, always, a Chaplin film is playing. He was called "the funniest man in the world." That wasn't hyperbole; it happened to be true. Chaplin was not only an incomparable comedian on screen, he was funny in real life. He would improvise hilarious scenes to amuse his friends, then use some of those impromptu bits in his movies.

We first met Chaplin during one of his visits to New York in the mid-1920s. At the time, Charlie and I were courting and working in the theatre. We had no idea that we would ever get involved in filmmaking, but we were eager to meet one of the screen's great talents at a party at Alice Duer Miller's house in town. Mrs. Miller was a well-known writer and a favorite among the Algonquin Round Table crowd. She was an elegant aristocrat from an old New York family, but quite unconventional for a blueblood: not only did she become a novelist and playwright, but she also conducted an "open marriage." She lived in the old Duer family mansion on Gracie Square, which later became the official residence of New York City's mayor.

We had gone to the party with Alec Woollcott, who grew edgy, crusty, as the evening wore on, annoyed because Chaplin had promised to join him but failed to show up. Alec was always temperamental, and his ego couldn't stand rejection.

It was quite late when we left Mrs. Miller's house and headed for home. Four of us—Charlie MacArthur and I, Alec Woollcott, and Irving Berlin—were walking along a quiet East Side street when a taxi careened around a corner and roared toward us. It stopped with a jerk and out tumbled Charlie Chaplin.

He explained that he'd been delayed elsewhere and urged us to get into the cab and go back to Mrs. Miller's with him. We protested that it was too late, that the party was over.

We went to Irving Berlin's place instead. This was before he married Ellin Mackay, and he was living in a little walk-up on West Forty-fourth Street, two flights above a store. We made our way upstairs, and Charlie, Alec, and I sat down and became the audience while Chaplin and Berlin entertained themselves and us. It was their first meeting, and they were bent on impressing each other. Irving played song after song on his small upright piano, which he could play only in the key of F♯. He changed keys by pressing a little lever. A tune he had just finished, called "Remember," which he sang in his reedy voice, became Charlie's and my special lovers' song.

That night at Irving's lasted till dawn. He and Chaplin fed on one another's talent, each trying to outperform the other. Chaplin mimicked an actor doing Hamlet's soliloquy. The actor, suffering from a hangover, absentmindedly picked his nose and was unable to remove from his finger what he had brought forth. Chaplin delivered the soliloquy as beautifully as I've ever heard it read, which made even more comical the actor's predicament.

Chaplin could be crude. He liked bathroom jokes. He'd been through the rough and tumble of English music halls, and though I didn't care for coarse humor, I couldn't resist his hilarious performance that night.

Years later, I was reminded of that night. I was at the Kennedy Center in Washington for the annual honors ceremony. A chorus sang "God Bless America" and "Alexander's Ragtime Band" in a tribute to Irving Berlin. Then two torch singers came on stage and sang "Remember." I began to cry in the middle of that crowd of people. It was embarrassing, but that tune, "our song," stirred up so many memories of the years with my husband, who had died long ago.

There was a time, before Chaplin married Oona O'Neill, when his life was plagued by marital and legal problems. To escape them, he came to New York and checked into a hotel. One night, he went out to some event and got word that he was about to be served with a summons. He rushed out and ducked into the first taxi that came along. Fearing the process server would be waiting at his hotel, Chaplin told the cabby to just keep driving around Central Park.

Every time they finished another circuit, the driver would ask, "Go 'round again?" Finally he complained. "It's getting late, sir," he said. "I have a family and I'd like to go home, if you don't mind. I have to work tomorrow morning. What's the point of all this, anyway?"

"I'll tell you," Chaplin said. "My name is Charlie Chaplin—"

The driver turned on the light and stared back at his passenger. "So you are!" he exclaimed in amazement.

When Chaplin explained his problem, the driver said, "I have

99

to go home and get some sleep. I live up in the Bronx. It's nothing fancy, but if you're afraid to go home tonight, I can take you to my place. You can sleep in my son's bed. He's only ten, so you'll have enough room. He won't bother you."

And that's what they did. When they reached the cab driver's apartment, they went to the son's bedroom. Charlie took off his shoes and lay down beside the sleeping child.

Worn out by the stressful night, Charlie awoke rather late. The little boy was gone, and so was the cab driver, but the cab driver's wife was in the kitchen. She offered him a cup of coffee, staring at him as if she couldn't believe her eyes. Charlie thanked her, but said he had to leave.

When he went down the stairs and out the front door, he was greeted by a milling crowd of children yelling, "Charlie! Charlie!"

The driver's son must have been astonished to find a stranger sleeping beside him. Either he'd recognized Charlie or his father had told him who the guest was, and the boy had rushed out to alert the neighborhood kids.

By the way, Chaplin eventually got the summons.

He once told me another story about an experience he had had in Paris. He was riding in a taxi when he felt a sudden urge to relieve himself. In broken French he told the driver he had to find a pissoir. No problem, said the driver, pointing to a little kiosk on the next corner and saying, *"Voilà!"*

Charlie was somewhat leery, but the cabby assured him it would be all right. As he ventured inside, Chaplin passed a number of men going in and out, and he kept saying, "I beg your pardon."

When he emerged, an applauding throng shouted, "Bravo, Charlot!" Charlie said he wasn't sure whether the ovation was for his artistry or the duration of the act.

We continued to see Charlie when my husband and I got to California. After our regular hitch there, we went back occasionally on some errand or for a movie or because I was touring in a play. We would catch up with old friends like Anita Loos, who served Sunday brunches at her house in Santa Monica. My husband and I, Aldous Huxley and his wife Maria, and Chaplin and his then wife, Paulette Goddard, were among the coterie that often gathered at Anita's.

Huxley, the author of *Brave New World,* was one of the eminent European refugees who had settled in California. He had come from England with his wife and their son Matthew in 1938. When World War II broke out the following year, they thought of going back. Although Huxley, a pacifist, couldn't serve in the army, he wanted to help his friends and relations back home, and decided he could best do this by working in Hollywood and sending them money and provisions.

Oddly enough, this outstanding writer was diffident about seeking a scriptwriting job, feeling that he might not be up to it. But Anita convinced him that he was far too modest. She recommended him to MGM, where he wrote scripts for literate movies such as *Pride and Prejudice.*

We used to visit the Huxleys at a house they had rented on a ranch in the midst of a redwood grove, a rugged place with big picnic tables and benches on the grounds. Charlie Chaplin joined us there on one occasion and treated us to a remarkable performance.

He was then working on his film *The Great Dictator,* and he wanted to try out a scene he was designing. He picked up a ball—I think it was a beach ball young Matthew had left on the ground. Then he leaped as light as a fawn onto a redwood table and began to dance around with the ball. In the film he used a globe instead of a ball. He held the globe in his hand and danced around, impersonating Hitler. Here was Charlie doing a graceful ballet on a shaky table on uneven ground. We all stood watching in awe.

The negative side of this comic genius was that sometimes

101

Chaplin could be an awful bore. I think he was convinced that he was a genius in *every* field, and he would lecture us unmercifully on his pet subjects and philosophies. One day at the Huxleys', his theme was "Why do they say a girl is 'ruined' by a man?" He left his chair and stood up to deliver an oration about how it never ruined any girl to have sexual relations with a man. "Why do they say she is 'ruined'?" he kept asking, but none of us thought he wanted an answer. He was defending the destroyers of young girls' innocence, their virginity, by saying nothing was destroyed, that in reality, the girls' lives were enriched. It sounded as if he was making an apology for his own behavior; his experiences with young women and girls were widely publicized.

We all sat there like eggs in a basket, unmoving, while he expounded this latest theory. Sometimes Charlie and I would plan in advance how we would escape from a party if Chaplin were there too and got wound up.

Chaplin was always a nonconformist, but as the years passed, his fame and his genius weren't enough to keep him out of trouble. He married young Oona, whose father, Eugene O'Neill, was so outraged he disowned her. Oona was eighteen; Chaplin, her father's age. In 1952, they went to live in Switzerland, leaving behind an array of charges against Chaplin that ranged from a paternity suit and a Mann Act indictment to being called a "fellow traveler" of the Communists. He was under investigation by the FBI and the IRS. Chaplin vowed never to return to the United States. He had remained a British subject, so he escaped the final indignity of having his American passport withdrawn. In 1975, in fact, he was knighted by Queen Elizabeth II.

The Chaplins settled in Vevey, Switzerland, where they raised a large brood of children. In 1972, an old man, he finally relented and returned to the United States to receive a special Academy award. He had never been given an Oscar, possibly because he was a sort of embarrassment to the movie colony. During his filmmaking years he was often in trouble over dating minors, paternity suits, divorces, back taxes, and those political charges.

I was among the people presenting awards on the night Chaplin was honored. It was sad to see him looking so aged and vague, completely unlike his former buoyant self. He remained backstage until he came forward to accept his award, and that was that.

After the ceremony, we all went to a hotel for the usual party. I was seated with friends when I spotted Chaplin and Oona, with some of their children, at a table nearby. For old times' sake, I felt like saying hello.

I went over to their table, introduced myself to Oona, and told her I'd like to say hello to Charlie.

"Charlie," Oona said, leaning over, "it's Helen Hayes."

He looked around blankly and blinked. Oona repeated my name.

"Oh, Helen Hayes!" Chaplin exclaimed. "I always wanted to marry you."

My head spun. How strange that I never knew anything about this, I thought. Then I realized that he probably made the same remark to any white-haired woman who spoke to him.

Another actor once made a similar crack on another occasion. It was at the Keeneland Racetrack in Lexington, Kentucky, where I was watching the races with the track president, his wife, and several other guests seated in the president's box. Someone saw Mickey Rooney sitting with a couple of men in a nearby box. Did I know him? I was asked. Only slightly; we'd met in passing at benefits and other events.

Our group wanted to meet Mickey, so they sent word, and he soon joined us. His greeting was effusive and we embraced, as actors invariably do—we hug whether we know each other or not. He was introduced to everyone, and he complimented the racing program. I'd been told that he loved horses and followed them everywhere.

103

Mickey soon excused himself, saying he had to get back to his friends. Then suddenly he whirled, squinted at me, and pointed his finger. "Was I ever married to you?" he asked.

I'm sure he made that remark often, but it tickled me just the same, as a good exit line always does.

Chaplin was one actor who seemed to enjoy life after leaving Hollywood. He lived quietly with his family in Vevey until his death in 1977. To those of us who knew him, his flaws were human, his talent divine. We all remembered what he'd contributed to our lives.

But he was not allowed to rest in peace in Vevey. Grave robbers stole his coffin from the local cemetery. We were shocked by the grisly news, and before his corpse finally was returned, various theories were aired about who had done it and why.

I heard the purported inside story from a friend, who said that Chaplin's family had hushed it up. God only knows where she got the lowdown—presumably from some "reliable source."

Four of us were sitting one afternoon in Dorothy Stickney's apartment in New York. Dorothy may be best remembered for acting with her husband, Howard Lindsay, in the long-running *Life with Father.* Dorothy had Lynn Fontanne as a houseguest, and Anita Loos and I had dropped in for a cup of tea with them. Anita always had a weakness for wanting to know the inside story about everything, and she proudly produced her offering for this occasion: the inside, unpublished story of the theft of Chaplin's corpse and how Oona got it back.

Chaplin had been buried in consecrated ground, she began, probably at the behest of Oona, who had a Catholic background. His grave had been dug up and the coffin stolen, as we had read in the newspapers. What we didn't know were the details.

Oona received a letter from the perpetrators, left in an envelope at the gate of their estate, Anita said. The letter told her the corpse would be returned on one condition: that Oona bury him on their own estate and not in consecrated ground. They—whoever had the body—thought Chaplin was a Communist Jew and they didn't want him in their cemetery. Following the terms set in the letter, Oona delivered her reply and left it on the gate. Yes, she said, she would bury his body on the estate. In the dark of night, the coffin was brought back and left just inside the gate to the property, to be buried, again, but this time quietly within the walls.

We were aghast, saying, "Oh, what a story . . . oh, how awful . . . oh, how terrible," keening over it.

After a pause, Lynn said with great elegance, as if she were delivering a line on stage, "And how is deah Charlie?" It gave us all another jolt, but she was then pushing ninety and it wasn't surprising that her mind wandered sometimes.

As a young actress on the London stage, Lynn was discovered by Laurette Taylor, who brought her over to the States to appear in a play with her. After Lynn met Alfred Lunt, whose career got off to a flying start in Booth Tarkington's *Clarence,* she became a regular stage-door Jane, picking him up every night.

In those days Lynn had no class whatever. Though tall, she was awkward and always looked bedraggled, somewhat like Eliza Doolittle. After she married Alfred and they began acting together, however, Lynn evolved into a stunning, suave, exquisitely groomed woman. Alfred and Lynn became the premier acting couple in the theatre, playing in sophisticated comedies like Molnar's *The Guardsman* and in more serious plays by Shakespeare, Chekhov, and Shaw.

Alfred, Lynn, and I became close friends and often saw each other when we lived in New York. While Charlie and I were courting and he would stop by the theatre to take me home, I'd often take him along to the Lunts' for supper. Like many of our friends at the time, they lived in a walk-up in a converted brownstone. The side streets near the theatre district, between Fifth and Sixth avenues, or Fifth and Madison, were full of such buildings.

One night Charlie stopped me in the hall just outside the Lunts' door and said, "If they go on talking shop like they always do, I'm going to butt in and tell them all about the trouble I had when my typewriter ribbon broke in the middle of a paragraph." He was speaking in a desperate whisper. "I'm going to dramatize that story and keep them silent for an hour while I tell them all about my typing problem."

"If you do that," I said, "I'll never speak to you again!" We stood there nose to nose, having a terrible argument.

Finally, he gave in. "All right," he said, "I'll listen to them one more night."

We went inside and, by God, Alfred and Lynn launched right into their usual rigmarole about what had happened at their show that evening. The theatre was their life, and they scarcely knew what was going on in the outside world. We used to joke about their having no home life: between shows they were hung up in their dressing rooms in cellophane bags to keep the dust out.

Years later, after they had more or less retired and settled in Genesee Depot, Wisconsin, I used to visit them for a week every year. Genesee was a one-horse town with a general store, a garage, and a railroad freight depot. The Lunts had a big spread where they played gentlemen farmers—it had been Alfred's family home—but there was nothing rustic about their house. It was elegantly furnished with antiques and mementos of their great stage hits.

As the years passed, Alfred's sight began to fail. He had taken up painting and was good at it, but he had to give it up. He and Lynn used to play a card game called "Spite and Malice," so I bought him some cards with large faces and figures, but he became almost blind and couldn't see even those. The only thing

106

he never gave up was cooking; he was a gourmet chef and actually wrote—or dictated—a cookbook.

Out of the blue one day, Alfred called me at my home in Nyack. "I have to tell you, Helen," he began, "that I've been laughing for a good hour about you and me. I've been recalling some of our times in *Clarence,* and laughing so hard that I had to call and tell you."

"What made you think of that?" I asked.

"You know I can't see anymore," he said. "I can't read or play cards or watch television. I'm tired of the radio programs, and I can't stand rock music. My cooking has gone to pot because I can't see the ingredients. But I found out what I like to do."

"What's that?"

"I just sit and remember."

After Alfred died of cancer, Lynn, who was about ten years older than he, stayed on in their Genesee house, with her memories and mementos. Except for the ailments and frailties of old age, she was able to live comfortably on what she and Alfred had set aside for their retirement. She survived into her nineties.

Mrs. Patrick Campbell, a close friend of George Bernard Shaw, was another British actress who came to Hollywood looking for a movie job. But she was in her seventies and had less foresight— or less luck—than Lynn. She was reputed to have been Shaw's mistress, but that claim was disputed, for he was known to be far more partial to the passions of the mind than to those of the flesh. However that may be, Shaw certainly was an ardent admirer of Stella Campbell. He had written *Pygmalion* for her, and she originated the role of Eliza Doolittle when she was in her forties. Many considered her too old for the part, but nobody ever played it better.

Mrs. Pat, as she was called, was capricious and had an acid tongue. Her performances were so unpredictable—marvelous one night, indifferent the next, depending on her mood—that producers were afraid to hire her. All the same, she appeared in many London hits and made several grand tours of the States.

She led a very tough life, supporting a feckless husband, two children, and some of her siblings. Once, when she ran short of money, she threatened to sell the love letters Shaw had written her. (He had written some to Ellen Terry too, though they were never lovers.) To stop her, the affluent Shaw grudgingly gave her some cash.

Finally, after several of her plays failed, she decided to try her luck in Hollywood. This was in the early '30s, when Charlie and I were out there. Our old friend Ned Sheldon, who knew Mrs. Pat, asked us to look after her, a daunting prospect. I feared that entertaining the formidable Mrs. Campbell would be more than I could handle, as I was still very shy and retiring. Still, we admired her, and her plight aroused our sympathy, so we decided to do whatever we could for her.

We had already met her in New York when she was the guest of honor at a dinner given by Herbert Bayard Swope, the editor of *New York World* and a wonderful, bumptious character whom we all loved. He used to serve fried egg and onion sandwiches at his place around midnight. We would eat, catch up on news and gossip, and sometimes play amusing word games.

Herbert was a nonstop talker. In fact, he didn't just talk, he bellowed. If you were tired, as I was after performances, you could just listen quietly while he boomed on.

At this particular dinner party, Mrs. Pat was seated at his right. He was in full voice, and she listened patiently with her elbow on the table, chin resting on her hand. Every once in a while she'd make a funny little warbling sound. Finally, Herbert paused and asked, "What are you doing?"

"That was a word trying to get in edgewise," she said. A tough and witty lady, not exactly lovable, but fascinating.

When Mrs. Campbell descended on Hollywood, I found there was no need to worry about entertaining her. Her fame had preceded her, and everybody was eager to meet her and give a party for her. A British celebrity had deigned to visit the colonies, and the natives were eager to show off their style. Mrs. Pat was not about to let down her side.

"Sit beside me and don't leave me," she said to me on the way to a party at Pickfair, the home of Mary Pickford and Douglas Fairbanks. I sat beside her, thinking that she might be a bit nervous, which was somehow reassuring.

As various guests approached our table to pay their respects, Mrs. Pat would murmur to me, "Who's this?" and I would name the person. "What is your name?" she asked when Harold Lloyd came to greet her. When he told her, she said, "Oh, are you in pictures?"

This routine soon began to annoy the other guests. Word spread, and they started to avoid her. Some of those stars were pretty self-important and were not about to suffer condescension from the likes of Mrs. Campbell. She may have been a great star herself, once, but now she was just a has-been. I could imagine the whispers behind her back. These people could be cruel. Bebe Daniels, who now came forward to beard the lioness, took another tack. "Bebe Daniels," I whispered to Mrs. Campbell, "a big star."

"What is your name?" Mrs. Pat asked.

And Bebe replied, "Mrs. Patrick Campbell. What's yours?"

Irving Thalberg gave Mrs. Pat the grand tour of the studio and a fancy luncheon. Then, one night, Irving and Norma entertained her at home. After dinner they screened one of Norma's films. When it was over, Mrs. Pat said to Irving, "Your wife is charming. Such a dainty little creature she is. Such tiny hands, a tiny waist, and tiny, tiny eyes."

This much-quoted remark did her in. It symbolized her attitude toward movie people. She wanted a job—that's why she was there. She had always been able to awe people with her acid tongue everywhere else, and she thought she could carry it off in Hollywood too. But Mrs. Campbell made two mistakes: she was catty about Norma to Irving, and she failed to realize how much competition there was from other acid tongues in Hollywood.

By that time Mrs. Campbell was well past her prime. She had grown fat and blowsy; only slight vestiges of her former beauty were left, and she could play only character roles. But she wasn't above joking about her appearance, and I liked her for that.

Finally, she did get a job. She appeared alongside Peter Lorre in a film of Dostoyevsky's *Crime and Punishment,* playing the old lady murdered by Raskolnikov. A sad comedown for a great actress who had made theatre history. She was a gutsy woman, willing to take what she could get. I felt sorry for her, yet privileged to have known her.

≫·9·≪

Before our adventures in Hollywood began, Charlie and I lived in an apartment on East End Avenue in Manhattan, and that's where we celebrated our daughter Mary's first birthday. We decided to give a buffet supper, a drink and a toast to the baby after the theatre. It was the zaniest party a child could ever have: while our baby slept in her cradle, the grown-ups carried on in the parlor. The guests were a smorgasbord of the people we knew—the Round Table crowd, artists, writers, actors, opera stars, and what-have-you.

Charlie was not satisfied with the invitation I composed, to be sent by telegram. "You can't invite all those people just for a baby's party," he said. "What we need is a guest of honor, a special guest." He decided to send a telegram inviting guests to a party to meet Mr. Al Capone, "Scarface." I protested, but Charlie insisted that everyone would know it was a joke.

Nobody sent regrets, and guests poured into our party. Charlie was posted at the door to deal with his own trickery: it was too much for me. He acted as though everyone should have known it was just a put-on.

Most people laughed it off. They knew that Charlie liked practical jokes, and if any of them felt let down, they soon rallied amidst the general hilarity. Except for Lucrezia Bori. The Metropolitan Opera star, who had been a friend of Charlie's before she adopted me too, was incensed. "I weel keel you!" she cried. Mme Bori insisted that she had been lured to the party by the promise of meeting Scarface.

Finally Charlie thought of a way to appease her. Howard Ellis, Al Capone's lawyer in Chicago, was a friend of his. He phoned Howard and said, "Can you get Al Capone on the phone for me or tell me how I can reach him? Lucrezia Bori is here at our baby's birthday party, and she won't be satisfied until she talks to Al Capone."

Charlie called from the phone in his den, but he asked me to listen on the extension in my room. Howard, of course, was astonished. Why in the world would Mme Bori want to talk to Al Capone—and at a baby's birthday party yet? Charlie explained the hoax to Howard, but Howard replied that he couldn't possibly call "the big boy" at that hour. "He goes to bed early." As if Scarface was a potentate needing his sleep before tackling important matters the next day.

But Charlie pressed on, and Howard finally relented. He was crazy about Charlie and, like most of Charlie's friends, was putty in his hands.

Pretty soon Capone was on the phone. Charlie had never interviewed him in his days as a reporter, since Capone never granted interviews. Yet the crime boss knew who Charlie was, probably because Charlie had written plenty of stories about him.

"I know you, Charlie MacArthur," said Capone. "And I know you don't have Lucrezia Bori there."

"I swear to God," Charlie protested. "She's right here and she wants to talk to you."

"Put her on the phone," Capone said. "If she sings the second aria from act one of *La Traviata,* I'll know if it's Lucrezia Bori. Only then will I speak to her."

It was a sign of the madness of our lives that America's top hoodlum would be talking opera with Charlie. Capone was reputed to be a great music lover who had a box at the Chicago Opera.

"Put her on," he repeated. "Have her sing 'Sempre Libre.' That's her great aria. If I'm satisfied it's Bori, I'll talk to her."

Well, Bori picked up the phone and sang like an angel. Capone recognized her voice, and they had a little chat. Then she made peace with Charlie.

The soprano, for years an idol of the Metropolitan Opera, was an elegant Spanish lady and a superb singer, but she had the reputation of being a cold, dispassionate woman. As far as anyone knew, she never had a lover. She once told me that Giulio Gatti-Casazza, the general manager of the Met, called her a Baked Alaska.

"He say, 'You are all warm and exciting on the outside,'" she recalled. "'But inside you are cold ice cream. Warm outside, freezing inside.'"

Bori spent her life cultivating her voice and called it her "lover." But later in her career, her only lover failed her. It was a sad irony that the dedicated Bori should suffer the kind of calamity that happens to singers who don't train or use their voices properly, as she did. The trouble began when she developed a node on a vocal cord. In those days there were no lasers to remove it; instead, doctors trimmed nodes surgically. A surgeon accidentally nicked the vocal cord during the operation.

Lucrezia was ordered to be silent for six months, forbidden to make a sound until the wound healed. She recuperated at her villa on the Riviera, and friends came to her aid. They took turns sitting up with her night after night, never leaving her alone, trying to keep her from falling asleep, because there was a risk

113

that she might cough and reopen the wound. They would let her doze off for a while, but if she got restless, they'd wake her up and keep her up with talk and music.

When the ordeal was over, Bori was triumphant. "I knew my lover would come back," she said, "I knew it—and he did!" Indeed, her voice was fully restored, and she went on singing beautifully at the Met.

Charlie and I led a fairly active social life, but we didn't throw big parties and stopped playing the kind of tricks that annoyed Mme Bori. Too often we were away from home, especially after we started working on movies.

During my semiannual reprieves I'd rush back to New York, alone or with Charlie if he could get away. We kept our apartment as a base and as a home for little Mary. We hated leaving her behind, in the care of a nursemaid and housekeeper, when she was too young to be trundled along on our travels.

Charlie would usually find a suitable house to rent in Hollywood before my six-months' movie stint began. One of those temporary dwellings was particularly well-equipped: it had a large master bedroom with twin beds, a dressing room, and bath; several guest rooms and baths; and downstairs, an elaborate living room, dining room, and kitchen, and even a game room with a big billiard table.

In the evening Charlie often went his own way, since he didn't have to rise at the crack of dawn to get to a movie set. I usually worked late, and it was a relief to get home, have a light supper, and go straight to bed.

One night Charlie went out with some of his cronies. When I awoke early the next morning and looked at the twin bed next to mine to make sure he was there, I saw a stranger with a very red face lying in Charlie's place!

It was Robert Benchley, Charlie's friend and roommate during their bachelor days in New York. Bob was now writing and acting in humorous movie shorts. Why was he sleeping in Charlie's bed? And where was Charlie? I pulled on a dressing gown and went around the house looking for him. I found him lying peacefully asleep on the billiard table, wrapped in its canvas cover.

As we grew increasingly disenchanted with filmmaking and with our nomadic way of life, we began to look for a way out. A solution came along at just the right time. Our agent, Leland Hayward, arranged for Charlie and Ben Hecht to make films at the Astoria Studio on Long Island. It was a dream of a deal: a million dollars to write, produce, and direct movies of their own choice. Ben said it was going to be "a two-year party."

A million was a lavish sum, worth, of course, far more in the mid-thirties than it is today. These days a bankable star can exact five million or more for a single picture. With wildly inflated production and distribution costs, is it any wonder that moviegoers get stung? They have to pay seven dollars to see a movie that may not be worth fifty cents.

Before we could head east, I had to finish another MGM film, *The White Sister,* with Clark Gable. Then, when we got home, Charlie and I began to long for a place of our own, a quiet house with a garden for Mary to play in, out of Manhattan but not too far from the city. Charlie already had a spot in mind.

His father had been an itinerant preacher, so the MacArthurs never settled anywhere long enough to put down roots. But from his boyhood Charlie had retained a special fondness for one town the family had lived in for a while: Nyack, along the Hudson River, twenty-seven miles north of Broadway, but a world apart.

The name Nyack is of Indian origin. The Nyacks were a tribe that lived in Brooklyn until they sold their land to the Dutch and moved to Staten Island, and then to Rockland County. By 1800 Nyack was a prosperous river port. It continued to thrive as a resort and commercial town until the 1890s, when river transport became obsolete.

Nyack is across the river from Tarrytown, the hometown of Washington Irving, whose tales so vividly describe the local landscape and history. Some of America's legendary estates are there, including Lyndhurst, the Gothic mansion once owned by Jay Gould, the nineteenth-century railroad tycoon.

The Goulds happened to be of special interest to my mother. As a young girl she had been fascinated by the lives of the rich. Even after she was married, she followed the activities of the Vanderbilts and the Astors and the Jay Goulds. Mother had a particular liking for Mrs. Gould, whose given name was Helen. In fact, she named me Helen after Mrs. Gould.

Many years later, the Goulds' home was opened for a charity event, and I was invited. After paying my respects to the hosts, I crept upstairs and found Mrs. Gould's bedroom. I stood there for a few moments, thinking this was where "Helen" Hayes had begun. It was a strange feeling, chilling yet satisfying, the way you feel when you tie up the loose ends of a story you hadn't fully understood before.

Nyack was only a village when Charlie, Mary, and I moved there in the '30s, with farmlands and great meadows along the Palisades. You could walk along the Hudson for miles without meeting a soul. We bought a white Victorian house on the heights, with eighteen rooms, lots of big windows, and porches that invited you to put your feet up and enjoy the view. We maintained an apartment in Manhattan, but from then on, Nyack was home.

Charles Lederer, Marion Davies' nephew, called our house "Pretty Penny," because that's what he supposed it had cost. It was very stately, with gingerbread decoration and magnificent grounds. We terraced the land, which swept down to the river. There was a rose garden on the first level, a pool and cabana on the second, and then a tennis court and a small orchard of apple, cherry, and peach trees. Below was a dock where Charlie kept his tiny boat, *The Anchovy,* christened with champagne by Ben Hecht.

Ben and Charlie lost no time setting to work on their first Astoria picture, which was really only a warm-up for their second, *The Scoundrel,* starring Noël Coward as an unscrupulous editor. The character was based on both Jed Harris and the publisher Horace Liveright, whose company had brought out several of Ben's early novels. Charlie and Ben appeared in the movie themselves as a couple of down-and-out bums in a flophouse scene. One critic described *The Scoundrel* as a sardonic and witty film full of "dazzling dialogue." It won them a lot of praise and an Oscar for best screenplay.

Meanwhile, Maxwell Anderson was trying to convince me to do his play *Mary of Scotland,* but I was apprehensive. I told him that I would be implausible as Mary, who had been perhaps the tallest queen in history. But Anderson dismissed my objection. "In this play I am not writing history's Mary Stuart," he said. "I'm writing *my* Mary Stuart."

Determined to have me play *his* Mary, he went along with me on a train journey to California and read me his entire script. But I still had misgivings.

Anderson was considered a great playwright. His first big stage success, *What Price Glory?,* written in collaboration with Laurence Stallings, had been a hit on the screen as well. When he began to write dramas in verse, we thought he'd become another Shakespeare. Theatre people knocked themselves out to get roles in Maxwell Anderson plays. But now he is almost forgotten, his plays rarely, if ever, revived. I have no idea why he has fallen into oblivion.

I was flattered when Max said that he had written *Mary* for me, but my doubts persisted. The play was a full-dress tragedy in blank verse. Up to then, my most serious role had been in *Co-quette,* and when I started reading about Mary, I found that Max had whitewashed her considerably. But it was a beautifully written play, so I thought that only sticklers for historical accuracy could object to Max's poetic license. In the end I agreed to take it on, hoping to do his Mary justice.

Helen Menken, the actress cast as Queen Elizabeth, was much taller than me. In the confrontation scene between Elizabeth and Mary—one of the liberties Max had taken with fact—I felt I should measure up to her stature. The four-inch lifts I added to my shoes made me nearly as tall as Helen Menken, though I still fell far short of Mary Stuart.

One night Dr. William Lyon Phelps of Yale University came to my dressing room after a performance. He asked me how I gave the effect of being so tall. I told him I wore lifts. "It can't just be that," he said. "You grow before our eyes and appear every inch of Mary's six feet."

"Well, if you must know," I said, "I *think* myself tall." I expected him to laugh, but he realized I was serious. Before going on stage I did think tall, but I hadn't expected it to come across the footlights.

The play proved to be a turning point in my career, convincing both critics and the public that I was more than an aging ingenue. Produced by the Theatre Guild, *Mary of Scotland* had a lengthy Broadway run, followed by a road tour.

When the tour ended, I was dismayed to learn that Hollywood wasn't finished with me yet. MGM insisted that I still owed them some pictures under my contract. They thought I had agreed to make a film called *Vanessa: Her Love Story,* while my impression was that the deal had been canceled when I left California. This misunderstanding led to trouble.

MGM threatened to sue me for ninety-six thousand dollars, the sum they claimed to have spent on a script and other development costs. I was daunted by the prospect of a fight and by the attendant unpleasant publicity, and I did not want to have to pay so much money for my freedom, so I gave in and went back to Hollywood to do *Vanessa.* The less said about that movie the better.

The truth is, I hated making those final pictures under contractual duress. None of them were very good, and one was a particular disappointment: an adaptation of James M. Barrie's *What Every Woman Knows.*

This play was very special to me. The role of the heroine, Maggie Wylie, had been all but the exclusive property of Maude Adams, the legendary actress who created the character. When I was cast as Maggie in a 1926 revival, many thought I was stepping out of my class. They still remembered Maude Adams' performance vividly, and I took pride in eventually being recognized as a worthy successor.

I remembered seeing Maude Adams one day back in 1909. I was walking with my mother past the Empire Theatre, then on Broadway at Fortieth Street. Suddenly, I darted away and crossed Broadway, threading my way through traffic, then mostly horse-drawn carriages and carts, with a few motorcars. Mother was frozen with terror at first, but she soon scurried after me, holding up her hand to stop traffic. "Helen, what in the world are you doing?" she asked. "You could have gotten yourself killed!"

"I saw Maude Adams coming toward us," I explained, "and I didn't want to get in her way."

That was what my mother had taught me: to get out of the way of important people, never to accost them, and to speak only when spoken to. She trained me well: I'm still not comfortable with celebrities, and I don't like being treated like one myself.

I was very nervous when I first played Maggie Wylie, knowing that I'd be compared unfavorably with Maude Adams, whom I venerated. But my love for Barrie's play and my empathy with the character helped me overcome my trepidation. *What Every Woman Knows* is probably my favorite of all the plays I've acted in. I revived it in 1954, and if it weren't for my age, I'd revive it again today, maybe for the sake of women overanxious for recognition in the world. Feminism has its virtues, but I think we're pushing too hard, upsetting ourselves too much. Marriage is now in a precarious state; half of them end in divorce, and that's a shame.

J. M. Barrie, a delightful writer, glorified a quiet woman who knew what every woman knows: that she can be the power behind her man. Maggie inherits a stubborn Scotsman in a peculiar marriage contract that she doesn't want but decides to accept. Ultimately, she makes him prime minister. She knows she is doing the bulk of the job, but would kill anybody who lets her husband catch on. I loved Maggie for her understanding and humor, and that was why I so enjoyed portraying her.

I was twenty-five at the time I played Maggie, in love with Charlie but wondering about his problems with his wife and his divorce. I was kind of wobbly about him, and this play marked a turning point in my young life. It garnered me more male admirers than any great romantic role I ever had.

Peter Arno, then a cartoonist-to-be, tried to "shanghai" me down to Gretna Green in Maryland to get married. I'd known him since he was a spear-carrier in *Caesar and Cleopatra,* and we went to supper one night after the theatre. When he drove me home, he became overbearing. "I'm not going to let you out," he said. "We can't go on like this." He wouldn't unlock the door of his roadster, but thank God, a guardian angel kept me from eloping.

Then there was the writer Percy Crosby, who drew the popular comic strip "Skippy." He got all worked up and invited Mother and me to come stay at his house—he was so eager and anxious that I would succumb—but I was obsessed with Charlie and nothing could break me loose of it.

120

The third suitor I attribute to Maggie Wylie was Herman Hupfeld, whom we all called "Dodo." I met him with Irene Castle in Chicago, where Herman lived. He wrote music occasionally for Irene when she performed at charity balls, so he was invited to all the Chicago parties and was quite a prominent figure. He began to get serious about me. I returned to New York, but he remained determined to marry me. He even took me to meet his mother, wanting her approval. I don't know if he ever married, but he wrote one fine song: "As Time Goes By" for the movie *Casablanca*. Sometimes when I hear it, I say to myself, "If I had married Herman Hupfeld, I'd be thinking, 'That's my husband's song,' " but I had no desire to switch from Charlie.

I had high hopes for the movie version of *What Every Woman Knows,* but they were dashed when I read the script. Barrie's delicate comedy had been torn apart in the most insensitive way. In the play, Maggie is content to sit in a chair by the fire with her knitting. The movie script had her barging into 10 Downing Street and singlehandedly saving the British Empire by taking England off the gold standard. Maggie was turned into an early women's libber, which went against the grain of Barrie's play. It was terrible!

I protested, but was told to stick to acting and let others worry about writing and directing. My mother had given me the same advice early on, but now I considered myself experienced enough to make suggestions about matters that reflected on my acting. After all, when a picture or play is lousy, the average ticket-buyer blames the star, not the writer or director, who have the advantage of being invisible.

There was really no alternative but to go ahead and shoot that travesty of *What Every Woman Knows.* Had I refused, I might have been put on suspension, which would have prolonged my indenture. I managed to persuade myself that it might turn out all right, but the first preview left me numb with despair. To make matters worse, it was shown on a double bill with *Red Dust,* starring Jean Harlow and Clark Gable. After the audience gorged itself on that one, here came this little piece of Scottish whimsy. I was with Charlie and Irving, and I was sick with horror. Irving said, "It's all right. Fundamentally, it's a good picture. We'll do some retakes."

When I showed up at the studio for the re-filming of some scenes, I learned that some stupid Scottish jokes had been added, all about being a tightwad and trying to avoid paying bills, the most trite kind of attempts at humor. I threw myself on the mercy of the director, explaining that it was wrong to put those awful jokes in a Barrie play. "Listen, baby," he said, "Barrie just laid an egg. Forget Barrie."

Thornton Wilder was in Hollywood, and Charlie and I and he and Ruth Gordon, who was visiting us, had dinner together one night to commiserate about the sad state of the film industry. Thornton always talked like a professor, patiently lecturing his students in clipped phrases. We avoided talking about the picture, and after a couple of highballs, Thornton became expansive. Taking in Hollywood with a sweep of his arm, he said, "God and nature created this as a desert. It was never meant to be a habitat for man. One of these days, God and nature are going to erase the whole thing, take it all back, and there will be nothing left of man but the little iron pegs the old men throw the horseshoes at in Pershing Square."

Having buried Hollywood and the movies, we all felt better.

When I finally finished my MGM contract, I told a reporter who interviewed me that I was leaving Hollywood permanently. "I don't think I'm much good in pictures," I said, "and I have a beautiful dream that I'm elegant on stage."

≫·10·≪

Back home in Nyack, I was happy to be reunited with Charlie and Mary. I had missed them and felt as if I'd been away for ages, stuck on a treadmill. At last I'd have a chance to relax, to put my feet up and enjoy the view of the Hudson. Not that there was much time to relax—I was too busy playing hostess. There is something special about a big, easygoing house: it attracts company, and we had plenty of it. Some guests were expected, some just showed up and spent the night or a weekend, and some stayed for weeks on end.

Our house had nine bedrooms, and most of the time we needed every one of them. I had hoped to fill those rooms with children, maybe because I'd been an only child, but that turned out to be impossible. Eventually we adopted a boy named Jamie—Jim, when he grew up. Mary's governess, Jamie's nanny, and our cook lived in that house along with our family of four.

I never cared much for modern furniture—all leather and glass and stainless-steel angles—so we chose traditional warm and cozy pieces with floral prints, plump chairs and sofas you could sink into. The living room was long, and wide enough to accommodate a small crowd. There was a formal dining room, a small parlor and library-office, and a big country kitchen. Sometimes we all sat around the breakfast table, talking the hours away. Bay windows opened the house to spring's greening, and there were fireplaces to tame the winter chill.

Downstairs was Charlie's domain: his private office and a recreation room, a clubby rathskeller with its own entrance to the garden. Over the years it served as a hangout for family and friends. It was furnished with odds and ends, including some seats from the first "Helen Hayes Theatre," which was demolished a few years back. One of my Oscars stood on the mantel; visitors who picked it up were surprised by its weight: it was the old, solid kind.

We had photographs of family and friends around, and pictures of celebrities only if they were friends. A producer once told me that he had visited a young actress' apartment in which the walls and furniture of every room were covered with autographed pictures of celebrities. "Don't you have any friends?" he asked the young woman.

When we first moved in, I saw no need for a decorator. The place was in pretty good shape by the time I went off to make another movie, but while I was away, Charlie called in a Dutch artist named Herman Rossi, a scene designer who had done Ben Hecht's house. Luckily, I got back in time to veto some of his schemes.

Rossi wanted to cover the walls of the front parlor with white lace. He decided that my dressing room should be carpeted with gray squirrel. Was gray squirrel durable? We got in touch with Revillon Frères, and one of the brothers came to discuss the project with me. I asked him how long a squirrel carpet would last with steady use. A couple of years, he replied. And how much would it cost? Five thousand dollars. That project ended then and there.

Rossi then turned his attention to our garden, which swept down in terraces to the river. Rossi wanted to build a six-foot-high brick wall about halfway down, not to enclose anything, just for visual effect. I had to stand there with my arms outstretched, shouting, "Not another brick!"

Charlie had bought a set of English posters of fruit and vegetables from the MGM art department, five dollars for the whole set. He sent them to Rossi, asking him to hang them in the dining room until we decided what to do with that room. When we got back, we found that Rossi had covered the walls and ceiling with canvas and pasted the posters to the canvas. A pair of artists, wearing smocks and berets, were perched on a scaffolding and painting the rest of the canvas with a trompe l'oeil of columns and Grecian urns. On the ceiling they had painted a glorious blue sky with soft clouds.

Another Rossi inspiration was a teakwood tub in Charlie's bathroom. It wasn't caulked, as it should have been, and soon it began to leak down the wall behind it.

I told Charlie that he'd have to choose between Rossi and me: one or the other would have to go. But we both stayed.

Then, one morning when Charlie was in California, a fellow in coveralls came to the door. "Who are you?" I asked. "I'm here to stucco the house," he said. "Mr. Rossi sent me." I phoned Charlie and said, "If you want to live in a stucco Victorian house, fine. But I'm going to look for someplace else to live." And that was the end of Herman Rossi.

One of our regular guests was Alec Woollcott, critic, Round Table wit, and Mary's godfather. He was one of Charlie's oldest friends; they had once shared a flat. Nearly every year we spent exactly two weeks—no more, no less—with Alec at his summer home on Bomoseen Lake in Vermont. Charlie called it "jury duty."

Then Alec came to visit us, always for an unspecified length of time. The Sheridan Whiteside character in *The Man Who Came to Dinner,* by George Kaufman and Moss Hart, was based on Alec, and it was a fair if not exactly flattering portrait. Alec was opinionated, domineering, and cranky. He made a lot of enemies. He could be excruciatingly irritating, but he could be very entertaining too, and he was the loyalest of friends.

His social manners were vile, but that was an act, part of the persona he created for himself. At bottom he was as sentimental as an old granny. And he was capable of enjoying a joke at his own expense. Monty Woolley was the first to play Sheridan Whiteside, but when the show went on tour, Alec took over the role. Life imitating art, I suppose.

Among our unexpected visitors were Laurence Olivier and Vivien Leigh, who arrived dripping and bedraggled one stormy night, hammering insistently at the door. They had been sailing up the Hudson on Jock Whitney's yacht, and when the downpour began, they asked the captain to put in at our dock.

We had met Larry before. Some years earlier, Sam Behrman had asked if he could use Charlie as the model for the playwright-hero of his new comedy, entitled ironically *No Time for Comedy.* Charlie told Sam to go ahead, and Laurence Olivier played the role based on Charlie.

Later, Charlie wrote the screenplay for *Wuthering Heights,* along with Ben Hecht. There was a search for the right Heathcliffe, until one day Charlie announced that they had discovered an actor with the appropriate gypsy allure. "But Charlie," I exclaimed when I looked at the actor's picture, "that's *you*! That's the actor who played you in *No Time for Comedy.*"

Larry had a glowering, Byronic appeal in *Wuthering Heights,* but I don't think he ever looked handsomer than he did standing there in the rain in Nyack. And Vivien was never more ravishing—a nymph in a yellow slicker.

There were so many special guests—the Lunts, Noël Coward, Bea Lillie, and Ruth Gordon, a very close friend. Ruth came to visit for a few weeks during an unhappy time in her life. She wound up staying with us four years.

"What do I do now?" Ruth asked me when she arrived. "My career has come to an end. My love life is over. What do I do?"

I didn't have any answers, so I just gave her a sympathetic ear. One never has the right advice for anyone that troubled, and a pep talk can easily sound falsely cheerful. Perhaps my reluctance to butt in helped to cement our friendship.

Ruth had always been a dedicated actress. Early on, she had read all of Shakespeare's plays, something I'd never done, even though I acted in some of them. Eventually Ruth pulled herself together and went on to greater acclaim as an actress and playwright and to more personal happiness than she had ever known.

Beatrice Lillie became a close friend, too. This may be surprising, because as I mentioned, Bea was once attracted to Charlie, and at first his friends viewed me as "Bea's understudy." But when she returned from a trip to Europe and saw what was going on between Charlie and me, she bowed out gracefully.

After Charlie and I were married, Bea and I became friends, and the three of us were inseparable. One day Bea and Charlie came to see me in the hospital after Mary was born. They stood at the foot of the bed grinning like a pair of children sharing a funny secret. "Bea is going to move in next door to us," Charlie announced.

At the time we were living at 25 East End Avenue, a building that had two apartments to a floor. Bea became our only neighbor, and there was a lot of trooping back and forth. She was such good company that she drew a horde of fans, suitors, and friends—Clifton Webb and Anton Dolin, among others. Our circles of guests often overlapped and overflowed into our adjoining flats. There was a party after the theatre almost every night, with alcohol flowing freely.

Bea joined in, but she couldn't handle too much drinking. Many a night I would end up undressing her and putting her to bed. Once she got stuck in a tubular dress as I was helping her pull it off. She stumbled around blindly, the tight garment drawn over her head and shoulders. It looked like a routine in one of her shows, and I couldn't stop laughing.

"All right, laugh," said Bea. "But I'm going to kill myself tonight." That stopped me. I was afraid she was serious. Liquor seemed to induce a suicidal urge in Bea: she had already made two or three attempts when drunk, God knows why.

It was very late and I needed sleep, as I was then a working actress. But I didn't dare leave her alone. I lay down on the edge of her bed and slept fitfully until morning. When Bea awoke and swallowed some coffee, she seemed all right. It was as if she'd forgotten all about her self-destructive impulse. Maybe the old saw about comedians concealing a morbid streak with laughter applied to Bea. I don't pretend to be a psychiatrist, but I'd had enough experience with alcoholics to know they could undergo a personality change when drunk.

Bea divided her time between New York and London, where she had a son and a husband, a member of the British peerage. In private life she was Lady Peel, and she was capable of pulling rank when the occasion arose—but her attempts to be regal were slightly absurd. After an evening of pub-crawling with Tallulah Bankhead in London one night, Bea returned to her hotel and asked the desk clerk for her key. When he eyed her suspiciously, she announced with a haughty air, "Lady Keel's pee, if you please."

Anything could happen when Bea got on her high horse. One hot summer day in New York, she called and said, "Let's get out of town." We couldn't go far, since we each had to perform in a show that evening. Charlie suggested that we take a ferry to Blackwell's Island. We could see the island from our windows overlooking the East River. Though it was the site of institutions for the mentally ill, indigents, and drunks, the island itself looked refreshingly green, with trees and shady walks, and the air might be cooler than in Manhattan.

We boarded a ferry at the East Seventy-ninth Street pier and spent several hours strolling around the island. Lunch was hot dogs, lemonade, and ice cream. We were about to board the ferry for the return trip after this pleasant outing when a guard asked us for our passes. What passes?

"Nobody gets off the island without a pass," the guard said.

"My dear sir," Bea replied in her toniest Lady Peel voice, "I am Beatrice Lillie, and this is Helen Hayes. We both have performances to give tonight, and we have to get to our theatres."

The guard was unmoved. Then she added, in her best British accent, "I am Lady Peel; Miss Hayes is the first lady of the American theatre, and this gentleman is the distinguished playwright Mr. Charles MacArthur."

The guard sighed wearily. "Listen, lady, we've already got some Lillies here, and several first ladies and maybe a couple of MacArthurs. So show me a pass or get back to the hospital and take tea with Greta Garbo and Lady Astor. There are a few of them there too."

He would have nothing more to do with us. Charlie tried to convince him, but to no avail. Finally he agreed to let Charlie make a phone call. He phoned Mortimer Rodgers, a doctor we knew, brother of the composer Richard Rodgers. Morty had some connection with the hospital on Blackwell's Island, or they knew his name, at least, so he got us released.

This contretemps delayed us for a quite a while. We got back to Manhattan with no time to spare, and Charlie bundled us into a cab to take us to our theatres. On the way Bea said, "One day

I'm going back to that island to confront those impostors claiming to be me."

Bea was always a welcome guest after we settled in Nyack, no advance notice needed. Usually she'd call to say she was coming, but if we happened to be out, she would just breeze in and we'd find her sleeping in one of the guest rooms.

Once, while Ruth Gordon was living with us, Bea arrived with a new beau in tow, Clifford Odets. Things soon got awkward. Clifford took an immediate shine to Ruth and started to ignore Bea. After she went back to town, Clifford stayed on, intent on wooing Ruth.

I've sometimes wondered what kind of play George and Moss would have written if Clifford had been their model for Sheridan Whiteside. Odets was the most appalling guest, a crashing bore. He would stand on the tip of the diving board, glance around, and announce, "I could have all this if I wanted it."

I suppose he meant that he could be a bourgeois success like Charlie and me if he weren't so committed to criticizing and correcting his fellow mortals' capitalist greed. Cliff's patronizing attitude was somewhat disingenuous, as he was earning lots of money as a Hollywood scriptwriter at the time. His admirers and friends from the Group Theatre, which had presented most of his plays, felt that he had sold out for movie lucre.

Finally Charlie had enough of Mr. Odets. He asked Mary, Ruth, and me to pack suitcases, then told Clifford that we had to return to New York and were closing up the house. We all went out, and Charlie locked the door. Cliff got into his car and we got into ours. He drove off for New York, and we rode around the block and came home. I doubt if a Stanislavsky would have been fooled by our performance, but Odets certainly was!

The last time I saw Bea was in the very elegant nursing home in New York where she lived after her health failed. She had suffered a stroke that left her unable to raise her head—unable to lift that proud, cocky carriage of her head that had so distinguished her. I went one afternoon for tea, and here came Bea, dressed to the nines, wearing her long, opera-length Peel pearls.

We sat on a small sofa and John Phillips, her companion, had a camera and wanted to snap a picture of us together. He said Bea would know who it was in the snapshot. I scooted over and spoke to Bea, but she didn't move, didn't respond.

"Bea, it's Helen, Helen Hayes," I repeated to no avail.

Trying one last time, I said, "Bea, it's Charlie MacArthur's bride that ever was." Slowly, Bea stretched a hand toward mine, took my hand, and touched it to her lips.

A writer of an entirely different ilk from Odets came to see us too: Scott Fitzgerald, who has become part of American literary legend. Scott and Zelda, his wife, were among the "beautiful people" of the '20s. Both were avid for fame, fun, and excitement during the jazz age, and both were heavy drinkers. Scott, like so many celebrated writers before and after him, used alcohol as a stimulus, until it became a stumbling block.

The Fitzgeralds had joined the expatriates flocking to Paris and southern France. Charlie had spent some time on the French Riviera, at Antibes, before we were married, and he became good friends with the Fitzgeralds and their friends Gerald and Sara Murphy. He knew that whole glamorous crowd of expatriates that traveled between Paris and Venice and the Riviera, occasionally returning to New York.

The first time I met Scott was an evening in New York when Charlie and I were sitting quietly in our flat and the doorbell rang. I went to the door, and knew immediately who it was from Charlie's description. He always said Scott looked like a "Catholic choirboy." There he stood, all even, chiseled features and blond wavy hair.

He asked me if Charlie was home, I said yes, and that began

a three-day stay in our apartment. Zelda had always been fun-loving and the perpetrator of nutty jokes, but then she became mentally ill, severely so. Scott had come to our apartment from Baltimore, where he had committed her permanently, at her own request, to a mental hospital. He came automatically to Charlie—as people often did when they had problems or were greatly troubled—knowing he wasn't going to receive advice or criticism or even consolation, as such. He knew Charlie would listen. He came for that.

The second night, Charlie and Scott had a rather bibulous dinner, then went off to see the reigning Broadway hit, *Dinner at Eight.* As the play progressed, Scott became more and more annoyed. Finally, in a loud, clear voice he asked, "Has this thing opened yet?" Whereupon, people around them complained, and Scott and Charlie were ushered out. That night, Scott slept soundly on our floor.

After that, he used to come occasionally to Nyack. He gave Mary her first book when she was a year old. It was a collection of Steichen photographs for children, things small fry could recognize, and Scott wrote a lovely little verse in it for her. We had a kind of sporadic intimacy with him, as friends will, being close when we were in one another's company but scarcely corresponding when we were all apart.

He went out to Hollywood, but he had a hard time adapting his skill to screenwriting. Overly proud, he was rebellious toward the studios and the system from the minute he got there. That was the trouble with him; he never gave Hollywood a chance.

One time, Scott said to me, "Every life changes and starts afresh every seven years. A snake changes its skin, we humans change our psyche." That was interesting, but I was not convinced. I think Scott made up things like that to encourage himself.

Eventually he quit drinking, but it was too late to recover his health and talent. When he came out to Nyack—it must have been in the late thirties—he was still very handsome, with chiseled features, deep-set eyes, a high forehead, and hair swept back. But he did look wan and sad.

Charlie, always a good host, offered to show Scott around. He suggested a spin in his new motorboat up the Hudson to Ossining, where Sing Sing is located. Charlie was fascinated by the old prison, and he liked to show it off to our guests.

Scott and Charlie were entirely different types, which made for a lively contrast. Scott was a romantic whose stories reflected a kind of wistful, jaded idealism. Charlie was an earthy realist. He had once been a crime reporter in Chicago and still had a taste for crime stories. I couldn't stand some of his grisly yarns and dubbed him "Charlie Macabre."

We took the boat out one evening before dark. Charlie kept up a running commentary about Sing Sing as he steered the boat. It was built over a hundred years ago and is a forbidding fortress. You would know it was a prison even if you hadn't been told.

By the time we got there, night had fallen and all the prison lights were on. Charlie explained various points of interest. "Those turrets are where the guards stand. If they suspect there's been a prison break on the riverside, they stand shoulder-to-shoulder up there with their shotguns ready to blast any escaping inmate out of the water."

He pointed in another direction. "That building with the very bright lights is the death house. Those lights are never turned off. But if they dim, that means the electricity is being used for an electrocution. If we hang around long enough, maybe we'll see it."

That was a sight I could do without. Scott peered through the night, quietly observing and listening to Charlie's spiel. Once he got wound up, Charlie went on and on, describing prison life in gory detail. It gave me the shivers. He was so engrossed in his story that he didn't notice the boat was drifting too close to the shore.

Suddenly a uniformed man on a turret began waving a shotgun at us. "Get back! Go away!" he shouted. I was scared, and even Charlie wasn't about to argue or make jokes. He swiftly backed the boat away, and we turned toward home.

"You know what it looks like?" Scott said, looking back at Sing Sing's blazing lights. "A carnival in Venice."

That remark, I thought, showed the difference between Scott and Charlie.

At dinner that night we were chatting about this and that, when the men recalled an incident I wished we could all forget. It was a troubling reminder of Charlie's temper. If someone insulted him, he'd charge, fists flying.

He, Scott, and Ernest Hemingway got together once when Charlie was on the French Riviera. Ernest started bragging in his usual macho way, putting Scott down, as he invariably did. Scott didn't defend himself, but Charlie became furious. Ernest challenged him, they squared off, and there was a terrible fistfight.

A crowd of onlookers gathered, Scott said, and let the two of them fight it out. I never knew who won—as if it mattered—though Scott said Charlie did. He admitted, though, that he grew sick watching the brawl and left before it ended.

This sorry subject came up again in 1956, when Charlie and I were in Cuba and visited Ernest and Mary Hemingway at their *finca* outside Havana. It was March, and we were surprised to see a Christmas tree still standing in their living room—a brown skeleton of an evergreen without a single needle but with bells and balls drooping from its branches. "We keep the tree because it still smells like home," Mary Hemingway said.

Well, I couldn't detect any piney smell, and to me that tall, dead Christmas tree told a dreadfully sad story of loneliness, homesickness, and yearning for a familiar celebration.

Pretty soon Charlie and Ernest got into an argument, and I began to feel uneasy. Mary, a small, attractive blonde who was Ernest's fourth wife, paid little attention to them. I suppose she was as accustomed to Ernest's ways as I was to my husband's. But we were guests in their home, and I didn't want an altercation to spoil our visit.

The men raised their voices, and I realized they were arguing about that fistfight on the Riviera, each contending that he had won and both threatening to come to blows again. "Oh, God, they're going to fight it out just to prove who won," I thought.

But it didn't come to that. I suppose neither of them felt up to a fight at the time. The bearded, bulky Hemingway still looked quite fit, but Charlie wasn't in good shape. I wished he could carry his liquor as well as Ernest still did, but in the end that wish proved futile.

They were people who brightened our lives, but sad endings came to so many of them. Zelda died in a fire in the mental hospital; Scott, of a heart attack at age forty-four; and Ernest took his own life rather than live with failing health.

≫·11·≪

After working off my movie contract, I spent some quiet time at home, looking over play scripts sent to me by Broadway producers. Opportunities to be lazy and enjoy home life rarely came my way, so I was in no hurry to go back to work.

The best script I had read so far was an adaptation of *Pride and Prejudice,* but I was reluctant to commit myself. Max Gordon was pressing me for an answer, and I felt guilty about stalling, for Max was an admirable producer and I liked him very much. Besides, I knew he was stringing other actresses along while I tried to make up my mind. It wasn't fair to Max or to the other contenders to delay a decision much longer.

When Max called one Friday, I told him that he would get a definite answer on Monday and that it would probably be yes. But I felt uneasy as I hung up the phone. I loved Jane Austen's novel, and the adaptation was well done, but I couldn't quite see myself as Elizabeth Bennet. Somehow the spontaneous instinct that I could play this role was missing.

Idly, I picked up another script from a pile stacked on my desk. It had been sent by the producer Gilbert Miller, the Charles

Frohman of the 1930s, highly regarded for his elegant productions of literate plays in both New York and London. Earlier I had tossed the script aside, because it seemed so unpromising. What could be more boring than a play about Queen Victoria? And how many queens could an actress play in one decade without appearing presumptuous or typecast?

I wandered down to the pool, sat down, and started to read. To my utter amazement, the script captivated me. I was overwhelmed.

I heard voices from the garden, friends asking the gardener where I was. I rushed to the cabana, locked myself in the bathroom, and went on reading. The play was so powerful that I couldn't bear to put it down.

I've come to believe that every actor has one role he or she can do better than anyone else. Real actors—which doesn't mean everyone holding an Equity card—give their best even to roles that may not be ideal for them. Sometimes they can turn in interesting performances even when badly miscast. And some really gifted actors never receive the acclaim they deserve, simply because the right role hasn't come their way.

But nothing can match the marriage between an actor and an ideal role. I had had good parts in the past, notably Maggie Wylie, but never was I so blessed as with Victoria. After all my years in the theatre, I can look back on only a handful of moments that met my own standard of perfection. When you transcend yourself and really get inside the character, it's like being touched by God. That happened to me once or twice while I was playing Victoria.

At first I knew little about Victoria, only that she was a powerful monarch who had ruled much of Europe personally or through relatives for over sixty years and ultimately gave her name to an entire era. But I had no sense of what she really was—how she lived, how she spoke and walked, what her political views were, her habits, her manners. I didn't know enough about her enduring love for Albert, who exerted the greatest influence on her life.

I tried to find out all I could, as though I were doing research for a definitive biography. I read history, memoirs, whatever I could get my hands on. The more I read, the more Victoria emerged not only as a powerful queen but as a sympathetic human being.

Her German mother had married solely in order to produce an heir to the British throne. But even though Victoria had been tutored from birth to play her role, she was still a naive girl, vulnerable and overly romantic, when she ascended to the throne at the age of eighteen. Before Albert came along, she had a crush on his brother, who was presented to her as a suitable consort but turned out to be a cad. Once she fell for Albert, though, she remained in love with him all her life.

At the start of her reign, Victoria was uncertain and too easily swayed. She was fortunate in the men appointed as her guides. The real ruler of the country was Lord Melbourne, her first prime minister and trusted mentor, a very romantic figure. Her later advisers were less to her liking. She couldn't stand William Gladstone, who "used to address me like a public meeting." Then came Benjamin Disraeli, who after Albert's death flattered and wooed her into doing whatever he wanted.

I felt great empathy for Victoria as a woman. At first it seemed impertinent to think of impersonating her, but I soon began to find the role comforting. It made me feel that my own weaknesses were pretty average, that even an exalted monarch was not immune to the kinds of problems all women confront as they try to sort out and deal with the issues of personal fulfillment, love, career, family.

The next stage of my preparation was a trip to England to soak up some of Victoria's life and culture. My daughter Mary and

Ruth Gordon came along, and we had an arduous but glorious time trekking around various Victorian landmarks, most notably the Victoria and Albert Museum.

I was fortunate enough to meet people who had actually known Victoria, and even one of her granddaughters, the dowager marchioness of Milford Haven. I asked her about something that had been puzzling me: did Victoria speak with an accent when she was queen of England? "*Ach,* no!" the marchioness replied. "She het no more eggzent den you or me."

So I decided to use a trace of a guttural accent, which would help prevent my own intonation from making Victoria sound too American.

Friends gave me some Victorian relics as gifts. One offered a piece of lace once worn by the queen. Vincent Price, who had created the role of Albert in London and would repeat it in New York, took me to an antique-jewelry shop near the British Museum, where I purchased jewels I later wore in the play. They were precise copies of those worn by Victoria or by members of the royal court.

My favorite gift came from Charles Laughton. It was a pair of Queen Victoria's own beautifully embroidered panties, with lace around the legs, which had been let out at least three times as her rear had expanded.

During our stay in London I got to know Rex Whistler, the British artist who was designing the sets and costumes for the play. We found we had an instant rapport. Rex had never been to America, and I told him I'd be glad to show him around if there was anything special he wanted to see or do when he arrived.

After a moment's thought he said that he'd very much like to see a Hudson River bracketed house, which typified one of his favorite periods and architectural styles in America. No problem, I said. But I hadn't the foggiest idea what he was talking about.

Back home, I asked everyone I knew where a Hudson River bracketed house could be found. No one seemed to know. Alec Woollcott said that such a house was in an Edith Wharton novel. But Rex Whistler wanted to see a house, not a book.

When he arrived in New York, Rex came to spend his first weekend in Nyack. I thought I'd have to fib and tell him that the style he wanted to see had vanished long ago. But when he looked up at the house, he smiled from ear to ear.

"Aren't you the sly boots!" he exclaimed. "You didn't tell me you actually owned a Hudson River bracketed house." All that gingerbread ornamentation was technically known as bracketing, Rex explained. It took an Englishman to tell Charlie and me what kind of house we lived in.

Victoria Regina opened the night after Christmas in 1935, and it was a spectacular opening in every respect. Everyone was there, including people from the British embassy in Washington and the most feared and widely read theatre reviewer in London, who gave us a great rave, saying, "No one in the British theatre could play the role so splendidly." We were spied upon by Guthrie McClintic and some of Katharine Cornell's staff who stood behind the orchestra seats for the last scene. Kit was having her big success in *The Barretts of Wimpole Street*, so her little coterie came over to see how I was going to fare. They kept trying to create competition that wasn't there. Kit later told me that one of them said to her, "When we left, they were still on their feet cheering. You'd have thought the real queen was on stage." We played on Broadway until May 1937, and then we went on tour for another year.

Around that time, I was dubbed "the first lady of the American theatre." The accolade was embarrassing, because there were several other "first ladies" around—Katharine Cornell, Lynn Fontanne, and Ina Claire, to name three. But since the label stuck, I began to feel an obligation to live up to it.

140

One day, as I was walking to a matinee in my somewhat curly nutria coat, I overheard a woman say to the man with her, "There's Helen Hayes." Her companion looked me over and said scornfully, "That's not Helen Hayes. It can't be." I had never cared much about what I wore offstage. In fact, I had once been called the worst-dressed actress on Broadway. (Elsa Maxwell came to my defense: "It's not that Helen dresses badly. She doesn't dress at all.")

Reluctantly, realizing that I'd have to improve my appearance, I went to a leading furrier of that era and ordered a sable coat for fifteen thousand dollars. It was very extravagant, but I figured it might be a bargain in the end; I could wear any old sweater and skirt under the coat.

Just then I happened to pass an art gallery with a lovely Renoir in the window. Wondering whether I could afford to buy it, I ventured into the gallery, and the dealer quoted a price of fifteen thousand dollars. I returned the coat and bought the painting. Furs go out of fashion, but a Renoir lasts forever.

In any case, I had a feeling that the public didn't really expect me to be glamorous, that they thought of me as a member of the family or as someone who lived down the block, which is pretty much the way the British felt about Victoria. Maybe some of her homey appeal rubbed off on me while I was playing the role.

The play covered the sixty years from Victoria's ascension to the throne to her Diamond Jubilee in 1897. People wondered how we managed the physical transformation from youth to old age. They wanted to know what I used to puff out my cheeks in the final scene. The question was asked so often that at one point I muttered "Oh, nuts!" to an interviewer. His article duly reported that I used nuts.

In fact I experimented with several things during the play's run. Charles Laughton suggested half an apple in each cheek, which was tasty, but the apples dissolved too quickly. In the end

I settled on wads of cotton wool moistened with a liquid antiseptic. It wasn't as unpleasant as it sounds.

After the two-and-a-half-year Broadway run, we took *Victoria* on the road. The fun and camaraderie of that yearlong cross-country tour are among my fondest memories. In the early *Pollyanna* days, a road tour meant less than luxury living. By the time of *Victoria*, I'd graduated to a compartment on our own special train.

Still, it wasn't exactly easy street. We'd roll into a town, set up in the local theatre, give our performance, and take off for the next stop that night or early the next morning. We played in forty-five cities and towns from Hartford, Connecticut, to Los Angeles, covering fourteen thousand miles in forty-one weeks.

If we were lucky, we had time to explore our surroundings. When we were in Oklahoma City, the British cast members were anxious to see a real Indian reservation. We all piled in a car and set off to see one. After about an hour of driving around, following various erroneous directions, we pulled into a gasoline station.

"We're looking for an Indian reservation," one of our group told the man pumping gas.

"Sorry. There aren't any."

"Well, in that case, could you tell us where we might see a real Indian," the Englishman said.

The attendant stopped filling our car's tank, straightened up, and said proudly, "I'm a real Indian. Look all you want." I think he was as impressed with seeing real Englishmen as we were by him.

One night, we were in a far western state, New Mexico or Colorado, and we were all back at the train, waiting for the scenery to be loaded aboard. We sat down on the tracks and had our sandwiches, our late-night supper, with us. Someone began to sing, and we all sat out there in the warm night beneath the stars, singing old songs. Pretty soon a brakeman came

142

over to us and said, "You better get off the tracks and get on your train. Another train is liable to come and not see you all sitting here."

As we began to stand up, reluctantly heading in, he said, "Do any of you know 'Long, Long Trail'?"

We all began to sing, "There's a long, long trail a-winding," and he stopped us with his raised hand.

"If you'll go ahead and sing all of that song, I'll put out flares so any train that heads this way will stop and you can stay outdoors."

It was thrilling to watch the landscape of America pass by my window. I remember one evening especially. We had crossed farmlands and plains and were chugging over that last mighty barrier to the West Coast—the Rocky Mountains. It was a blustery, snowy night, and the train stopped to take on an extra locomotive to haul us through the last mountain pass.

I was preparing for bed, hair in curlers, face smeared with cold cream. When I turned out the lights and raised the window shade, I saw a breathtaking sight. The black sky was filled with stars that seemed close enough to touch. The moon's pale light shone on the mountains, where snow sparkled like diamonds. It was an exquisite, silent scene, with not a soul in sight, not even a house or a light. It was so awesome that I felt I couldn't watch it alone. It had to be shared.

Forgetting that I looked a mess, I rushed out of the compartment and into the corridor. The other actors were sitting around, singing or chatting, having a last drink before bedtime. "Look out there!" I shouted.

They ran to raise the shades and were enthralled by the scene. Except for one of them, an English actress named Bunty Cobb, whose gaze was fixed on me. "One quick click for *Pic*," Bunty said, "and I'll die happy." Even then there were magazines that paid a lot for pictures of well-known people looking their worst.

I'd always been a pushover for a good wisecrack, and Bunty and I became friends for life.

There were a lot of laughs on that tour, many at my expense. Having no sense of direction, I kept getting lost—even on the train. One of the actors pinned a note on the door of the men's room: "The ladies' room is at the other end of the car."

On New Year's eve in Philadelphia Charlie came down from New York and talked me into a little surprise for the cast. Dressed as the elderly Victoria during curtain calls, I pulled a red tin horn from beneath my black capelet and gave it a couple of toots. Yes, I did step out of character, but it was New Year's Eve.

There were many benefits from playing Queen Victoria, among them being raised up on high and called "the greatest living actress," by Noël Coward, and other wonderful rewards. There were also some comical complications, including off-balance meetings with real royalty. *Victoria Regina* endeared me to all of the foreign royalty that found its way to the United States in those years, and there were a whole lot of them. They used to cluster at my dressing room door, and it was a bit nervous-making for me, who had been trained to leave important people alone.

Sam Woods, an English expert on royalty, was hired by the producer to give everybody in the company pointers in how royalty acts and how people should act around them. He knew exactly what you should do and how you should do it.

One night, Ruth Gordon was sitting in my dressing room after the performance, waiting to go back to Nyack, when the second-in-line to the Spanish throne was announced as wanting to come in. Sam hadn't told me about this one. I said, "Oh, my God, Ruth, how do I introduce this man to you?" She didn't know either, so I pushed her into the bathroom and locked the door. I was in a blind panic and didn't know what else to do. Then I graciously met the gentleman and we had our little visit. Let me tell you, Ruth was pretty indignant by the time I let her out.

144

Then we had former Queen Ena of Spain. I was to call her "Your Majesty," Sam said, and I was never to ask her a question. I was not to say, "How are you?" or "Did you like the play?" or anything like that. Don't ask questions, answer them, Sam told me. My head was filled with so much of that stuff, it took all the crumbs of poise I possessed to be presentable. I was a dithering fool by the time she came in, but she stayed only briefly, so I got through with some degree of success.

The bad part was, she asked me to come to tea at her daughter's apartment on Park Avenue. The theatre was my territory, but now I was going to hers. I wished I had never heard of *Victoria Regina.* I stood up when Queen Ena entered the room, and I think maybe I did a little bow. We began a halting conversation which was interrupted when her daughter, the Infanta, came in, carrying on her hip a small baby, one of the heirs to the throne. She put the baby down, and he immediately crawled to a table near my chair and pulled it over. The table was covered with a collection of small Battersea and French enamel boxes, and down they all clattered to the floor. I stared in misery at Her Majesty, who suddenly dropped to her knees and began scrambling for the boxes. Down I dropped too, except I went down almost on my stomach. Sam had said, "You must not be higher than she is." She was on her knees, so I had to get lower.

Another royal encounter with about the same amount of seriousness was with the grand duchess Marie of Russia, who was a great friend of Alec Woollcott and had had a crush on Charlie. She had tried to take him home one night in Europe, before we were married and when he was roaming around the Continent alone. In Paris, they had dinner in the Bois—Charlie, Mary Harriman Rumsey, the grand duchess, and her brother. Charlie had a touch of mayonnaise on his formal white shirtfront, and he happened to notice the grand duke's eyes riveted on it.

Trying to laugh it off, Charlie said, "You see, sir, I'm wearing my decorations tonight."

Unamused, the grand duke shot back, "Doubtlessly from the night before last."

Charlie's Scottish pride stiffened, and he waved for the maitre d', saying loudly, "Waiter, the grand duke's hat and kiddie car. He's leaving."

The grand duchess loved that and took an instant fancy to Charlie. He gave her a ride home that night, but when she invited him up for a nightcap, he didn't want to go. Never one to be caught without a good line, he sadly explained that he had suffered war injuries that left him impotent. With that, he escaped.

When the grand duchess arrived in the United States a few years later, Charlie and I were invited to a dinner for her. We were married by then, and I was about eight months pregnant, my stomach standing out like a balloon. When I was introduced to her, the grand duchess slowly looked me up and down, then said, "Naugh-ty, Charlie."

She did have something that set her apart from the other ex-royalty I'd met: she worked for a living. She was hired by Machiavelli's perfume department at Bergdorf's, mostly for promotion. One night, she was coming to see me perform and, as usual, Sam coached me on the rules for royalty. By this time, I was a little bored with all of his instructions, but he pumped my head full of them again. When Marie came into my dressing room, she sat down on the sofa and gave me a bottle of perfume. Before I could stop myself, my first utterance was, "Is Your Serene Highness still working at Machiavelli's perfume counter?"

I didn't come off any better with British royalty. Charlie and I took one of my vacations from *Victoria* to visit all the lovely places in Europe which, he said, "would never be the same again." He was right. Hitler was already making his moves. We traveled in Holland and France and went down to Austria, where we were houseguests at a *schloss.* Our hosts told us that the duke of Kent and his wife were expected for the weekend, and after supper, we were asked to stay up to greet them.

I told Charlie I was too tired to wait. "I'll meet them in the morning," I said, but he insisted I stay with the group. I lasted as long as I could and was getting a little testy. "If the duke wants to see me, he can come up and see me," I said as I left. I retired to my room to put cold cream on my face and roll my hair in curlers, preparing for the great moment the next morning when I was to meet this most handsome and charming member of the royal family.

I was lying in bed with the light out when I heard, from far away, footsteps coming down the corridor. I couldn't believe it, but as they came closer, I could tell it was two men, and it sounded as though they were coming to our door. I ducked under the covers and grabbed a corner of the sheet to wipe the grease off my face while I tore down the curlers.

The footsteps stopped. The door opened. The light went on. "Helen," Charlie said sweetly, "the duke of Kent wants to meet you." God help me, at that moment I could have murdered Charlie. They came in and I lay in bed and the duke pulled over a chair to sit beside it, like a visiting doctor. What he wanted was to show me his big trick, something he had become famous for doing: he could put his handkerchief on his head so one of the points was in the center of his brow, like the pointed white muslin cap Queen Victoria wore, and blow out his cheeks and make a sour face to become a dead ringer for his great-grandmother, Queen Victoria. He wanted to do that for me, and he did it, and it was quite a sight.

As late as 1976, when Queen Elizabeth came to the United States for our bicentennial, I was still getting *Victoria* fallout. One morning, I received a telephone call from a voice saying it was the British ambassador, something "Ramsbottom." It all sounded like one of my practical-joker friends, but I kept listen-

147

ing. "I'm speaking for Her Majesty, Queen Elizabeth, who wishes you to come to dinner on the royal yacht, *Britannia,*" on such-and-such a night.

"Who is this?" I said. "Is it you, Johnny DeVries? This isn't funny, you know."

I went through all of that, and of course it was Lord Ramsbottom, the British ambassador, and I was invited to dine with the queen. Subdued by the terrible gaffe I'd made, I very meekly accepted. *Victoria Regina* was ancient history by then, but I was still garnering honors from it. Queen Elizabeth was charming; I was silent.

The negative side of the tour was that it kept us away from our families and friends for a long time. Although *Victoria* provided us with jobs and folding money, and we became a closely knit company, I sometimes resented my work for separating me from Charlie and our children.

One night in Boston, on my way from my hotel to the theatre, I paused on Beacon Hill at dusk and watched the lights go on in nearby houses. I'll never forget how homesick I felt.

Sometimes I became so melancholic that I felt all actresses should be spayed so they couldn't have children. It's so very difficult to balance the careers of motherhood and the theatre. I can't honestly say I ever managed it—at least not in a way that measured up to my own standards. At times I thought of giving up work to concentrate on raising my children, but I couldn't bring myself to do it. It's a tough balancing act for any working woman, but even more so, I think, for women in the theatre, with all the rehearsal time and odd hours, even when they're working close to home and are not away on tour.

When our tour ended, I thought we had finished with *Victoria,* but instead we reopened on Broadway for another run of several months. It is remarkable that in our country, which had rebelled against monarchic rule to create a republic, people were so taken with a play about British royalty. I suppose audiences were attracted not only by Victoria's character, but also by the drama of Laurence Houseman's play.

Although I had to report to the theatre every night, and some days for matinees, at least now the theatre wasn't too far from my family, which had recently acquired a new member, James Gordon MacArthur, our adopted son. Adoption is never easy for the surrogate parents or the child, but for us it proved to be a great blessing.

A few years after Mary was born, we had decided to have another child. Charlie came from a large family, and he wanted a brood of our own. I readily agreed, knowing as I did the heavy responsibility an only child can be asked to bear. We certainly didn't want our Mary to be so burdened, as I had been.

Unhappily, I wasn't able to conceive a second time. I knew that some women were envious of my career, but I envied their pregnancies. When I passed a pregnant woman on the street, I would begin to cry. I became edgy and suffered from blinding headaches that lasted a day or more. All the while I kept on acting, forcing myself to go through the motions.

Charlie was deeply concerned. At the time I didn't understand why I was so despondent. Only with hindsight did I realize how frustrated I was at being unable to do what came naturally to other women.

Charlie sent me to a doctor he knew in Los Angeles, a good internist, for a general checkup. He gave me a thorough examination and a battery of tests, which showed that there was nothing wrong physically. The doctor then questioned me about my emotional health.

"Something is worrying you," he said, "and I think it would help if you could talk about it."

149

"I can't think of anything," I replied. Then, almost as an afterthought, I added, "I would like to have another child. We have been trying."

The doctor smiled. "So that's it. It's the most common cause of nervousness and headaches in a marriage." He suggested we consider adoption. "This might ease your tension and help both of you to relax. Sometimes after a couple adopts, the wife finds she can conceive again."

After talking it over with Charlie, I told the doctor we might be interested. One of his patients, an unmarried young woman of good family, had placed her child in a foster home, but still brought the baby to him for regular checkups; if we liked, the doctor said, he could arrange for us to see the baby. Charlie and I decided it would be better if he went alone; we were afraid I might be recognized.

The doctor phoned the mother and told her it was time for a checkup for the baby. Then he called Charlie, who went to the doctor's office. I sat home, gnawing at my fingernails, while Charlie studied the baby. Only it was the other way around.

"Helen, he's a beautiful baby, and he never took his eyes off me—they were glued to me the whole time he was there," he said. That sealed our decision.

I didn't see the baby until later, when everything was arranged and ready. I had taken a room in a small, out-of-the-way hotel for several days, and the doctor's office called and set up our rendezvous. I went to a certain street corner near the hotel, and the doctor drove up in a taxi, jumped out, and handed me the baby, who was wearing only a hospital sheet. I went to my little hideaway hotel, and the baby and I were alone together for two or three days.

At first he was fussy and out of sorts. This was all new to him, too. I gave him some orange juice, and I guess he'd never had any, because he spit it right back out at me. The second day, after a

150

sleepless night for both of us, I was walking him up and down in the little room, rubbing my face against his and talking to him. I didn't notice the mirror until I looked up and was confronted with the two of us, our faces together. I looked in the mirror and smiled. He looked for a long time and then smiled, too. That was when my baby was "born." He was seven months old.

Later, when I took Mary in to meet him, I said, "Mary, this is your little brother." She looked down at him and then her little hands flew up to her face, and she said, "Did he come out of you?"

"No," I said, "he came from God." I felt sure that God's hand was in on the adoption of Jim. Mary always adored her little brother, as big sisters often do. She was protective of him and eager to pass along what she already knew. She took him right into her heart, as Charlie and I did. Some evenings Charlie would take out his old clarinet and entertain us with traditional Scottish ballads. It was a happy time for us, though war was already imminent in Europe, and like all Americans, our lives would be changed by it.

My own involvement began shortly after England went to war, nearly two years before America joined the Allies. Bunty Cobb, my friend from the *Victoria Regina* tour, had a young son, Charles, and I was very worried about him. I wrote to her in London, suggesting that she send Charles to live with us. Many British families were sending their children to stay with friends or distant American cousins.

Bunty replied by cable. Charles was only four, she said, too young to come alone. So we invited both of them to come to Nyack as quickly as possible. Pretty soon we were a family of six.

I had imagined Charles as a sweet English lad with curly hair, rosy cheeks, and a shy voice—a latter-day Oliver Twist or David Copperfield. What we got was an irritable, skinny kid with big ears.

151

My husband immediately dubbed Charles "The Artful Dodger." He was a bully, forever teasing and pinching our Jamie, and he had the most awful Cockney accent, picked up from the nanny who had taken care of him while Bunty was appearing on stage.

Thinking that Charles might be homesick, I bought a Union Jack to hang over his bed and gave him a picture of the king and queen. That didn't help much. One day Maurice Evans came to visit, and I thought another Englishman might be comforting to Charles. They spoke more or less the same language, at least, though Charles' cockney was a far cry from Maurice's Oxonian English.

I took Maurice upstairs to Charles' bedroom. "Hello there, old chap," said Maurice, his eyes twinkling as he smiled at the boy.

"Bugger! Bugger! Bugger!" Charles yelled.

Maurice and I fled. Apparently "bugger" was the only dirty word the boy knew. He hadn't tried it on me or Charlie, perhaps figuring we wouldn't know what it meant.

Gradually, he allowed us to get closer to him. When in 1945 the time came for him to go back to England, he didn't want to leave. He sobbed and clung to me. It was painful to put him on the boat and watch him sail away. I kept track of Charles, and he turned out well. He's now an artist living in Greece.

Another change in my life after the outbreak of war was that I began to make speeches, something that's occupied a good deal of my time in recent years. Though I've never pushed myself forward, if I'm asked to speak for a worthy cause, I do it. At first, however, the idea of talking in my own voice, not as a character, gave me more jitters than I'd ever felt on any opening night.

My first speech was at Far Rockaway Beach, and the audience was a bunch of wet and sandy swimmers. A plan to take forty American ships out of mothballs and send them to Britain, which badly needed them, had aroused public controversy, because we were still officially neutral. My speech was a plea of support for the plan. Robert E. Sherwood, a playwright and later a speech-writer for FDR, was keen on taking us out of isolationism. It was he who persuaded me to deliver the speech, which he had written himself.

I climbed to the top of a lifeguard station and started lecturing the people on the beach, who seemed bewildered as they stared up at me, shielding their eyes from the sun. I felt like a fool, especially when I heard a voice demand as I climbed down from my perch, "Who does she think she is? Queen Victoria?" It isn't easy to run in sand, but I got off that beach in record time.

Besides making speeches, I also promoted the cause on Broadway, in Maxwell Anderson's *Candle in the Wind.* It was the first time that Alfred Lunt directed a play in which neither he nor Lynn Fontanne appeared. The first-rate supporting cast included Lotte Lenya in a small role, and my costumes were designed by Valentina. It was hard to see how any production with so much talent could fail. But it did, dismally.

The story was set in Nazi-occupied Paris. I played a glamorous actress who comes to France and falls in love with a Jew who is deported to a concentration camp. The actress proceeds to confront the Nazi commandant of Paris, arch-villain of the piece. Oh, it was a grand tragedy!

Max's intention was to shake America out of its complacency and to build support for Britain and France. Charlie had read Max's script. "Don't do it, Helen," he warned. "No war has ever been won by a bad play." But I didn't listen. My heart was fired, and I was every bit as passionate as Max about getting America into the war.

Perhaps Max's passion was the problem: he wrote the play at white heat. He usually spent at least a year on a script, but he wrote *Candle* in a matter of weeks. During rehearsals I sensed that Alfred wasn't entirely happy with the play; he suggested revisions that Max was either unable or unwilling to make. So we opened and flopped. The reviews were scathing but for one exception: everybody praised Valentina's costumes.

The night after the opening, Max drove me back to Nyack after the performance—he was a Rockland County neighbor. It was pouring rain, which certainly didn't lighten our mood after the awful notices. We were silent for a long while, watching the windshield wipers slosh back and forth.

Finally Max spoke. "You know that Lonergan . . ." he began. Yes, I knew about Lonergan, who was much in the news at the time, having bashed in his wife's head with a candelabrum during an altercation in their Sutton Place apartment. The papers referred to him as "the alleged murderer," but still called him *Mr.* Lonergan.

That *Mr.* really irked Max. "The papers attack me as 'Anderson,' with no Mister," he complained. "So it looks as though murdering your wife isn't as grievous a crime as writing a play nobody likes."

I laughed and commiserated. The reviewers had been rough on me too, but at least they deferentially called me "Miss Hayes." *Candle in the Wind* was not a complete fiasco: it managed a run of more than ninety performances, closing not long after the attack on Pearl Harbor. By that time, whatever propaganda value the play may have had was moot.

When America entered the war, the view from our porch in Nyack changed dramatically. We watched ships sail up the Hudson to Iona Island, where they were loaded with ammunition. Then they sailed back down and out to sea. It was a fascinating but frightening sight.

A friend of Charlie's was the captain of a destroyer. One day his ship stopped near our dock, and he came over in a launch. He invited Charlie to go for a ride. All of us were waving madly on the dock as the destroyer came by, but nobody aboard seemed

154

My mother, Catherine Hayes

I smile at the world

My father with "Bean," our Boston bulldog

My first New York appearance: Little Mimi
in *Old Dutch*

My debut·with the Columbia Players, at
age five

Father and I

At twelve: part seasoned actress, part
dreamy child

In the title role of *Pollyanna*

During my *Pollyanna* days, 1917

Bab opened when I was twenty,
the youngest "star" ever

As Bab

In *To the Ladies,* at twenty-one
Otto Kruger was the piano salesman

Coquette, 1927 to 1929,
the play I was in when Charlie proposed to me

Charlie MacArthur

My daughter, Mary

Mary and I studying for our
roles in *Alice Sit by the Fire*
at New Hope, Pennsylvania.
Her theatre debut

The Sin of Madelon Claudet, with Neil Hamilton, 1931. My first movie and first Oscar

With Gary Cooper in *A Farewell to Arms*, 1932

What Every Woman Knows, 1926. Seated left to right: Kenneth MacKenna, Dennis Cleugh, Eugene Weber, and Jack Terry

Reviving *What Every Woman Knows* in 1954, I played with Kent Smith

As Mary Stuart in *Mary of Scotland*, 1933

As tipsy, lovestruck Adie in *Happy Birthday*, I won the Tony award for 1946. Playing with me, left to right: Dort Clark, Louis Jean Heydt, Philip Gordon, Lorraine Miller, Jacqueline Page, Jack Diamond, and Jean Bellows

My biggest success was in *Victoria Regina*, in which I played Queen Victoria, both as a teenager, when she assumed the throne of England (right), and near the end of her reign (below)

In *Anastasia*, with Ingrid
Bergman, 1956

Backstage with Richard Burton and Susan Strasberg during
Time Remembered, 1957

Charlie and I at home in Nyack, on Edward R. Murrow's *Person to Person*

In 1955, the ultimate tribute from New York City

There's no reason to stop at sixty-five

to notice us. We were getting discouraged, when Jim's nanny whipped off her skirt and waved it over her head. That got their attention!

Charlie felt impatient about staying in Nyack. He always wanted to be where the action was—no, he *had to be* where the action was. Ben Hecht said that Charlie's hyperactivity dated back to their days as rookie reporters in Chicago. Most men outgrow the need for continual action and excitement as they get older, but not Charlie. It was in his blood.

Charlie was over forty-five when the war started. The only way he could get into uniform was as an officer. General William Porter, in charge of Army chemical warfare, offered him a job involving duties ranging from courier to escort to battlefield observer.

So Charlie became a major, and his friends had great fun at his expense. When the screenwriter Nunnally Johnson was told that Charlie had been assigned to chemical warfare, he asked, "My God, aren't they afraid he'll drink it all up?" Herman Mankiewicz, another writer friend, suggested that they could fly Charlie over Berlin and hold him by his heels outside the plane. "His one-hundred-proof breath would knock everyone out."

Charlie had been mainly a social drinker, but his frustration over being seen as "a slacker" while other guys went off to battle led to heavier drinking. To Charlie, the war wasn't a joke, despite his friends' ribbing. When he came home on leave, he'd just sit and complain of depression. He didn't know anything about chemical warfare when he joined up, but he got an awful load of it before the war ended.

Much of the time Charlie was posted to the Pentagon in Washington, which may not sound too arduous. People thought he was just one of those desk majors, pushing papers around and looking handsome in his uniform. One of his special duties was to escort scientists to rest homes or mental institutions. These were people previously dedicated to healing, to saving lives, and now they were working on mass killing. The change was too drastic for some to manage. They lost their bearings and had to be given time off for rehabilitation. Charlie was deeply depressed by their suffering.

Meanwhile, like so many others, I did what I could on the home front: making speeches, selling war bonds, helping to raise funds for war victims, working at a USO canteen. And I kept on acting at a time when people needed distraction.

A producer sent me Thornton Wilder's magnificent *The Skin of Our Teeth,* possibly the best script I was ever offered. But as I read the part of Sabina, I kept hearing Ruth Gordon speaking the lines. Ruth was a close friend of Thornton's, and I was sure he had written the part with her in mind, so I turned it down. Perhaps that was foolish, for the first Sabina wasn't Ruth but Tallulah Bankhead—who, let me add, was splendid.

In the spring of 1943 I decided to do a play about Harriet Beecher Stowe, the author of *Uncle Tom's Cabin.* It was a solid piece of craftsmanship rather than a great play, but Charlie and I both felt that its spirit of patriotism could bolster American morale.

Before starting rehearsals, I felt the need for a vacation, and I went off to Mexico with Mary for a short holiday. We had heard that a new volcano was forming near the village of Parícutin in the Mexican state of Michoacán, and that was something we thought we'd like to see.

Mary and I went to Cuernavaca and stayed with Charlie's older brother Alfred and his wife at their winter home. Everyone we met sounded like an expert, advising us on how to prepare for our venture to Parícutin. Mary and I simply accepted what we were told.

Everyone insisted that the air would be laden with lava dust and that any exposure to it would be dangerous. So we went to the market and bought pith helmets, engineer's gloves, long socks, bandannas, and goggles. We looked like beekeepers.

The town closest to the volcano was Urupan, where we spent the night at a small hotel. The next morning a guide picked us up in a jeep. He took one look at us and broke up laughing. I've played some pretty high comedy in my time, but never have I received such an immediate response from an audience. The poor man couldn't stop laughing at our volcano-watching costumes.

After he composed himself, we set off cross-country, passing a village where molten lava was flowing. When we started up the slope of the volcano, we were engulfed in a black landscape—everything was thick with lava dust. A church steeple poked up out of black soil in what was left of a village.

The guide stopped when some fierce-looking horsemen raced toward us, but they explained meekly that they only wanted to rent us their horses. We couldn't go any farther by jeep.

We continued on horseback. We heard Parícutin long before we saw it—a titanic roar from deep in the earth. We observed the eruption from a low hill, at a safe distance. The air was full of smoke, and enormous rocks flew out of the crater and crashed all around us. "Rocks as big as Chryslers," people standing beside us said. I don't know why they singled out Chryslers, but those boulders were certainly as large as any car I'd ever seen.

A little Mexican boy came up to Mary and said something in Spanish. She understood from her school lessons, and asked if she could go with him.

They ran down the hill, scrambled across a flat strip of land, and started up the side of the volcano. I shouted to Mary to come back, but she couldn't hear me. The boy picked up two rocks, using them as mittens, and started to gather up chunks of lava. Mary had better sense than to try it, and she soon came running back to me, much to my relief.

As we were preparing to leave, I heard an unmistakably American woman's voice say with a broad twang: "Are you girls about ready to go and eat now?" I whirled around and saw three American women dressed in cotton dresses and comfortable shoes. No helmets, no gloves, no long sleeves or pants; they were in what they wore for traveling in Mexico, and they weren't going to deviate for anything.

Mary and I had a grand time exploring Cuernavaca. We found the best ice cream shop, took in a band concert, looked at jewelry in the tiny silver shops lining the main shopping district. An ornate fountain in the plaza spewed water from a lion's head. The spray was refreshing on a hot day, and Mary and all the children loved it.

At sundown, people would come out of their houses, sprinkle down the dust in front of their homes, and carry chairs outside to sit and watch the sunset. This was part of their life, like the Sunday evening *paseos,* when young boys would walk one way while girls strolled arm in arm in the opposite direction, circling in a subtle courting ritual.

There were other rites that I found fascinating too. One morning I awoke to an ominous beating of drums. It sounded like a dirge and a march combined, a regular thump-thump-thump that started far away and drew steadily nearer. I had the wild notion that someone was about to be stood up against a wall and shot. It was that kind of drumbeat. I dressed and hurried to the front door.

The drums seemed to be coming from around the corner on Morelos Avenue. Fearfully, I visualized some downtrodden character in a guayabera shirt stumbling along between ranks of soldiers prodding him on. I probably heard a Max Steiner score too, for the scene I imagined came straight out of a movie about the Mexican revolution.

But it was only a group of children in uniform, on their way to school. There were no school buses, so the children were being marched up the roadway; the drums kept them in step, and perhaps reminded them that education was a kind of military discipline.

A few days later, I heard the lugubrious sound of drums again, this time in a funeral procession. Men were carrying a coffin down Morelos Avenue, while women followed with tuberoses, calla lilies, and lighted candles, which they carefully shielded from the wind. The man had been killed in a duel the night before, I learned.

Trying to pack as much as possible into our holiday, Mary and I went sightseeing in Mexico City, and then took an excursion to the Pyramids of the Sun and Moon at Teotihuacán. Mary wanted to climb up and I, determined to be a good sport, agreed.

We were teetering halfway up the steep steps of the Pyramid of the Sun when suddenly we were surrounded by a group of Mexican boys. They were not threatening, but they had appeared out of nowhere and had us at a disadvantage. We clung to those stairs like flies on a windowpane, unable to go up or down.

I happened to be wearing some gold jewelry. I had quite a nice collection, and why own it if you can't wear it? But it was surely careless to be sporting such jewelry on an excursion like this.

Thinking the boys really wanted money, I told them I had none with me. That was all right, they said. They would swap the silver trinkets they were peddling for my gold. I saw only innocence in their faces, but I knew they meant business.

A sudden downpour saved us and my gold. It was the rainy season, and the shower fell as though someone had turned on a faucet. The boys just melted away: one minute they were there, the next they had vanished.

Soon after we got home, I plunged into rehearsals for *Harriet*, which was staged by Elia Kazan, who had switched not long before from acting to directing. To my mind a director should be as unobtrusive as possible, never trying to give the performance himself or showing you how to do it. On the other hand, he shouldn't be so subtle that you forget he's there; he should help you, guide you, give you the feeling that he appreciates you, that he is pulling for you to achieve the performance you're after.

There has to be a good balance, and Kazan—or Gadge, as he is called—found it. He was skillful in many ways. He would squat at the feet of the actors rehearsing a scene, listening as intently as a child hearing a fairy tale, his eyes glued to the actors, his head moving from one to the other as they spoke their lines. He never said, "Do it this way," or, "Try it like that." The force of his attention and concentration inspired the cast with creative freedom.

Gadge was less than satisfactory in only one respect. I had always relied on directors to watch a performance about once every six weeks during a play's run, for I had a terrible fear of slipping into the trap of overacting, of which I'd been accused early in my career. My *Harriet* contract stipulated that Gadge would return to see an entire performance every so often. The producer, Gilbert Miller, paid Kazan a fee for this service in addition to his director's percentage of the weekly gross.

After a few visits, however, Gadge vanished. No one seemed to know where he was. The play was full of young actors playing sons, daughters, and friends of Harriet Beecher Stowe, and many of the men were drafted for war service. There were constant cast replacements, and only a stage manager who was terrified of the job was on hand to rehearse the newcomers. We needed Gadge desperately, but no one could locate him.

Finally I said to Gilbert, "Don't pay him that extra salary. He hasn't come near us, so he hasn't earned it." Gilbert followed this advice, whereupon Gadge threatened to sue for the money. I was shocked. Kazan was being totally unprofessional, but he got what he wanted. Gilbert gave him the money in order to avoid a legal battle.

At first I took Kazan's neglect personally, thinking he had stayed away from the play because he didn't like my work. Later I learned that he always lost interest in a show after it opened, and rarely returned to see it again. If this is true, then it is easy to understand why he prefers film-directing to stage work, as he has said he does.

≫·12·≪

Fortunately, despite our trials, *Harriet* was a solid hit that ran for over a year in New York. We were on tour with the play when Germany surrendered on May 7, 1945. What a day that was! All of Broadway turned out and cheered, and after the years of blackout, Times Square was its old shining self again. I longed to be there but wanted to come back in a play different from those I'd been doing for the past few years, preferably something light and amusing.

The British actress Maggie Smith once told an interviewer why she was temporarily giving up Shakespeare for a modern comedy: "I'm tired of wearing a wimple." I knew exactly what she meant. All that time as Victoria and Harriet taught me what a heavy toll makeup and hoop skirts can take. I yearned to kick up my heels a bit.

When I was at the end of the tour, in Los Angeles, Anita Loos, an old friend, asked me to stay with her at her house in Santa Monica. These were the pre-freeway days, and I really didn't want to stay clear out there and have to go all the way into Los Angeles every day, but she had just quit MGM and we were all concerned about her, so I gave in. Everybody loved Anita because of what she had contributed to America: *Gentlemen Prefer Blondes* and the ultimate gold digger, Lorelei Lee.

So I stayed with Anita, and every night when I came home from the theatre, there would be a little stack of manuscript on the table by my bed. In the morning, she would come in and say, "Did you read it?"

She was writing a play called *Blue Lounge,* and I thought it was awful. I finally got through the three weeks that I stayed with her without committing myself one way or another on her play, and then I went up to San Francisco with *Harriet.* After a few days, she phoned me. "Helen, the most wonderful thing has happened," she said. "Oscar Hammerstein is crazy about my play, and he wants to do it if you will."

I didn't know what to do. "Really? Oscar?" I said. She said that he wanted to put it right into production as soon as I finished *Harriet.* I acted on impulse and said I would do Anita's play. I didn't know how else to answer, and sometimes, when people catch me like that, I answer without thinking.

The play, renamed *Happy Birthday,* was Anita's attempt to rescue me from the stuffiness of those other ladies I'd been playing. She undertook to get me out of hoop skirts, and she did. But the play didn't start out well. I thought it was an amateur mess during rehearsals, and when we opened in Boston, it was a disaster.

Oscar and I were riding back to the Ritz Hotel together after the opening, and I said, "Oscar, how did we ever get into this?" He said, "I got into it because you wanted to do it, Helen." I said, "Oh, God, Anita told me that *you* wanted to do it." That's the way she was.

Happy Birthday is about Addie Beamis, a mousy librarian in love with a bank clerk. With the help of a few glasses of champagne, she loses her inhibitions, starts to sing and dance, and wins her way into his heart. The show was beautifully produced by Rodgers and Hammerstein, and was staged by Joshua Logan, one of my favorite directors.

Josh had a way of dropping a phrase on you that would stick in your mind; all through the run, whenever you'd reach a particular line, that phrase would guide you, coloring your whole approach to a scene.

At one point, Addie, tipsy, launches into a torrid tango with a professional dancer in a seedy Newark bar. When she reaches clear back, doing a back-bend, she catches sight of Mr. Bishop, her secret love, sitting at a table with another woman. Addie gives him an embarrassed little wave, which brought a big laugh at every performance.

"It's the first time Addie's ever seen Mr. Bishop upside down," Josh said to me when he was staging this scene. I thought of that every time I did the back-bend, and it enabled me to keep the moment fresh and funny. Josh's direction was full of tips like that.

I had a ball as Addie Beamis. The critics and public seemed surprised to find me in such a lighthearted role, but, after all, my career had started with Lew Fields. We opened in autumn 1946 and ran for a year and a half. My transformation from British queen to Newark party girl won me a Tony award.

After *Happy Birthday* I went to London to do a play I had misgivings about—*The Glass Menagerie.* Though I recognized the quality of Tennessee Williams' play, I wasn't drawn to the role of Amanda Wingfield, maybe because she was too much like the aging Southern belles I'd known in my youth in Washington. And something else bothered me about the assignment. One of my idols, Laurette Taylor, had originated the Amanda role, and her performance was legendary. Would I be able to follow her without stumbling?

I had witnessed Laurette's skill in the Williams play at first hand. She and I had become friendly back when George Tyler sent me to observe her. I knew that after the death of her husband, the playwright J. Hartley Manners, she had gone on what she called "the longest wake in history." Manners had been able to keep her under control by tapping her on the shoulder after the second drink, but he was gone. Her career nose-dived, and her role in *The Glass Menagerie* was a daring attempt at a comeback at age sixty.

The play's pre-Broadway engagement opened in Chicago while I was there acting in *Harriet*. Laurette and I would get together after work every night. Tennessee often joined us, and we'd go to a State Street bar where we could all relax. Laurette could handle one or two drinks at most, and she stayed within that limit.

One night the phone was ringing when I returned to my suite at the Ambassador. It was Laurette. "I can't go on tomorrow," she said in despair. "My throat hurts, and I'm losing my voice. If I don't go on, everyone will think I'm drunk. If they say I'm drunk, I *will* get drunk and stay drunk till I die."

Her cry for help galvanized me. I always carried a croup kettle when I went on tour, an electric steam kettle to which you could add medicine. It had been helpful when I came down with bronchitis or laryngitis. I told Laurette I'd come right away with the kettle. I dressed quickly and taxied downtown to the Sherman House.

I stayed with her through most of the night, making sure she was breathing properly and that the kettle didn't dry out. The next evening she gave a magnificent performance.

Laurette remained in the role for a year and a half, suffering from various ailments, among them a growth on her vocal cords and high blood pressure. She was silent all day, trying to save her voice for the evening performance, and audiences never guessed she was seriously ill. The play had been scheduled to open in

London, and she told me that she wanted me to replace her if she was unable to go on. I promised I would, never expecting it would come to that.

But perhaps Laurette knew. She once asked for my photograph to hang in her hallway gallery of people she liked. I said we would make an exchange. On mine I wrote: "To Laurette, my guiding star." On hers she wrote: "To Helen, who knew how to follow her star, with affection and admiration, Laurette."

When Laurette was dying, Audrey Wood, Tennessee's agent, reminded me of my promise. Despite my trepidations, I decided to honor Laurette's wish and went to London in 1948 to start rehearsing for the production, which was directed by John Gielgud and presented by H. M. Tennent, Britain's leading company. Charlie, Mary, and Jim came over for the opening some weeks later. It was my first stage appearance in England, and they wanted to lend moral support.

While I was learning the part, I had Laurette's understudy from New York come over to coach me on all the ad-lib lines and business Laurette had done. Laurette and Tennessee had fought over what he called her ad-libbing, but her improvisation clearly hadn't hurt his play's success. The understudy had stood in the wings and written down Laurette's every variation in the script. I tried to emulate her, though of course I couldn't be a carbon copy. We were different persons, after all.

From the outset I was uneasy about being directed by John Gielgud, a superb actor whom I'd known and admired since he'd played Hamlet in New York in 1936. We got along fine then, but the prospect of working with him was somewhat unnerving. I imagined that British actors looked on their American cousins as provincial hayseeds.

My anxiety was shared by three fellow cast members, two Americans and a Canadian. As we waited for Gielgud's arrival at the first rehearsal, we were as nervous as a bunch of colonials anticipating a visit from their Lord Protector.

Binkie Beaumont, head of H. M. Tennent, opened the rehearsal by announcing that Gielgud wished to say a few words to us. John himself was something of an anticlimax after Binkie's buildup. He looked terribly impressive, every inch the Savile Row gentleman, but his welcoming address might as well have been in Greek. It was a jumble of swallowed consonants and elongated vowels, delivered at breathtaking speed.

When he finished, we applauded, but the moment he left, I asked Binkie Beaumont if he could please translate for us.

"Mr. Gielgud was saying," Binkie explained, "that the British have difficulty with American speech patterns, so please speak distinctly and slowly in the play."

Rehearsals went quite smoothly. John was courteous, patient, and helpful. But my English friends kept hinting there might be trouble ahead. Disturbed, I went to Binkie again for clarification.

"John always has a blow-up on every production," Binkie said. "I suppose it's nerves, but it always happens and we're all a bit apprehensive until it does."

But we managed to get through rehearsals without incident, and our tryout in Brighton went well enough. I was convinced, however, that *Menagerie* was too American to go over in England. When I confessed my doubts to Tennessee at the Brighton opening, he told me that he was "not afraid of critics or bad reviews." That sounded like bravado to me, and I sensed that in fact he did care about his play's reception here, especially since it had been such a hit in America. The English press somehow got wind of our exchange and blew it out of all proportion. Perhaps I should have known better than to voice my apprehension to Tennessee.

John Gielgud's nerves finally gave out at the worst possible moment: at the full dress rehearsal before our West End premiere in London, he decided the lighting wasn't right at the start of the second act. We were stopped after every line, while filters were changed and spots were repositioned. The changes made no difference in the play's dramatic impact, but last-minute jitters drove John to keep us rehearsing until dawn. How we ever found the energy to go on that night, I'll never know.

Tennessee failed to show up at the London opening. He later explained that during the two-week run in Brighton he'd flown to Paris to spend a few days with friends—Gore Vidal, Truman Capote, and Carson McCullers and her husband. He got drunk, passed out in their apartment, and missed his train for London.

But his mother and brother did show up and made me realize why I felt uneasy about playing Amanda. Tennessee called *Menagerie* "a memory play," and after meeting his mother, I understood what kind of memories he was drawing on. When she introduced her son Dakin to us she said, "I want everybody to see that I have one son who's a gentleman." She was everything I disliked in an aging Southern belle, but in the play she was portrayed in a soft focus of compassion.

I suspect that it was fear of his mother as much as dread of the critics that kept Tennessee away from the opening. But later he came to London and basked in the attention he got from the press.

Menagerie had a decent run in London, but nothing like the success it had won in New York. You don't win many friends playing Amanda, but I think I was right about why it didn't go over in London: it *was* too American. None of Tennessee's plays was initially well-received in Britain; only after his death did English critics award him the respect he deserved.

I wasn't happy about my performance as Amanda, and about ten years later I had the chance to improve on it. In 1955 I received a desperate phone call from Jean Dalrymple, an old friend then in charge of the drama division of the New York City Center, which also presented ballets and operas at low ticket prices. She said the opera company was in financial straits and might have to fold that week unless I helped out. I was astonished. Did Jean expect a loan or contribution from me?

"We've just had a meeting at a bank," Jean explained. "They'll give us a loan if we can use your name as collateral. If you agree to do a three-week run of *Glass Menagerie* this fall, we can use your contract for a loan to bail out the opera company."

Charlie used to say that my name was on every sucker list in the world, and maybe he was right, but this was one request he agreed I couldn't refuse. We both loved Jean and admired what she was doing: quality revivals of worthwhile plays at modest ticket prices. We knew how important the New York City Opera was to New York, providing a training ground for young singers like Beverly Sills and Placido Domingo and staging operas too risky for the Metropolitan.

But why *The Glass Menagerie*? Jean explained that although the play was already regarded as a classic, it hadn't been staged since the original production.

"I know Amanda is not your favorite role," Charlie said. "But you did it in London, and it went all right. Take a chance." As usual, he was right.

At City Center I played Amanda more my own way, trying to ignore Laurette's performance as much as possible. That gave me more self-confidence. The *New York Times* critic Brooks Atkinson originally had reservations about the play, but said that he now considered it Tennessee Williams' finest achievement. He also said that I was "at the peak" of my career.

That made me feel pretty grand, but Charlie brought me back to earth. "Once you peak," he said with a glint in his eye, "there's nowhere to go but down."

≫·13·≪

Charlie and I never wanted theatrical careers for our children. We never pushed them in that direction or gave them any special encouragement until they decided for themselves. Mary did make a definite decision, but for Jim, being an actor started out as an accident.

The theatre was an inescapable part of our daily lives even in Nyack. My bathroom was my favorite spot for studying a script, because it was the only place I could be alone. I would sit and read on a little sofa, memorizing, taking notes. But even there, the family would soon come barging in. First Mary, all legs and full of gossip about what had happened at school. Then Charlie, then Jamie; and, trailing after him, Camille, our French poodle. I would order them out, but before long they would creep back in to read over my shoulder.

When we were in London with *The Glass Menagerie*, Jamie hung around the theatre so much that one day he gave a letter-perfect reading of Tom's opening speech. I began to realize that we had two budding actors in the family, Mary having already informed us that that was what she wanted to be.

A producer offered her a role in a film adaptation of Paul Gallico's *The Snow Goose* when she was only thirteen, but Charlie and I felt she was too young. She was very disappointed, and naturally argued that at her age I had already been a veteran of several years on the stage. Fortunately for us, the film project fell through, and Mary forgot about her ambition—for a while.

At seventeen Mary again told me that she was determined to be an actress, and this time I knew she had to be taken seriously. She had been a beautiful child, with an unusual poise and serenity. She was even lovelier as a teenager: intelligent, self-confident. "Mary is the most perfectly adjusted person I've ever met," our actor friend Kent Smith once told us. If she wanted to be an actress, I knew she must have carefully considered her decision and felt that it was within her reach. She deserved our support, I thought.

But I wasn't sure Charlie would agree, so I painstakingly planned a speech to convince him. "Mary sees you as a successful man because of the plays and movies you've written," I said. "She sees me as a successful actress. Our lives are good. We have a charming house, wonderful friends, many comforts. So how can we tell her, 'No, don't go into show business, it may break your heart'? How can we say that, when our lives tell her something different?"

Charlie made a stab at rebuttal, but soon gave in. He was crazy about Mary and wanted her to be happy. "Maybe once she tries it, she won't like acting," he said hopefully. If theatre life didn't suit her, she'd be the first to know and would give it up.

So in the summer of 1946, just before *Happy Birthday* opened, I agreed to appear in a summer-stock tour of James M. Barrie's *Alice-Sit-by-the-Fire*. Mary, cast as my daughter, would be able to get a feel for what being a professional actress was all about. We were fortunate to have Joshua Logan, a good friend who was very fond of Mary, as director.

171

We were both jittery before the opening, I more than Mary. I flubbed a line early on, and she covered for me so skillfully that I doubt the audience knew anything was wrong. Charlie was out front and probably would have died if his daughter had shown no promise, but she came through beautifully. After the performance he presented her with a bouquet of violets with a rose in the center. He had brought a similar bouquet to the hospital the day she was born and had continued to give her violets on Valentine's Day and other special occasions.

Later, on the opening night of *Happy Birthday,* I was unusually nervous. Mary, who was waiting in my dressing room before the curtain went up, asked what was wrong. I explained that I had to dance in this show, something I hadn't done in years. What if I stumbled and fell? "Well," said Mary, echoing an Ira Gershwin lyric, "pick yourself up, dust yourself off, and start all over again." I was so amused that I forgot my jitters.

After graduating from Rosemary Hall in 1946, Mary enrolled at the American Academy of Dramatic Arts, where she worked diligently to learn her craft. She didn't want anyone to say she got ahead because her parents pulled strings.

But Jim's acting career came to him. I was making *The Skin of Our Teeth* for television, and he came over to the studio with his girlfriend one day. He was at Solebury School in Bucks County and all of seventeen years old. The producer took one look at him and said, "Oh, the all-American boy." He said he'd been looking for an actor with Jim's looks to play in a new movie, and he asked me if Jim had any ambitions to act. I told him I didn't know. That didn't stop the producer from coming back and asking Jim if he could do a picture on his summer vacation. It wouldn't interfere with his schoolwork at all, he was told, and he could make some real money. The picture was *The Young Stranger.*

After it came out, Jim's life was never the same again. He

finished high school as president of his graduating class and editor of the school paper. He also almost singlehandedly dug the school's new swimming pool, since that was the punishment for a student caught smoking and Jim had a smoking habit he couldn't quit.

I went to see his school's production of *A Christmas Carol*, in which Jim played Scrooge. At the end, the repentant Scrooge takes a big basket of Christmas goodies to Bob Cratchett and his family. Jim was handing out the goodies, and when he got to Mrs. Cratchett, he said, "And here's a big goose for you, Mrs. Cratchett." It broke up the audience. He was an incredible free spirit, quite wonderful and adored by his fellow students.

Jim went on to Harvard, and he kept getting acting offers, so many that they were disrupting his life. At the end of his second year, he told me he was leaving the university for a while. I argued against it, but when he said how exhausted he felt and how torn apart in different directions, I told him I would much rather have a healthy son than a diploma on the wall. Despite his best intentions, he never went back.

His best-known role was Dan-O on "Hawaii Five-0," one of the most popular television series ever. He played it twelve years, and I'm sorry he stayed in it so long, because he became associated with that one role, and it's been tough on him ever since. All actors get crazy after a while in a series. Nobody enjoys it: you're doing the same character, the same thing, all the time. And usually, when you leave a series, you have trouble working again right away. Until recently, Carroll O'Connor couldn't get anything after he left "All in the Family," and poor Mary Tyler Moore is still struggling.

I always regretted that my Mary didn't live to have a full life as a wife and mother, but Jim has given me three wonderful grandchildren: the older ones, Charlie and Mary are in their twenties, and little Jamie is four. My Jim told me when he was

173

fourteen that his name was Jim, and he didn't want to be called Jamie anymore. Well, wouldn't you know—he's named his younger son Jamie. Not Jim, not James: Jamie.

During the run of *Happy Birthday,* Josh Logan told me that he was writing an adaptation of Chekhov's *The Cherry Orchard,* set in Louisiana in the 1900s. The symbolic cherry trees were to be replaced by wisteria, and that would be the title: *The Wisteria Trees.* Josh had grown up in Louisiana, and his idea was to fuse Chekhov with legends about the post–Civil War South that he had heard as a boy.

He asked whether I would like to play the lead. I had loved the original play, but wondered if I would be believable as the Louisiana counterpart of a Russian beauty. If he thought so, I said, I would read the play when it was finished. But Josh soon got involved in something else, and I assumed he had abandoned *The Wisteria Trees.*

The Theatre Guild then asked me to go on a summer-stock tour of a comedy called *Good Housekeeping.* The play looked promising, but the Guild wanted to test it to see whether it was ready for Broadway. I agreed, partly because it had a good role for Mary.

We opened in Westport, Connecticut, in June 1949. Charlie couldn't be there, because he was hospitalized for an ulcer that had bothered him for years. We missed him, especially on opening night, which went splendidly. How proud he would have been of Mary, I thought. The show was so well-received that the Guild discussed opening it on Broadway that fall or the following spring.

After the Westport engagement, Mary suddenly came down with a cold, and I took her home. I was disturbed by her extreme lethargy and finally brought her to Lenox Hill Hospital, where Charlie was being treated. The doctors didn't seem unduly alarmed about Mary's condition, and she urged me to get back to *Good Housekeeping.* She promised she would join me before the week was out.

The next day, just before the opening in New Hope, Pennsylvania, Charlie called and said the doctors were now gravely concerned. I chartered a plane and rushed back to New York and was shocked to find Mary in an iron lung. In the summer of 1949 the country was suffering the worst polio epidemic in history, and somehow Mary had contracted the disease. She was heavily medicated, and Charlie and I were at her bedside constantly. One day she looked at us through the haze of medication and said, "Let's the three of us get out of here." A few days later, we lost her.

Nothing is more difficult to accept than the death of a child. My mother was also sick at the time and died soon afterward. Her death was a sad loss, yet it seemed somehow natural, for she was old and ill. But Mary was so young, beautiful, talented. We could not understand why this had happened to us. What had we done? Despairing questions with no answers.

Letters of sympathy poured in from all over the world, from the famous and the unknown, from parents who had suffered the same fate as we. Eleanor Roosevelt told me of her grief at losing a son, and Dwight Eisenhower, then president of Columbia University, wrote to us about the death of his firstborn child.

Jonas Salk later told me that press coverage of Mary's death helped him gain financing for his research. This helped me to understand that Mary's death had meaning. She had had a wonderful life. Her coming into the world had been a blessing, and her departure brought aid to countless others.

But it took time for me to see it that way. The first months after Mary's death were horrible. The main discipline of the theatre is never to show how hard you are working—your performance must never seem labored. Some of that discipline now carried over into my private life: don't let the suffering show, it isn't professional.

Theatre friends kept urging me to get back to work; that was the best remedy for grief, they insisted. I was offered many roles, but I didn't even want to appear in public, much less present myself on stage. The first time, after we lost Mary, that I went for a walk, at the insistence of a young friend, people smiled at me—it had always been a delight to me that when people recognized me on the street, they smiled—but now their smiles quickly changed to expressions of pain; they looked away. This I couldn't bear, so I became housebound.

One evening, as Charlie and I were sitting in our apartment in New York, numb, waiting out our lives, the phone rang. It was Tallulah Bankhead, calling from Connecticut. "What are you doing with yourselves?" she wanted to know.

"Nothing," Charlie told her. "We're just sitting here."

"My God, you can't be alone," Tallulah said. "I'll come stay with you."

"No, Tallulah," Charlie said. There was terror in his voice. "Don't do that."

But Tallulah ignored him. "I'm on my way in the morning— packing right now."

After he hung up, Charlie looked at me and said. "We have to get out of here." Perhaps Peter Hurd, the painter, could put us up at his place in New Mexico.

And that was what happened. We "eloped" to the Hurd ranch, where Henriette Wyeth Hurd made us feel like family for a week. Then we continued westward to Hawaii.

In Honolulu, we intended to be private, incognito, but the press got wind of our presence, and the next thing we knew, it was in the papers.

The Jimmy Stewarts immediately called us at our hotel. Although they were on their honeymoon, they picked us up, took us in tow, and during our stay there never let us out of their sight. They even took us deep-sea fishing off the coast of the Big Island in a boat they had chartered—this, on their honeymoon. I credit Gloria and Jimmy for helping me back to life—and Tallulah, too, in her own fashion.

Charlie, in the deepest despair himself, wanted to help me, so he called Josh Logan and asked him to go ahead with *The Wisteria Trees*.

We went into rehearsal in December 1949, well before Josh had had time to polish his script. There was a lot of rewriting, with new lines to memorize every day. I tried hard to be cooperative, but I must have seemed remote and irritable at times. The continual revisions didn't help my concentration. I managed to get through rehearsals, and the habit of professionalism drove me to give it my best at every performance.

It was that discipline that saw me through, and *The Wisteria Trees* was well-received. But I had lost my taste for work, and I was haunted by the thought that audiences were being kind because they didn't want to see me hurt again.

That first Christmas without our Mary was unbearably sad. We couldn't face the prospect of a holiday banquet with company and the usual festivities, so we decided to have a quiet dinner at home. With a cookbook lying open on the kitchen counter, I roasted a turkey with stuffing and fixed sweet potatoes and creamed onions.

Charlie and Jim sat at the table, and I served the first course, a fruit cup. Before bringing in the bird, I told them that I didn't want to hear any teasing if anything was wrong—if it was overdone or underseasoned. In that case we would just put on our coats and hats and go to our local restaurant, the St. George's Inn.

When I came back in from the kitchen with the turkey and trimmings, I found Charlie and Jim, silent and deadpan, bundled

177

up in overcoats, caps, mufflers, and mittens. That completely broke me up.

Jim was a bastion of strength. I can't imagine what he must have gone through. It must have been hard to take, especially for a boy as sensitive as Jim. In fact, early on I feared he might be too serious and hypersensitive, but he turned out fine: he is good-humored, generous, and very kind.

Years before, when I was still very young, I had met an actress who was married to a charming British actor. One day she told me that her son had been fathered by another man. That didn't surprise me—June was a pretty loose-living lady—but I was shocked to hear that she'd told her son who his natural father was. The boy loved her husband and they were great friends, so it seemed cruel to have told the child the truth. "Well," June said, sensing I disapproved, "there's one thing that's going to see him through—he knows he is loved." That made good sense, and later I thought it applied to Jim as well. Through all the hard times, he knew he was loved.

Charlie's wit served us well in those days. He tried to overcome his depression and to cheer us up, but I knew that Mary's death had sapped something vital inside him. Ben Hecht once used Murger's description of the poet-hero of *La Bohème* in writing about Charlie: "He walked backward through life looking at the day he was twenty-one." Ben was right. It was part of Charlie's charm. But after Mary's death, his youthfulness faded.

He began to drink more than ever. In the '20s Charlie had lived in a world where heavy drinking was considered a kind of emblem of revolt against the enforcers of puritan American values. Many writers and artists—John Barrymore, Dorothy Parker, Scott Fitzgerald, Robert Benchley—suffered from the effects of alcohol. And Charlie was among them. He didn't know when to say enough.

The problem was aggravated by his writer's block. He wanted

to write something for me. In the early '40s I had appeared in *Ladies and Gentlemen,* a Hungarian comedy that he and Ben Hecht had adapted for Broadway. But that was only a supporting role, and Charlie wanted something better—a play of his own with a role for me that would overshadow *Victoria.*

When he drank too much, Charlie became argumentative and even boring, like many drinkers—and quite unlike his old self. I remember too many nights when I met him at '21' after the theatre and sat and waited while he downed one nightcap after another. As we drove back to Nyack, he'd repeat the same old stories again and again, too befuddled to realize what he was saying. "Please, not again!" I'd think, my nerves on edge.

Until Mary died, the drinking was only sporadic. But then Charlie set about killing himself. It took seven years, and it was harrowing to watch. I longed to help, but everything I did proved wrong. Looking back, I feel sure that there was no right thing to do, but at the time I was frustrated, always trying and always doing something wrong.

Charlie agreed to join Alcoholics Anonymous, but it didn't work for him. Maybe he was too proud. I went to some AA meetings with him, and so did friends who wanted to lend support. But I sensed that he felt that this was reducing him to a *nobody* when he had always been *somebody.*

Fearing that he felt diminished by my career, I offered to give it up. That was a mistake: he wanted no sacrifices on my part, and he kept searching for plays for me to do. After *Wisteria Trees,* Leo McCarey offered me a role in his next film, *My Son John.* I wanted to refuse, having finished with the movies more than twenty years before, but Charlie insisted I accept. McCarey was a fine director, he said. It was a good script, and a few months in California would do me good.

Jim went with me, and we rented a house in Beverly Hills. We waited for Charlie to join us, but he never did. I think he was glad to have me out of the way. He knew it was torture for me to watch him destroy himself; he couldn't live with my need to help when he knew he was beyond helping himself.

When we finished shooting, Charlie urged me to accept roles in what were planned as limited engagements: a revival of *What Every Woman Knows* at the City Center and a new play for producer Robert Whitehead, *Mrs. McThing,* by Mary Chase, the author of *Harvey.* Mrs. Chase had written her play for children, but it was so popular that it was transferred to Broadway and then went on tour for several months.

One of the leads in *Mrs. McThing* was young Brandon de Wilde, who had made his mark in *Member of the Wedding* a few years before. After a time, Brandon left the show and was replaced by a boy from what would now be called a disadvantaged background. He was discovered by Robert Whitehead. I took him to Nyack.

That proved to be a mistake, and I should have known better. When Bunty Cobb's son left us, Charlie and I had made another attempt to extend our family, and that too had been a disaster. We took in a bright girl from the Appalachian hills, recommended to me as a poor but very gifted child. She had an excellent record in school and wanted a career in the theatre, but there was no chance for intellectual or artistic nurturing where she lived. I talked to Charlie about her, though we both knew it wouldn't make much difference what he said.

The girl stayed with us and finished high school in Nyack. Then we sent her to the American Academy of Dramatic Arts for professional training. I introduced her to theatre people who might help launch her on stage when the time came. She was smart, attractive, and talented, but she had one dreadful flaw: a backwoods mentality as narrow as a ribbon. She was overflowing with that old-time religion.

She made life unpleasant for everyone, accusing us of all the sins she had ever heard of or imagined. My secretary, a very nice girl, she called a Jezebel who shouldn't be allowed near Mary and Jim, lest she contaminate them. Every day brought another accusation, another superstitious fear. Finally she fell in love and announced that she was leaving. That was a happy day for us.

The boy from *Mrs. McThing*—I'll call him Tommy—presented another problem. He was an able actor and a nice kid in many ways, but he had a childish habit hard to accept: he took things. Not that he was a kleptomaniac. He just helped himself to whatever he wanted. Neither the show's cast nor my household could curb his appetite for illegal possession.

Among the things he appropriated were cigarettes. Ten years old and already smoking! I couldn't believe it. Since I never actually caught him smoking, I assumed he was hiding out somewhere and puffing away.

I was confident I could straighten him out, and I prepared a firm but mild little speech. Perhaps the stealing and smoking were just signs of rebellion. I sat him down one day and told him calmly that everyone said he was taking cigarettes from their dressing rooms. I warned him against petty thievery and the evils of smoking. I told him he was too good an actor to get into trouble and risk his career.

"If you want a cigarette," I concluded, "just ask me and I'll give you the money to buy a pack." I hoped he'd never have the nerve to ask.

Tommy looked me straight in the eye and said, "I don't smoke."

That was that. End of wise counseling. Also the end of Tommy for us. The show soon went on tour, we both left Nyack, and someone else took charge of Tommy.

In the winter of 1954, I thought a warm climate and a change of scene might do Charlie some good, so we accepted a joint engagement at the Royal Poinciana Playhouse in Palm Beach, Florida. Charlie was to direct a production of *Twentieth Century*, and I was to appear in *The Glass Menagerie*. We rented a bungalow and went to work.

Charlie had been working with Ludwig Bemelmans on a comedy based on the life of Elsie de Wolfe Mendl, which Bemmie had chronicled in a memoir, but then Bemmie slipped away and Charlie was stuck with the project. Anita Loos asked if she could work on it with him. "It's my kind of play," she said. "I know those people." Charlie acquiesced, and she joined us in Florida. The role of Lady Mendl was intended for me, but I had my doubts about playing the acerbic, high-falutin' decorator.

One evening, when I was at the theatre, Charlie became so ill that Anita called a doctor. The doctor quickly had him admitted to a local hospital, which happened to be Catholic. It was the custom of the admitting personnel to ask the patients' religious preference so they could get necessary help if they needed it or wanted it. Anita was asked, "What is his religion?"

It was Charlie who responded. "I'm a phallic worshiper."

By the end of the week, when my contract was up, Charlie looked fine and the doctor dismissed him. He, Anita, and I went off to Havana for a few days' holiday, which Charlie insisted would perk us up. That's how he was then: he could be deathly ill one day and seem to bounce back the next. But a lot of it was show.

The following summer I got another chance at *The Skin of Our Teeth*. ANTA and the producer, Robert Whitehead, were underwriting an international theatre festival in Paris, and I was offered the role of Mrs. Antrobus. Sabina, the role I had turned down in 1942, was played by Mary Martin, and other cast members included George Abbott, Don Murray, and Mary's daughter, Heller Halliday. My son Jim was assistant lighting director.

Charlie was happy to be in Paris again, and there was a procession of old friends coming by our apartment at the Lancaster to see him. Irwin Shaw, the writer, was constantly there, and Art Buchwald, then a columnist on the *International Herald-Tribune,* told him that Charlie and Ben's play *The Front Page* was what sent him off to seek his career with newspapers.

After the Paris engagement, we opened for a few weeks on Broadway. By then, the late summer of 1955, Charlie was sick and he didn't want me hovering around, helplessly watching him go downhill. He wanted to stay in our New York flat, but thinking he'd be more comfortable in Nyack, I decided to renovate the house so he and I could sleep on the first floor. Climbing stairs had become difficult for him.

When I showed him the plans, Charlie stared at them and shook his head. "I'll never go back there to live," he said.

"Charlie, you don't mean that!" I gasped. But he did.

"I'll never live to see these changes," he went on. I was heartsick.

He spent the last months of his life at the Manhattan apartment, working occasionally and keeping up with his friends, who wrote to him and paid visits. On the first warm day of 1956, Ben managed to get him out of bed for an annual spring rite of theirs: a leisurely stroll along Fifth Avenue. A month later, Charlie was gone.

We had wonderful, unforgettable times in our marriage, but there were also moments when I prayed that we could be released from each other. We had some bad times because we were both people of passion and high spirits: we went from high to low. And we were both public people, with others almost constantly around us. But the bond between Charlie and me was too strong ever to be broken. If it wasn't a perfect marriage, well, what marriage ever is? There was never a time when I thought Charlie was unfaithful, which would have been the worst thing I can think of, and there was never a time when I had an urge to be unfaithful to him. It was a happy marriage, as happy as marriages of people in our way of life can be. It certainly wasn't a bland marriage.

In our courting days, Charlie once said to me, "Helen, I may never be able to give you contentment, but I promise you'll never be bored." He was true to his word. There were times when I was anxious and moments when I despaired, but there was so much fun and laughter, and so much love, in between. Though we had our rough periods, they never came from the boredom that eats away at many marriages.

After Charlie's death, I was torn by guilt and self-recrimination. Should I have stopped acting when we married? Could I have said or done anything to stop his drinking?

But Charlie would not have wanted a *Good Housekeeping* wife. And what can be said to make an alcoholic seek help unless he himself decides he needs it? With time I came to see that I had not been to blame, but in the months after Charlie's death I was overcome by the most terrible sense of failure I've ever known.

I was aware, too, that now I would be shouldering responsibilities alone. Jim was a great comfort, but he was only eighteen when Charlie died, too young to be burdened with my cares. My mother had guided me through my early years; then I had Charlie to advise me. But now there was no one to fall back on. I was on my own.

≫·14·≪

With our family so depleted, Jim and I rattled around in the large house, which was full of reminders of Mary and Charlie. The first Christmas without Charlie loomed before us as a sad ritual. Even spending the holiday with old friends daunted us, because they too would remember him and Mary. Sometimes too much sympathy can be an aggravation.

What we needed was a complete change of scene. And for my part, I also needed a respite from the world of the theatre. The awful self-consciousness I had felt after Mary died returned with a vengeance after Charlie's death.

We decided to spend Christmas in Cuernavaca with my in-laws, Alfred and Mary MacArthur. God bless them! They were thoughtful and generous hosts, as they had been to my daughter and me in the past. They got Jim and me out of our misery.

It was a great relief just to walk around town without being recognized. I was completely free of the self-conscious feeling that bothered me in New York. Then, as I became more aware of my surroundings, I realized anew why Mexico was so appealing to me. It reminded me of those carefree days when I would return to visit my father in Washington after my mother had launched me in the theatre. I would relish our ordinary home life, and I didn't miss the theatre world at all. Similarly, in Cuernavaca I could relax and shed the identity that oppressed me back home. Among the major attractions were the sidewalk cafés. Everyone had a favorite café—mine was the Universal, on the plaza in the middle of town. You could sit there and sip a *limonada* or a cappuccino and watch whatever was going on. It might be a ceremony in front of the Government Palace or the *campesinos* in their sparkling white clothes, sitting around and enjoying a Sunday evening in town. Or there might be one of the band concerts I loved despite the terrible cacophony.

I was also drawn to Mexico because I like places with a lot of history. Towns like Palm Springs, Palm Beach, and other fashionable resorts where people spend the winter simply have no background.

It hadn't occurred to me that I'd ever reside in Cuernavaca. The possibility arose by chance. One of the guests at a dinner party given by my in-laws was a fascinating and handsome man named Eduardo Rendón. He was a Mayan with a finely chiseled face that resembled the great Mayan head in the National Anthropology Museum in Mexico City.

In the course of our conversation I learned that though he wasn't a trained architect, he had restored some of the old Spanish colonial homes in town, making them habitable for present-day residents. When I waxed enthusiastic about the charm of the town, he mentioned that he knew of a house for sale. Would I care to see it? Well, why not? No harm in looking, I thought.

It turned out to be the stodgiest, most unattractive house I'd ever seen. Eduardo and my brother-in-law stood by as I looked around in disbelief. "You must buy this house," they kept saying.

"Is this a place you think I'd be happy living in?" I asked. "Is it the kind of house you think I deserve?"

"You must imagine the way it can look," Eduardo said. "I will fix it for you. If you buy it, I will pour poetry into it."

And that's what he did. He turned it into the most exquisite little jewel of a house, removing all the ugliness and making it a magical place. He put in wide doorways, opened it to the sun, and brought in three young Indian artists to paint the walls and ceilings. They would laugh and sing as they worked on their scaffolding, while I sat and watched, feeling like a de Medici. But the cost of the renovations was hardly princely: a grand total of fifteen hundred dollars.

I stayed while the house was renovated and decorated. It had come with some furniture which, when stripped, revealed a beautiful, light-colored wood. Everything else I needed was made by a master cabinetmaker, who built everything to my specifications at a cost of less than thirty dollars per piece.

Before the house was completely refurbished, I had to return to New York and make a decision about further work. Earlier I had turned down the role of the Russian dowager empress in the film version of *Anastasia*. I didn't think the part of a domineering Romanov suited me. But, then, I can't remember ever playing a role that didn't seem, at first, more suited to someone else. Even in the case of Victoria, despite my enthusiasm I thought an English actress would have been more appropriate. On stage the dowager empress had been played magnificently by Eugenie Leontovich and by my close friend Cathleen Nesbitt, and I didn't think I'd be nearly as good as either of them.

But friends kept urging me to get back to work. They all believed the wounded soldier had to return to action, never mind the bandages or the morphine. And the attitude in the theatre world has always been: "The show must go on," whatever the personal cost to the actors.

Josh Logan implored me to take the *Anastasia* role, saying it was my duty to use the talent God had given me. Anita Loos and Lillian Gish also encouraged me, Anita going so far as to say she would accompany me to London, where the film was to be shot. Eventually I gave in.

That was a mistake. Going back to work so soon after Charlie's death set me back several years in getting my personal life sorted out. A period of mourning and introspection is necessary, and trying to skip over it only prolongs it.

I still occasionally felt the guilt and remorse that had overwhelmed me right after Charlie's death. I suppose most women experience this after the death of a husband. You are disoriented, unsure that you can function on your own. It is as though you have been cut in half; as though you are not a complete entity.

And there is the added weight of blaming yourself for the words that weren't spoken, for the times you might have been there but were not. You assume the guilt not only for your failures but for his too, and that guilt can be a great burden until you reach a distance and the past falls into the proper perspective.

But something else bothered me about *Anastasia*. I couldn't figure out why the producer kept coming back to me, why he wouldn't take no for an answer. He already had Ingrid Bergman and Yul Brynner for the other leading roles, so why did he want me so desperately? Then, after a talk with him one day, I suddenly realized that he needed me *because of* Ingrid.

Anastasia would be Ingrid's first American film since her widely publicized love affair with the Italian director Roberto Rossellini. She had had a child with Rossellini while still married to another man. This caused a terrible scandal. Ingrid had generally played very virtuous characters—Joan of Arc, the nun in *The Bells of St. Mary's*—and the American press and public turned against her when she made no secret that she was living with Rossellini. They felt betrayed. Preachers denounced her from the pulpit and pickets tried to keep people from attending her movies.

188

Charlie and I had written her a note of sympathy and support at the height of the scandal. I remembered all too well the hurt I had felt when the press treated me unkindly at the time of Mary's birth and "the act of God" controversy.

We had known Ingrid from the time she first came to the United States from Sweden. She was preparing to do *Liliom* on the New York stage with Burgess Meredith, a fine actor and a Nyack neighbor. He and Ingrid came over regularly to play tennis on our tennis court, and we became good friends.

Now I had an opportunity to help Ingrid in a more significant way. The producer of *Anastasia* wanted someone with a moral and upright reputation to costar with Ingrid. Someone like me. I was meant to lead the way to public reacceptance of her. And I guess the ploy worked. Ingrid's return was a triumph, and she won her second Oscar for *Anastasia*.

I felt a trace of a Russian accent was needed for my role, so I called on a Nyack neighbor and friend, Countess Alexandra Tolstoy, daughter of the great Russian writer. Since 1939, when she emigrated to the United States, she had run a center for exiles from the U.S.S.R. She had a farm with several cottages and dormitories where they could live until they felt secure enough to move on.

One of her guests was a teacher, a courageous woman whom the Soviets had arrested in the States and had been holding against her will in the Russian consulate on Park Avenue. Somehow she managed to jump out of a window and make her way to Countess Tolstoy's farm. The Soviets pursued her to the farm, but local police threw up roadblocks all around the area.

This charming woman, a very fine teacher, became my tutor. She made tapes on which she would read a line from the script, then I would repeat it. I listened for hours, tuning my ears to her accent, trying to pronounce each word as she did.

The day came for Anita and me to leave for London. The

producer wanted me there early, perhaps because he was afraid I would take as much time to show up as I had taken to decide to do the role. Anita and I sat around the Dorchester Hotel for several days, waiting for them to call me. Halfway through the second week, I suggested we go to Brighton for a holiday.

Off we went, delighted to be free of that awful waiting around. We didn't tell anyone we were going, since I was sure they wouldn't need me for a while, but they found us and called the next day, putting an abrupt end to our escape.

Later we learned there was pandemonium at the studio when I couldn't be found at the Dorchester. God knows how they traced me to Brighton. Perhaps they talked to the concierge who had booked our rooms or the doorman who got the taxi to take us to the railroad station. In any case, they summoned me back to London at once, not to begin filming but to undergo a sound test for my Russian accent.

The advisor on the set was another Russian countess or some such who, gossip had it, had been one of H. G. Wells' mistresses. She declared that my Russian accent was the best she'd ever heard from a non-Russian. Well and good. But she hovered beside me throughout the shooting, making sure I didn't stray from her idea of perfection.

Once production started, I realized that I wasn't quite ready to get back to work. I plodded along as best I could, often ill at ease and morbid, feeling as though I'd been anesthetized. Though I had been friendly with both Ingrid and Yul in the past, now I didn't mix much with them or with anyone else. At the end of the day I'd go back to the hotel, crawl into bed, and close my eyes. The next morning I'd report to the set and go through the motions like a robot.

It seemed to take forever to finish. The director, Anatole Litvak, was a tough taskmaster, though he did turn out good films. When *Anastasia* was wrapped up, I staggered home, not at all happy with the work I'd done. It was a relief to get back to Nyack, but soon the same melancholy I'd felt before came over me again. All the little demons of memory, guilt, and remorse were waiting to pounce anew. I was in a continual fog and can't recall how I managed to fill each day.

One thing I do remember is the birthday party I gave for Jim at the '21' Club. In the middle of it, a waiter told me I was wanted on the phone. It was Anatole Litvak, who had tracked me down and wanted me to go with him to the opening of *Anastasia* at the Radio City Music Hall that very evening. He had already asked Ingrid and Yul, but both had declined. I was number three.

Playing third fiddle didn't bother me as much as walking out on my son's party. When I told Litvak why I couldn't make it, he urged me to leave for a while and then return to the club after the premiere. I refused. Though I didn't say so, I thought his audacity was unwarranted.

Playing in *Anastasia* wasn't exactly a gratifying experience, but at least I believed my accent was pretty good—after all, it had passed muster with two ex-members of the Russian nobility. But Judith Crist, the *Herald-Tribune*'s movie critic, wrote: "Helen Hayes will remind you of your old aunt in Vermont."

Sometimes you just can't win.

After that job I needed a breather. Staying at home was just keeping me depressed, so I took off for a short holiday in Cuernavaca. My friends couldn't understand why I'd bought a house in Mexico. Why Mexico? And why of all places "that cocktail town," Cuernavaca?

They had the wrong impression. Cuernavaca has been a tropical winter retreat since the fifteenth century, when Aztec chieftains left the rigors of the capital to enjoy the climate of the mile-high resort. But the permanent residents didn't start the day with a vodka gimlet. I told my skeptical friends that a house in

Mexico was a good investment. It could be rented when I wasn't there. I had already found a tenant, Julie Carpenter, who had lived all over the world with her father, a career Army officer. She was thinking of settling permanently in Mexico. Whenever I needed the house, Julie would take a room at the Hotel del Parque, leaving her two West Highland terriers with me. This arrangement worked out very well.

My vacations in Cuernavaca, always too brief, were a mixture of pleasure and frustration. "How wonderful to be here!" I'd sigh as I arrived. But at the same time I would realize that soon I would have to return. Anticipating my departure spoiled my fun.

In typical fashion, I had already committed myself to another job, in a play I was not even eager to do: *Time Remembered,* by the French playwright Jean Anouilh. It was about a rich and dotty countess determined to prevent her nephew from pining away for the love of a woman he'd lost years before. The countess comes up with the bizarre idea of employing a shop girl to impersonate *la belle dame sans merci,* but the scheme leads to endless complications.

It was a highly theatrical and delicate comedy. But I was not ready to work just then. When the role of the countess was first offered to me, I turned it down, and probably wouldn't have changed my mind but for a request from a most unexpected source.

Susan Strasberg had been signed to play the shop girl. It was her first stage role after her great triumph in *The Diary of Anne Frank* two years earlier. She had become a star in that role while still a teenager, and now she would surely be scrutinized by critics who might feel her stardom had been won too easily. *Time Remembered* was going to be a ticklish moment in her career.

It was Lee Strasberg, of all people, who asked me to help his daughter. I say "of all people" because Lee was one of the founders of the Actors Studio, which I blame for many of the things wrong with the American theatre then and now. Lee must have been aware of my opinion, because I had made no secret of my disapproval.

All the same, Lee wanted me to help Susan, and I felt I had to hear him out. Whatever I thought of his method, he had given me good advice on how to make Amanda my own performance when I played *Menagerie* at City Center.

When we met to talk about Susan, I found we agreed on one important point: it wasn't necessarily an advantage for an actor to be put on stage as early as Susan had been. Child actors tended to pick up bad habits and tricks that had to be quashed swiftly lest they became ingrained.

Susan was in roughly the same position I had been in forty years earlier, when I opened in *Bab*. We had both become stars without acquiring the experience or technique to merit that status. Lee wanted someone to guide Susan, and he felt that that someone would have to be in the show with her.

Lee, himself a renowned coach and star-maker, might well have seemed to be the right person to instruct Susan, but I understood why he stepped aside: parents, no matter how highly qualified or well-intentioned, often make the worst tutors. They are too quick with praise and too cutting with censure.

Susan was definitely talented, so I said yes. I felt obligated to repay the kindness that so many people had shown me when I started out, and to pass on what I'd learned about the tradition of the theatre. But had I been able to foresee the consequences, I doubt I would have been so willing.

To begin with, I wasn't comfortable in the part of the countess, and the director wasn't giving me any helpful hints. It was only when we opened in Boston on the tryout tour that I realized how the role should be played. It happened purely by accident.

I was listening distractedly to the radio in my hotel room one morning when suddenly I heard a madrigal played on the virginal—or one of those Renaissance instruments. That's it! I thought: the countess should be as light, dainty, and tinkly as that music. Up to then I'd been playing her all oom-pah-pah, as though she were a tuba, akin to Oscar Wilde's Lady Bracknell.

As my performance improved, however, things backstage began to deteriorate. Richard Burton, playing the countess' nephew, fell in love with Susan—or, more accurately, Susan fell in love with him, and he wasn't about to turn her down. My God, what a mess! In her memoir, *Bittersweet,* Susan describes the toll their affair took on her, and I can only add that it was nearly as distressing for the rest of the company.

In New York, Susan and I had the only ground-floor dressing rooms at the Morosco Theatre. She and Burton would make noisy love in her dressing room between the matinee and evening performances on Wednesdays and Saturdays. I was the unwilling voyeur—or auditeur, if that's the word—of their intermission couplings.

I often felt ill during the run, and my doctor prescribed a nap between shows, but the moans of ecstasy reverberating through the walls kept me awake. Even my radio turned up full blast couldn't drown them out.

In more than fifty years as an actor I had never seen a theatre used that way. For me, theatres were temples, and this one was being sullied. Couldn't they have rented a room in a Broadway hotel? The Morosco was particularly hallowed, home to more prizewinning plays than any other New York house. It was a real actor's theatre, which we all deeply loved and mourned when it was torn down a few years ago despite our protests.

When I say "we," I exclude Richard Burton, who, as far as I could see, cared only for himself. As we came offstage after the curtain call at one performance, I saw Richard's wife Sibyl, who had just come over from England, standing there holding Kate, their firstborn child. Sibyl had probably heard what was going on

194

and hoped she could stop it by coming to New York. After all, she'd been through this before. "What are you doing here?" Richard snarled when he saw her. Without waiting for an answer, he started climbing the stairs to his dressing room. Sibyl looked stunned. I took her into my dressing room so that she could compose herself before confronting Richard and Susan.

Had Burton and I been on speaking terms, I might have asked him why he was doing this to Susan. I guess he would have replied that he was only trying to help her with her performance, or some such malarkey. But I believe he was only trying to help himself.

We had once had a long conversation that ended on a note of bitter self-revelation on his part. "How would you feel," he asked, "if you had a pockmarked face like mine?" I was too startled to reply.

When Burton first came to America with John Gielgud in *The Lady's Not for Burning,* we thought he'd be the next Olivier, not only because of his rich Welsh voice but also because he projected the brooding glamour of a Heathcliffe. But apparently he felt deficient because of his blemished skin. Conquering every woman who came within reach seemed to be his way of compensating for that liability.

Susan was not the first to help Richard convince himself that he was an Adonis, and she would not be the last. But all those conquests cost him what had been easily within his grasp: unstinting recognition as a great actor.

Time Remembered got middling reviews, but it ran through the season. A respiratory ailment that had plagued me for years flared up during the run, and there were moments when I wanted to pull out, but it was a costly production, and I felt obligated to see it through.

When it was over, I returned to Mexico for what I hoped would be a long vacation, with nothing to drag me away. After the strain and conflicts of the Morosco, it was a relief to sit quietly on my terrace and relax. The view of the two volcanoes, Popocatepetl and Ixtaccihuatl, looming in the distance, held an eternal serenity. There is a romantic story about them far more edifying than the one played out backstage during *Time Remembered.*

According to Eduardo Rendón, before the Spanish conquest the volcanoes were worshiped as deities, and many Mexicans still believed they were spirits, not just masses of rock, lava, and snow. Ixta (for short) had been a princess who fell in love with Popo, a young warrior. Her father, who disapproved, sent the warrior into a battle where he was sure to be killed, and news of his death sent Ixta into a depression from which she never recovered.

The volcano named Ixtaccihuatl is shaped like a woman reclining, while Popo suggests a guard watching over her. Once a year, legend has it, the star-crossed lovers ascend to heaven for a holiday, and the rainy season begins while they are away. Clouds make the volcanoes all but invisible.

I suppose Popo and his girlfriend might be classified as primitive archetypes of Romeo and Juliet, but I don't think the mystery and enchantment of old legends should be explained away. We need a touch of poetry and magic to lift us above the tabloid reality of everyday life. Maybe that's why Mexico clings to the old myths: there is a lot of reality to transcend in Mexico.

You could see the enchanted volcanoes from my terrace; walk out my front door, and you were in a dirt road. I had the street paved with cobblestones and erected a barricade to discourage wayward cars. A good neighbor, I reasoned, should improve the surroundings. But I can't say my good-neighbor policy worked out any better than Roosevelt's did in 1934.

An open-air market opened down the block almost as soon as the last cobblestone was in place. The stall-owners camped out in the area; they spliced wires into our electric lines and lived in their booths with their wives, children, and pets. Of course there were no facilities for sanitation.

I liked the spice vendors with their strings of dried *chiles,* piles of parsley and cumin, stacks of cinnamon sticks, and great brown mounds of *mole* powder. Just as appealing were the colorful and artfully arranged fruits and vegetables. But it was my bad luck to have the butchers just across the street from my front door.

Their specialties included innards, goats' heads, and the generative organs of bulls dangling prominently in the sun. The aroma was pungent early in the day, and by late afternoon it was nauseating. When the market closed, whatever had gone unsold was tossed to the stray dogs, who had begun to congregate in the area for just this special treat.

I would rush out and try to clean up the offal when I was expecting guests. But how to get rid of it? Dumping it in a trash bin would have put it out of sight but not out of smell. On one occasion, I am ashamed to say, I threw the sweepings over the wall of an adjacent house. When I confessed this to a friend, she told me not to worry. "You were only adding compost to your neighbor's shrubs," she said.

The Lunts paid me a visit around this time, and Alfred couldn't understand why the market distressed me. He found it "picturesque," and the unusual cuts of meat aroused his culinary curiosity. He even suggested we sample some local fare for dinner. "Oh, no!" I protested. "I'll eat Spam before I take one bite of that dog chow."

Eventually, city officials set up a spacious covered market, but the vendors refused to relocate. They couldn't live and sleep in the indoor premises, and their earnings were too meager to pay for even a small apartment.

The standoff was finally resolved while I was away. On my return with some friends, I warned them to hold their breath and noses as we approached my house. But when we turned into the street, there was no market, no fetid scent, no dogs, not even a bone.

Later I heard that two trucks had rolled through the outdoor market a week before, demolishing the flimsy structures and routing their inhabitants, most of whom moved to the covered market in the heart of the city.

I was pleased that the market was gone, but concerned about how it had been done. Eduardo Rendón explained this was the way things happened in his country. "Mexicans move slowly," he said, "but once they get going, watch out!"

≫·15·≪

The first American production of Eugene O'Neill's *A Touch of the Poet* was presented in 1958, and I was offered a part in it. Years before, early in his career and in mine, O'Neill had turned me down for *The Straw*. He went on to become America's leading playwright, and I'd become seasoned enough to play the mother in *Poet*.

O'Neill had written the work some twenty years earlier as part of an unfinished cycle of eleven plays, which he had decided to destroy. But he had completed *Poet*, and it was saved from burning after his death in 1953. It was published several years later and had recently been staged in Sweden.

The New York production was directed by Harold Clurman, who was one of the founding members of the Group Theatre, which had staged the major Odets plays. The Group was also responsible for adapting Stanislavsky for America, and this became the basis for The Actors Studio's Method.

Clurman was debonair, witty, and intelligent, with a thorough knowledge of theatre history. He moonlighted as a critic. But something that helped him in this second career was not at all helpful in the first: he talked too much.

After listening for several days to his explanations of why O'Neill had written this or that, or what was suggested in some character's subtext, I grew impatient. His analyses may have been brilliant, but he was conducting a college seminar, not a rehearsal.

Eric Portman, the splendid English actor who played my husband, was equally unnerved. "I don't understand all this," he whispered to me. "We've had our scripts for months and presumably have done our homework. We should be getting the play on its feet, but Clurman keeps on talking and talking."

When we finally got around to walking our way through the play, another problem cropped up. The third major role in *Poet* was played by one of the Actors Studio's great prides and joys. There was no question that Kim Stanley was gifted, and she drove herself mercilessly to discover "the dramatic truth" of whatever character she portrayed. She wouldn't say or do anything she thought did not ring true. If she couldn't find the truth, the fault had to be the playwright's, not hers.

One line gave her particular trouble. It contained the word "cute," and she explained to Harold that she had never uttered that word in her life and didn't feel comfortable saying it now. Besides, it was anachronistic, wasn't it? The play was set in New England in the early nineteenth century, and "cute" was no older than Shirley Temple's dimples.

We took a break while someone went in search of a dictionary. *Cute,* it turned out, was an Irish-Americanism for *acute* and had entered the language long before the period of the play. Nevertheless, Clurman gave in and the line was changed.

The whole fuss was offensive to me. Like other actors of my generation, I felt that we should respect the text. If the author was alive, of course, then he could be asked to make changes. But O'Neill was five years dead, and I doubt he would have accommodated our stickler for verisimilitude anyway.

There is a certain irony here. It was around that time that Lee

Strasberg made an infamous remark about the Lunts, saying that they were superb actors and great technicians, but that they had frittered away their talent on star vehicles by Noël Coward and Terence Rattigan. I was bewildered by Lee's comment. Why this reverence for great dramatic literature when an Actors Studio disciple felt no hesitation about rewriting O'Neill to express her own personality?

And what was wrong with Noël Coward, anyway? New generations of playgoers continue to be entertained by revivals of his witty works. And the Lunts had acted in plays by Shaw, O'Neill, Chekhov, and Shakespeare too, which was more than you could say for most Method graduates. But Lee wanted to sweep away the past in favor of a Brave New World on Broadway where there would be no stars, just Strasberg actors, and no star vehicles, just great plays tailored to fit the idiosyncrasies of Strasberg actors.

Lee's influence was widespread, and his admirers—actors, critics, and the public—parroted his views almost mindlessly. Actors of my generation, such as the Lunts, Katharine Cornell, Maurice Evans, Ina Claire, and myself, were considered derrière-garde— all technique and no emotion.

"Technique" was becoming a dirty word. When our son Jim decided definitely on an acting career, I suggested he might benefit from formal training. A friend recommended a good coach, and Jim took a few lessons, but soon quit. "Mom," he complained, "too much technique might rob me of my natural charm."

I tried to hold my tongue, though there was much I wanted to say. For instance, that charm won't project across the footlights unless you can send it flying toward that customer in the last row of the balcony night after night. And that takes perspiration, not the inspiration that the Actors Studio and its Method promised.

Some critics, however, had good words for old-timers like myself. Walter Kerr of the *New York Herald Tribune,* for example, wrote: "Though Helen Hayes may never have appeared in a masterpiece, she is a masterpiece herself." Charlie clipped this from a review and handed it to me, saying, "We'll put this on your tombstone." I was flattered by the comment, but questioned its accuracy. No actress is better than her material, and some of my material has been damned good. After all, I have appeared in plays by Shaw, Chekhov, Pirandello, O'Neill, Wilder, and Williams, and I've had more than one brush with Shakespeare.

As a young actress, I wasn't drawn to Shakespeare, perhaps because he was presented in school as someone you had to study to appreciate, and that intimidated me. I'm sure my experience wasn't singular: Shakespeare has been spoiled for countless students by the reverent approach of too many teachers.

I had read and seen only a handful of Shakespeare's plays when I was suddenly tricked into playing one of his greatest heroines. It happened back in the 1930s during the tour of *Victoria Regina.* I suggested to Abraham Sofaer, who was playing Disraeli, that we might work on a new production and put it on for a few matinees so we wouldn't get bored doing the same play night after night. We had been performing *Victoria* so long that we could have played it underwater; in fact, some nights I felt that was exactly what we were doing.

"Let's do *The Merchant of Venice,*" Sofaer said. He had always wanted to play Shylock, and he thought I would make a wonderful Portia. I said I didn't have the energy or aptitude for anything that strenuous. But Sofaer pointed out that Portia wasn't a long part and that most of her lines were in prose. He thought I could handle it easily. Finally he cajoled me into giving it a try.

Our *Merchant* was cast entirely with actors in the *Victoria* company, and I financed it as an early Christmas present to the cast. It cost under five thousand dollars. We got nice reviews, and my delivery of the famous "quality of mercy" speech was praised. Many people had been forced to memorize those lines in school, but some members of the audience told me they had never really understood them until I spoke them as simply as I felt they should be said—not as an aria but as a spontaneous expression of Portia's inner being.

There had been no thought of taking *Merchant* to Broadway. The production had fulfilled its purpose, and it was right for it to end there.

This was when Ruth Gordon was living with us, trying to pick up the pieces of her life. Her acting career had faltered, and she had had an affair with Jed Harris and bore his son. Jed wasn't the marrying kind or the faithful kind; he treated Ruth as shabbily as he had treated all his lovers, abandoning her and their child. We thought she was well rid of Jed, but Ruth had to come to her own conclusions in her own time.

An offer to play Margery Pinchwife in Wycherley's *The Country Wife* came her way from a summer stock theatre, and I urged her to take it. She did, and her performance was so brilliant that I thought the play should be taken to Broadway. I talked to Gilbert Miller, who produced *Victoria Regina,* about staging *The Country Wife* for Ruth. Gilbert was the classiest producer Broadway had seen since Charles Frohman. His productions were always impeccable, of the highest order, and his perfect taste extended to the smallest detail.

"Nobody wants to see Restoration comedy," he said of Ruth's play. "I love Ruth, but I don't think she's a big enough star to sell tickets to a seventeenth-century play." When I offered to back the production, he shook his head. "I can't let you waste your money."

I wasn't ready to give up; there had to be another way to go about it. I happened to know Oliver Messel, a British set designer highly acclaimed for his settings for the Sadler's Wells Ballet.

Oliver was a friend of Bea Lillie's and often visited her, so the next time he was at her apartment, I joined them and related my conversation with Gilbert Miller. If I could get the play staged, would Oliver be willing to design the production? He said he would like to do it.

His consent gave me a needed lift. I wanted the production to be something special. Most modern productions of Restoration plays failed, Messel claimed, because they always looked so tacky. They were staged on a shoestring because the producers were convinced they wouldn't run. We hoped to prove them wrong with *The Country Wife* starring Ruth with Oliver's sets.

To work in New York, Oliver had to join the scene designers' union, one of the toughest of all theatrical unions to crack. He took the examination and, to our surprise, failed. Believe it or not, he was unable to name five master set designers. He could only come up with a couple. When we passed the news to Bea Lillie, she said she could name five without any trouble. Closing her eyes, she put her fingers to her temples and began chanting, "Master set designer, master, master . . . Masturbation." Any others she planned to name were drowned out by our roar.

I was disheartened by Oliver's failure to make the union, but he had another idea. "Don't worry about it. We'll get the Old Vic to do the play."

The Old Vic was then London's foremost repertory company, and Oliver sent a message to its managing director, Tyrone Guthrie, asking him to meet me as soon as possible.

I was appearing in *Victoria Regina*, but Miller let me have a six-week summer vacation during the long run so I could rest up and recharge my creative batteries. I didn't tell Ruth why I was going to England, because I didn't want to get her hopes up in case things didn't work out. As soon as I could arrange passage, I sailed for England. That, in itself, was a vacation.

At Claridge's, a maid unpacked my luggage, and I was surprised to see a bottle of Scotch in my steamer trunk. In those days, we didn't have to travel light, but bringing Scotch to England was like carrying coals to Newcastle. We had a houseman then, Chatters, working for us in Nyack. Maybe Chatters had put the Scotch in my trunk, thinking I might need a stiff drink to get over the rigors of my journey.

When Guthrie came to see me, I was a bit in awe of him. He had a formidable reputation, and he looked very important and powerful: a tall, angular man, he towered over me. He had a lean face, a beaky nose, and a cool, aristocratic air. He proved to be gentle and friendly, as many big men are, but I was put off at first. After we exchanged amenities, I offered him a drink and he accepted. I fixed a Scotch highball for him and one for myself, but I didn't touch mine until we finished our business.

The Old Vic had not had much success with Restoration plays, Guthrie began. The year before, a Congreve comedy had played to an empty house. While Wycherley was raunchier than Congreve, he wasn't as witty. Guthrie had heard about Ruth's wonderful performance, but the Old Vic had no precedent for using an American star or for employing an outside designer like Oliver Messel. Still, he liked the idea and would discuss it with Lillian Bayless, who administered the Old Vic, and with the board of directors. I told him I would finance the production, and he said we would have to find out what the others thought.

During our talk, I kept replenishing his drink, but left my glass standing. I was afraid I would get addled and forget what I had to say. After Guthrie departed, I took a sip of my highball and nearly gagged. What I swallowed wasn't Johnnie Walker. It took me a few seconds to identify it as a mint julep. Apparently, Chatters, who was famous for that concoction, had mixed a batch for me and sent it along in the empty Scotch bottle. Let me tell you, mint juleps don't benefit from ripening for six days.

What a polite man Guthrie was to have swallowed those awful

drinks without comment! Maybe he thought it was the latest American cocktail. Whatever he thought, I've always believed that that mint julep was the key to *The Country Wife*'s success. Guthrie didn't walk very straight when he left, but he must have pulled a lot of weight with the Old Vic, because they decided to present the play with Ruth Gordon playing the lead. Bravo Chatters!

It was a rousing success, and Gilbert Miller later ate crow in the nicest way: he brought the production to Broadway, where it did very well. After that, Ruth went back to England to do Thornton Wilder's *The Matchmaker*, again directed by Tyrone Guthrie. It, too, was a big success in London and later in New York.

The Country Wife brought Ruth out of her doldrums, and she went on to even greater success on stage and screen. Then she launched a second career as playwright and memoirist. For more than ten years, we remained the best of friends—until *Twelfth Night* came along.

In 1941, the Theatre Guild approached me about doing a Shakespeare play. I talked it over with Ruth before committing myself. Unlike me, Ruth was familiar with all the Bard's plays, so she urged me to go ahead. "Tell them to do *Twelfth Night.* You'll be Viola, and I'll play Olivia."

Lawrence Langner and Theresa Helburn, the heads of the Guild, were delighted to have Ruth join the cast, and I was pleased when they suggested Maurice Evans for the role of Malvolio. I had known Maurice for years, and our friendship was long-standing.

Maurice had been brought over from England by Katharine Cornell to play Romeo to her Juliet in her 1935 production of *Romeo and Juliet.* The next year, he was the dauphin in Kit's staging of Shaw's *St. Joan.* He stayed in New York to start his own Shakespeare company, and that, to my mind, is his greatest achievement. Almost singlehandedly, he made Shakespeare popular with the American public. Audiences were enthralled by the experience of living through Shakespeare instead of having him whittled away to fit the whim of a star actor or explained away by pedantic teachers.

Maurice agreed to play Malvolio on condition that the production be staged by Margaret Webster, who had worked compatibly with him in the past. That was fine with me. Peggy Webster was the daughter of two celebrated British actors, Ben Webster and Dame May Whitty. She was probably reading Shakespeare sonnets when most children her age were struggling with Mother Goose. Her successes at the Old Vic were rivaled in number only by Tyrone Guthrie's.

Everything seemed to be falling easily into place, and I signed the Guild contract, confident that my first major Shakespearean production would be shaped by expert hands. But almost at once we hit a snag. Langner asked me to drop by the Guild office for a chat, and when I got there, he said Webster had refused to direct the play if Ruth Gordon played Olivia. Why? I gasped. I didn't pretend to be an expert, but I had read the play several times and couldn't understand why Ruth was unacceptable.

"Peggy feels Olivia is the antithesis of everything Ruth is," Langner said. He was obviously quoting accurately what he had been told. "Everything Ruth has given to the theatre is the opposite of what Olivia is." What did that mean? Langner threw up his hands. "That's what she said, Helen, and she means it."

There was to be no arguing. If we kept Ruth, we lost Webster, and with her went Evans. I was terribly distressed. Whenever I was faced with a problem I couldn't solve in those days, I went to Ned Sheldon.

"Lay it on the line to Ruth," he advised. "You've already signed the contract, and you should live up to that commitment. You can't force Ruth on Webster. Even if you could, no actress would be happy working with a director who really doesn't want her."

When I told Ruth what happened, she said, "You tell them you won't do it without me."

"You want me to force them to take you on?"

"Yes," she said. "It was my idea in the first place."

Never in my life had I been so knee-deep in a mess. I felt I had proven my friendship to Ruth in the past and shouldn't have my loyalty tested now.

When I talked it over with Charlie, he gave me much the same advice as Sheldon's. "You can't back out. It would be wrong for everyone."

So I stood firm. Perhaps it had been heedless of me to sign a contract before Ruth had signed, but it didn't occur to me that she wouldn't be offered one. "I'm sorry," I told her, "but I have to go through with it."

Unhappily, that ended our friendship. I phoned Ruth and tried to keep in touch; we spotted each other at parties, and at the end of Charlie's life she came to see him in the hospital, but we never were close friends again.

One day, not long before her death in 1985, we both happened to be lunching at Sardi's. When she caught sight of me, she bolted out of her chair and came toward me.

"Helen!" she called in a very loud voice. "Helen, I just want you to know you did more for my career than anyone else."

"Thanks, Ruth," I said.

"I just want you to know that," she added, then returned to her table. She had already said as much in a memoir, and I couldn't understand why she felt the need to repeat the same thing in such an ostentatious way. I was glad to see she'd got over her hostility, but it was too late to pick up the pieces of our friendship.

There was something good that came out of all that: our

Twelfth Night was very festive in design and costume, and it received favorable reviews. After we played in New York, we took it on the road and had the intoxicating thrill of learning that the length of our run was the longest single run that *Twelfth Night* ever had, dating back to its very first performances, in which Will Shakespeare himself appeared.

Looking back, I now wish I'd had more opportunities to do the classics when I was young. There were certain areas of the theatre in which, for all my experience, I didn't know the right approach—Shakespeare, for instance, or the Greek dramatists, or Restoration comedy. That approach must be acquired either through training or from an ongoing tradition, which didn't exist in this country when I was coming of age as an actress.

I always had a hankering to play Hecuba in *The Trojan Women.* I once visited the famous Epidaurus amphitheater in Greece with two friends. They sat in an upper row while I stood on stage and read Hecuba's great lament for her grandson. It was a thrilling experience, but not one I would risk repeating for an audience larger than two good friends.

In the past decade or so, American actors have begun to be schooled in the appreciation and understanding of the dramatic conventions of past eras. And they've had a chance to appear in productions of works by playwrights whom actors of my generation may have read but never thought they would perform: Shakespeare, Sophocles, Sheridan, Schiller. I hope that enough young people seize the opportunity. It will benefit them as well as our theatre, which needs all the help it can get.

The Broadway theatre began to decline in the 1960s. Production costs soared, and producers came to rely on blockbuster musicals and British imports, steering clear of anything controversial unless it happened to be salacious too. After my experiences with *Time Remembered* and *Touch of the Poet,* I was less

209

and less eager to get back on stage. I traveled a bit, relaxed, and caught up on reading, either in Cuernavaca or in Nyack.

Unhappily, the early '60s also saw a decline in Nyack's fortunes. Indecisive town management had run the village down. Streets were ill-kempt, and thugs began infesting the small business district. At the same time, I began to have trouble with my neighbors' son, who had taken to hanging out with the local toughs.

I had always invited children in the neighborhood to use my pool when I didn't have guests, and there had never been any problem. But this boy started bringing his hoodlum friends around for late-night swims. I would hear splashing out there at two in the morning and would call the police. The police would always make a big racket pulling into the driveway, more or less announcing their arrival. Apparently they didn't want to pick a fight with the boys, but only meant to scare them off.

I had spoken to my neighbors, but they couldn't seem to keep their son under control. Since I couldn't think of anything else to do, I had the pool drained. The gang returned that very night and, enraged at finding no water, threw the teak garden furniture into the deep end of the empty pool, smashing it into splinters.

I decided I'd had enough and put the house up for sale. I was living alone at the time, since Jim had married and moved away. I couldn't sleep at night, and the local law officers couldn't help me.

There were immediate offers, and I took the best of them, though it was much less than I thought the property was worth. The prospective buyers were real-estate developers who planned to pull down the house and build garden apartments. Nothing in the local zoning ordinance prevented them from doing that, but the town board kept postponing action on their application. I was disturbed by the prospect of Pretty Penny being razed, but I saw no other way out.

When local residents got wind of what was happening, they held protest meetings, wrote letters to the town paper, and even picketed my house. The prospect of having an apartment complex in their midst prodded them into action. And perhaps, as someone speculated, they suddenly realized that they didn't want to lose me as a neighbor. "You know why they're doing this?" a reporter from the *New York Herald Tribune* said. "Because you give this town a certain distinction. They want to keep you as a captive celebrity."

I certainly felt like a captive. Because of the opposition and the delays, the developers eventually backed out, and I resolved to stay put. My neighbors' son had somehow been persuaded to stop his marauding, so I felt more secure. But I had already bought a five-room apartment in Manhattan and had announced an auction of everything that I wasn't planning to take with me. I felt that the auction had to go on, as the profits were promised to the American Academy of Dramatic Arts and its Mary MacArthur Scholarship fund, which Charlie and I had established soon after Mary's death.

Before the auction, the second weekend in October 1963, there were exhibitions of the discardable and unused items I had accumulated in my life—furniture, jewelry and clothing, curtains and dishes, books that I'd read and didn't consider worth saving, all the stuff you buy and years later wonder why. The first preview was at an invitation-only cocktail party attended by many of my friends. Then came a two-day public display at which browsers paid a dollar to look over the clutter on sale.

A striped tent was put up on the front lawn on the day of the auction, and the atmosphere was festive—or so I heard. I had planned to be on hand, but decided at the last minute that I couldn't face it, so I went off to visit a relative in Virginia. While the gavel was banging in Nyack, I was in bed with the covers pulled over my head. I had written blithely in the auction catalogue that for me the act of acquisition was a greater joy than possession, but now that others were acquiring my possessions, I wasn't so sure. Still, the news that the auction had netted over fifty-seven thousand dollars, more than double the expected profit, bucked me up. It wasn't a fortune, but the Academy could put the money to good use, renovating its theatre.

I had put aside special gifts like signed books, but some slipped through. I was upset to learn that an autographed copy of Edith Hamilton's *The Greek Way* had been sold. In her inscription Hamilton had written: "To Helen Hayes, whose life is a search for excellence." That message had helped keep me on my toes for years, and I couldn't believe that I'd somehow let the book slip away.

The buyer, I learned, was a dentist from New Jersey, and he agreed to sell the book back at the price he had paid. It was the quickest, least painful transaction I'd ever had with a dentist.

Most of the belongings I cherished were put aside to take to my New York apartment. In a moment of panic years ago, after Charlie's death, I'd sold our collection of French Impressionist paintings at a fraction of what they were worth, but I had kept our pictures by the Hudson River school of painters. I loved the river so much that I wanted it indoors as well as out.

Jasper Cropsey is my favorite among the artists of that school, because his work has so much luminosity. Another favorite is an unsigned depiction of the *Half Moon*, Robert Fulton's steamship, sailing up the Hudson as a group of Indians peer down with astonishment from a high cliff. (I had a little brass nameplate put on that one: "There goes the neighborhood!") I also have a painting by Thomas Cole, father of the Hudson River school, but it's even darker than most of his other murky riverscapes.

With these pictures and other prized possessions back in their old places, I doubt if anyone even remembers that there was once an auction at the house. It looks pretty much the same as before, and it's still a comfort to be there. In time I made my peace with the townspeople, who seemed as happy as I was that I had not left Nyack.

My little rebellion, if it can be called that, stirred the town board to take action to stop the deterioration. Nyack today is spruce and prosperous, an attraction for tourists shopping at boutiques and antique stores. On weekends the streets become so crowded that I stay home, but there are still five days a week to enjoy the town's quiet and charm.

≫16≪

Celebrity has always struck me as a dubious and transitory claim to achievement in our society. Status seekers and other so-called glitterati stand precariously on shifting sands, ever in danger of being swallowed up and then replaced by a fresh throng of famous or notorious stars. This does not apply, of course, to those who make real contributions to science, art, and literature; to them fame can be a nuisance that interferes with the work they are born to do.

I'm well aware that had it not been for my career, nobody would have pursued me, put my name on every sucker list, as Charlie used to say, or opened doors that are closed to most people. Though I was born in Washington, if I hadn't left Washington for Broadway, I doubt I'd ever have passed through the White House door except as a tourist.

The theatre provided me with a ticket to 1600 Pennsylvania Avenue. What I saw there was in many ways unsettling, suggesting a life far more stressful and lonely than I had ever imagined. No doubt a good many men driven by "fire in the belly" to seek that office wished they could escape once they got there.

My first invitation to the White House came in 1938, when *Victoria Regina* played in Washington during our national tour. Eleanor Roosevelt asked me to lunch, and it was a pleasant occasion—until Mrs. Roosevelt, whom I greatly admired, made a special request. Would I return a week later for dinner with the president and join them after my performance for a diplomatic reception on the same evening?

I wanted to decline—what an exhausting day it would be!— but felt I couldn't. President Roosevelt was under heavy strain, and I'd been told that his wife was trying to arrange visits by people who could help him relax by taking his mind off politics and world affairs. I guessed that that was the reason for my invitation. As it turned out, my guess was right, but I'm sorry to have to report that I muffed it.

I was seated next to FDR at dinner that night. At one point he turned to me and asked, "Well, Queen Victoria, what do you suggest I say in my next State of the Union speech?"

Perhaps he was only trying to put me at ease, but I was confused and tongue-tied at being identified with the role I was playing. I babbled some nonsense and felt like an idiot.

I was still blushing at my stupidity when Roosevelt began grumbling about the diplomatic reception to be held later that evening. "Oh, Franklin," Mrs. Roosevelt interjected, "it's the big night of the year for those people. They look forward to it as the high point of their stay in Washington."

"I'm not going to do it again after tonight," the president countered. Mrs. Roosevelt sighed as though there were nothing more to be said to a man so stubborn and petulant. Then she announced that we would have coffee in the sitting room.

Two hefty men appeared from nowhere before we could rise from the table and picked the president up as if he were a child. I knew, of course, that he was disabled, his legs made useless by polio, the disease that would later kill my own child. But the intimacy of that moment when his attendants lifted him into his wheelchair was so startling that I bolted from my place and was halfway across the room before I could collect myself. Then I noticed that no one else had moved: to them what had happened must have seemed routine. I felt mortified.

Eleanor Roosevelt greeted me warmly when I returned for the diplomatic reception. "Go upstairs and visit with the president before the other guests arrive," she said. I crept upstairs like a lamb going to slaughter.

FDR was alone in the family sitting room. "I'm having a beer," he said. "What'll you have?" The same, I answered. We sat drinking beer and chatting about this and that. All I remember is thinking that once I downed the beer I'd be free to disappear among the throng of foreign diplomats arriving downstairs.

FDR had a lot of charm and great courage, as even his political opponents acknowledged. He evidently liked folksy chitchat, otherwise his wife wouldn't have sent me up there. But I was still embarrassed by my earlier gaffe, and I feared he might consider it a reflection on his disability.

When I came to my senses back in my hotel room, I realized I was being ridiculous. Roosevelt had far more important matters to worry about. The diplomats the Roosevelts entertained that night came from countries on the brink of war, and the president was already thinking about preparing the nation for the end of neutrality, if worse came to worst.

I was more at ease with Dwight and Mamie Eisenhower. I felt I could unbend and forget about protocol with them, though there was a subtle shift in our relationship after Ike went into politics and was elected president.

A few weeks before his first inauguration, Ike and Mamie were in Denver visiting Mamie's mother. I happened to be there too, and they asked me to come and see them.

When I arrived, Ike jumped up and grabbed me in a bear hug. Instinctively I stiffened, though he had often greeted me that way in the past. He was an old and devoted friend who had been very supportive when Mary died, but now he was president-elect, and the old welcome seemed somehow inappropriate. He pulled back too, as if to say, "Oops, I can't do that anymore."

I visited the White House several times during Ike's two terms. I had a warm friendship with Mamie, almost as informal as with other friends. On one occasion her sister and I were sitting in the family room while Mamie packed for a short vacation.

"Do me a favor," Mamie said to me when Ike looked in. "Tell him to come to Phoenix with me. I'm going to Elizabeth Arden's Maine Chance, and he could play golf while I'm being beautified."

"I don't know anyone in Phoenix who plays golf," Ike said.

Mamie said with seeming seriousness: "I'm sure you could find someone soon, Ike."

An extraordinary conversation to take place in the White House.

When I left that afternoon, Ike escorted me to the front door of the White House, about a mile from the family quarters. I mentioned I had seen him leaving a meeting the day before. "Why didn't you say something?" he asked.

There was a big crowd, I explained, and he was surrounded by Secret Service men. "How was I supposed to get your attention? Yell 'I like Ike'?"

"I wish you had," he said. "I was talking about socialized medicine, and afterwards I got my brains beaten out. A shout of approval might have helped just then."

What went wrong? I asked.

"I deviated from the text prepared for me," he answered. "I improvised, I said, 'We don't want to be the pooh-bahs of medicine.' My aides were furious because I ad-libbed like that. I tell you, Helen, I'm so fed up, I can't wait to get out of this place."

I was taken aback by this confession. Imagine this great general getting a tongue-lashing from his subordinates!

Dwight Eisenhower's successor was his antithesis in background, politics, and style, and their first ladies couldn't have been more unlike. The Kennedys brought youth, beauty, and glamour into the White House, and Mrs. Kennedy embellished the venerable mansion with good taste. Only after President Kennedy's tragic death did we gradually learn that Camelot wasn't all that it was cracked up to be.

My first meeting with John Kennedy was at a state dinner for the grand duchess of Luxembourg. I was seated at the president's table, directly opposite him. The duchess was on his right, and the woman at his left was a cabinet minister of Luxembourg. Also at the table were Robert Wagner, then mayor of New York, and a businessman friend and financial backer of the Kennedy clan.

Just before dessert, Kennedy asked Wagner if he had a pen. No. How about the businessman? No. I suppose gentlemen don't carry pens in their tuxedos. You don't ask a grand duchess if she has a pen, so Kennedy skipped her. But I happened to have a small gold pen, a gift from the producer of one of my shows, in my evening bag. A waiter passed it to Kennedy, who immediately started to scribble on the back of his menu. He was making notes for his after-dinner speech, and I was amazed at how small a part of his concentration it took. He would jot something down, then turn and pick up his conversation with the duchess.

When he began to speak, he barely glanced at his notes, which was especially astonishing, since he spoke entirely in French! But when the dinner ended, he forgot to return my pen. Though it had some sentimental value, I thought it was well lost if it helped cement American-Luxembourg relations. As we all left the dining room, I felt a tap on my shoulder. "Thanks for helping me out," said Kennedy, returning the pen.

218

A few months later the president repaid my little loan in a very special way. He conceived the idea of sending a group of actors on an international tour, both as a goodwill gesture and as a sign of his administration's commitment to fostering the arts.

Lawrence Langner of the Theatre Guild was asked to organize the company, and he proposed that I play Mrs. Antrobus in *The Skin of Our Teeth* again. I was delighted. I love traveling as much as acting, and now I could combine my two favorite activities.

The company was to present three plays on a rotating basis. Langner asked whether I had any ideas for the other two plays. I suggested *Death of a Salesman.* A fine play, Langner agreed, but it might be interpreted as an attack on capitalism. How about *Long Day's Journey into Night*? Too bleak a portrait of American family life, Langner thought. *Our Town*? Two plays by the same author would give Thornton Wilder undue prominence.

I asked what he had in mind. *The Glass Menagerie.* I groaned, but finally agreed to play Amanda once again. I've always felt that Williams and O'Neill are our finest playwrights, and certainly one of them should be represented on our tour.

The third play selected was *The Miracle Worker,* William Gibson's drama about the young Helen Keller and her teacher, Annie Sullivan. There was no role for me, so I had a free evening when it was performed.

The tour lasted for almost two years, with a few months off in the middle for a vacation. We did six performances every week, visiting Europe, the Middle East, and Latin America. There were fifty-two people in the troupe, forty actors, the rest technical and management people. The actors included June Havoc, Leif Erickson, James Broderick, and Barbara Barrie.

President Kennedy gave us a gala send-off at the White House, and the tour was one long adventure from the very outset, with grand hoopla wherever we performed.

One of our first stops was in Lebanon. The theatre in Beirut was part of a large complex built by a local millionaire on a hilltop in the city. It was a bizarre mixture of Lincoln Center and Atlantic City, with a theatre, an opera house, a gambling casino, and a cabaret modeled on the Lido in Paris.

The Lebanese entrepreneur hosted an opening-night party for us and a couple of hundred of his best friends. He was a sinister-looking character, enthroned at the head of a U-shaped table around which leading players of our troupe were interspersed with members of the American diplomatic corps. I asked one of the embassy people how our host had made his money.

"Did you notice the little Arab cafés you passed on your way up here?" he asked. "He owns them all. That's how he got started. Then he branched out. He made his real money by selling little girls in the Persian Gulf."

My jaw dropped. "Where did he get the little girls?" I asked.

It was simple, my informant replied. Parents sold their daughters on the cheap—that released them from the worry of having to accumulate a dowry and marry them off—and our host resold them to the brothels along the Persian Gulf.

I glanced at the man who was busy charming June Havoc. I couldn't wait to tell June she had been turning on the allure for a child-slave merchant.

The next day brought another startling revelation. I was taken to a beautiful house that had recently become a semiprivate museum. The main attractions were intricately woven rugs and an elaborate ironwork gate that separated a section of the house from an interior courtyard. The gate was a particularly fine example of Arab craftsmanship. It led to the deceased owner's harem, our guide explained. His concubines used to peek through the grillwork to catch a glimpse of their lord and master as he hobnobbed in his courtyard with other local potentates. "Did he leave a large family?" I asked, trying not to sound ironic.

"Many wives, many children," the guide replied. Then he

lowered his voice to a near-whisper and added, "Late in life his taste changed. He found comfort in little boys."

That Lebanon wasn't entirely a man's world I learned a little later when I visited Madame Sirsuk, Beirut's grande dame deluxe. In her youth—long gone, though she still looked splendid—she had caught the fancy of the French novelist Pierre Loti, who modeled the heroine of *The Chatelaine* after her. Loti had always been a favorite of mine, and I was eager to meet any lady who had inspired one of his best books.

June Havoc went with me to Mme Sirsuk's villa outside the city. We were greeted by a tall majordomo wearing a turban and a high-collared tunic cinched at the waist by a brocaded sash. "Punjab!" June whispered as he ushered us into his mistress's presence. What a sight she was! I wondered how she could stand erect under the weight of so many jewels, so much enamel and lamé. But there was intelligence and wit beneath the paint, and I could see why Loti had found her irresistible many years before.

She was now close to seventy-five and not, I was later told, at her best. Several years before, an incident had changed her life. "Her secretary and her chauffeur got into a row because each mistakenly believed he was Mme Sirsuk's only lover," an American embassy official told me. "There was a duel. One died, the other went to prison. In a matter of seconds Mme Sirsuk lost a secretary, a chauffeur, and two lovers. She hasn't been the same since. At her age it isn't easy breaking in new help."

After Lebanon we went to Israel, and in Tel Aviv we chartered a bus to take us to Nazareth, which I, as a Catholic, hold sacred. I would be stepping, I felt, on hallowed ground. But we pulled into a huge terminal where a mob of hucksters peddled cheap souvenirs, hollering, "True cross! True cross!" In their midst danced a demented-looking man in a sackcloth. He had dirty, stringy hair and cried, "I am the new Messiah!"

I put my hands to my face and moaned. "Oh, dear! What would Jesus say if He could see this?"

" 'Oops, I saved the wrong world!' " answered Billy Miles, our company manager and a dear, amusing man.

We were taken to the place where Mary was visited by the angel. Like every ancient site in Nazareth, it was dank and lay below ground level. Apparently everything had sunk in the two thousand years since Jesus had lived there. It would have been dispiriting unless you clung, as I do, to the belief that Jesus the Nazarene actually did live there.

From Israel we traveled to Turkey and opened in Ankara with *The Glass Menagerie.* After our performance, there was a party at the American embassy. A very elegant Turkish lady told me she was both moved and disturbed by the play. "I have a son, and I wonder if I could be like that mother in the play without knowing it."

As we went on chatting, this very chic, cosmopolitan woman confessed that she missed some aspects of the old days, before Kemal Ataturk's program to westernize Turkey. "Many Turkish women miss the mystery of the veil," she explained.

For better or worse, Ataturk's policy had touched nearly every area of Turkish life, including the stage. Local theatres were doing peculiar versions of American plays: *The Zoo Story, Toys in the Attic,* and, weirdest of all, *Life with Father.* All the family members in that play were redheads, and so the Turkish actors sported pink fright wigs. The men looked especially strange, bristling with five-o'clock shadow under their cotton-candy coiffures.

After a short break back in the States, we set off on the second part of our tour, in Central America and Mexico. Our last stop was Mexico City, where we opened at the Bellas Artes, the Palace of Fine Arts. What a stately but strange theatre it is! Built at the turn of the century on what had been a lake bed, it sinks a little every year, and by the 1960s the stage entrance was below street level. But when you came offstage, you were reminded that Mexico City is thousands of feet above sea level: someone was always waiting in the wings with an oxygen mask if you needed it, which many foreign actors do.

We were all weary after that tour, but any one of us would have happily done it again. It was an exhilarating experience. Our shows were treated as cultural events by the host countries. Audiences seemed to appreciate our plays, and if they didn't always understand everything, they could at least follow the action. English is a lingua franca around the world, at least among the educated classes that go to the theatre. In America, after all, people have flocked to see the Moscow Art Theatre company performing in Russian, and Ingmar Bergman's Swedish *Hamlet*, and performances of other foreign troupes using their own language. Foreign audiences responded to our American-language plays with similar interest and curiosity.

I never saw Jack Kennedy again after the White House reception at the beginning of our first tour for the State Department. But, like most Americans, I remember exactly when and where I heard about his assassination. I had left Cuernavaca in November 1963 with a friend and Vera Benlian, a friend and companion, for a trip to the Yucatán. On the way back, we stopped at a hotel in Oaxaca for the night. We checked in and agreed to meet in the lobby for dinner that evening.

When I came downstairs, Vera rushed up to me, looking distraught. "President Kennedy has been shot," she sobbed. "They don't know if he will live."

"Don't be silly," I snapped. I can't explain my reaction, why I got irritated with Vera. Perhaps I wanted to believe it was a bad joke; maybe I felt the need to punish the bearer of bad news. In any case, I sidestepped Vera and proceeded into the lobby, where a group of people were gathered around a television set, many weeping openly. My Spanish is not fluent, but I understood the news report. President Kennedy was dead.

We went outside and sat at a sidewalk café, too numb to think or speak. A Mexican placed a small transistor radio on our table. "It's tuned to an English-language station," he said.

We thanked him, but I didn't want to hear the grim details about the terrible event in Dallas, all I wanted at that moment was to get back to Cuernavaca as soon as possible. I wanted to be behind the walls of my house, because I felt full of shame. For all Americans, I think, Kennedy's assassination carried a mark of shame as well as horror and grief.

We left Oaxaca very early the next morning. At home, the cook was waiting at the gate, tears streaming, arms outstretched. We embraced and wept together.

Unable to sleep that night, I looked for a book to read, something light and far-removed from what had happened. I picked up a biography of Max Gordon, a darling man and a great producer. It looked as though it would have lots of amusing show business anecdotes—just what I needed then.

The first pages were a lively description of Max's early years as a gag writer for his brother, a popular vaudeville monologuist. Some of Max's best one-liners were quoted, most of them pretty corny, but one, more than fifty years old, took my breath away: "In Mexico presidents have to run twice—once to get into office and once for their lives."

What was once a bad joke about Mexico was now a reality for America. I put the book down, went out to the garden, and gazed at the distant mountains. Somehow the horizon held more solace than any wit or wisdom my bookcase might contain.

≫17≪

In the 1960s I probably announced my retirement more often than any actress since Sarah Bernhardt. Each farewell was truly meant but was postponed by some irresistible project or other. One was the APA-Phoenix Repertory Company, with which I was associated for two years.

The APA had been founded about a decade earlier. Ellis Raab was the leading director, and Rosemary Harris, Nancy Marchand, and Eric Berry were among the roster of actors. In the early '60s it merged with the Phoenix, another troupe dedicated to presenting a mixture of classics and the best modern plays. The very diverse program had everything from Sheridan to Kaufman and Hart to Ionesco.

Everyone worked for minimum wages. I took home two hundred and twenty-five dollars a week after deductions, but felt I owed the theatre something for the wonderful life it had given me. Of course I was gaining something too. I had never done repertory work before, and I loved it. This was an opportunity to play character parts, those cameo roles that often demonstrate a playwright's gift for characterization more subtly than do his heroes and heroines.

A particular favorite of mine was Signora Frola in *Right You Are! (If You Think You Are)*, perhaps the most engaging of all Luigi Pirandello's plays. The philosophical discussions of the nature of reality are lightened by a commedia dell'arte spirit, and we tried to emphasize the giddiness of that spirit. It was great fun. Another of my roles for the APA-Phoenix was Mrs. Fisher in *The Show-Off*, a delightful 1924 comedy by George Kelly, a neglected playwright best known as Grace Kelly's uncle. Its successful New York run was followed by a brief tour ending in California.

I then announced my retirement again, and this time I was determined to muster the willpower to resist any offer. Not even the discovery of a lost Shakespearean tragedy would change my mind.

While playing *The Show-Off* in Los Angeles, I had stayed with my dear friend Lari Mako, a Beverly Hills decorator with many show business connections. On the nightstand in my room was a copy of Arthur Hailey's *Airport*, a best-seller recently sold to the movies. That was thoughtful of Lari, though I would have preferred a dish of chocolates.

It turned out that the book had been provided as bait. Lari invited some people for dinner one night, and among the guests was Ross Hunter, a Hollywood producer who specialized in vehicles for actresses like Lana Turner, Doris Day, and Susan Hayward. Many of his films began with flawless diamonds, emeralds, and rubies cascading down the screen as the credits rolled by. Ross was pretty swanky himself, but he was charming and intelligent too. I liked him from the start.

I found out from the table talk that he was to produce *Airport* for Universal Studios. Had I read it? No, I said, though Lari had supplied a copy. She had done so, Ross confessed, at his request. If I looked through the book, I'd find a few underlined passages that he'd like me to consider carefully. They concerned Mrs.

Quonsett, a sly grandmother who stows away on a plane that's carrying an insane passenger whose briefcase contains a bomb timed to explode during the flight.

That night I more than nibbled at the bait. I read the whole book, not just the sections marked by Ross Hunter. It was a gripping story, but I wasn't convinced that I'd be the best possible Mrs. Quonsett, however much Ross, Lari, and other friends were conspiring to make me think so. I resented being prodded, but finally I had to admit that it was a juicy part, and those are not easy to come by on stage or screen, whatever age you are.

In developing Mrs. Quonsett I didn't use anyone I knew as a model, as I had often done in the past. While working on Victoria, for example, I had Graddy Hayes in mind. They were contemporaries, they dressed alike and probably thought alike. Graddy had a singular walk, measured and regal, as though she were in a royal procession. Mrs. Quonsett, on the other hand, is pretty much me, though of course I took some hints from the writers.

Airport was a big-budget picture with an all-star cast—Burt Lancaster, Dean Martin, George Kennedy, Jacqueline Bisset, Van Heflin, Maureen Stapleton, Jean Seberg, and myself. My scenes took fifteen weeks to shoot, more than I really cared to spend in Southern California, though there were some compensations. An unexpected one was Dean Martin, who wasn't at all what I imagined from the TV appearances in which he crooned away with a whiskey in his hand, indifferent to everything and spoofing what he was doing.

I soon discovered that Dean was a dedicated professional. We started to chat during one of those interminable waits on the set. I preferred theatre to film, I said, because if you flubbed a line in a play or if your performance was below par, you had a chance to improve it the next night.

After a thoughtful pause, Dean said that when he left the

studio each night, he realized how he might have changed the inflection of a word or altered a gesture to better his performance that day. "I always wanted to turn around and go back to the studio and ask them to let me do it again," he said. That kind of dedication is the mark of a real pro.

Another compensation for the long shoot was a chance to spend some time with Jim, who divided his time between Los Angeles and Hawaii as one of the stars of "Hawaii Five-O." Though Jim did appear in one play in the 1960s—Arthur Laurents' *Invitation to a March*, with Celeste Holm and Jane Fonda—most of his career has been in movies and television.

The Young Stranger, his first film, was a success, and Charlie was so proud of Jim that he bought a print of the film to show to his friends. My pride in Jim was mixed with a touch of envy. He knew instinctively that the key to screen acting is not to project too much, and that's why my screen acting has never looked right to me: I don't know how *not* to project.

But most people seemed to like my Mrs. Quonsett in *Airport,* and audiences loved it. It was one of the top-grossing pictures of the year and got a number of Academy Award nominations.

Trivia experts should try this one: Who is the only actress to be nominated once in the best-actress and once in the best-supporting actress category and to win each time? The answer is Helen Hayes: best actress for *Madelon Claudet* in 1932; best supporting actress for *Airport* in 1969.

But I must confess that I didn't see all of *Airport*—just as I failed to see the remake of *Madelon*—until years later. During a recent trip to Australia, shipboard friends talked me into joining them in the liner's theatre, where *Airport* was being screened. They surrounded me and marched me in like a prisoner, and made sure that someone sat on either side of me, so I couldn't escape. I hadn't been on the screen more than two minutes when I was seized with a sneezing fit. After twenty sneezes, they hus-

228

tled me out: I was disturbing the rest of the audience. I continued to sneeze until I was safe in my cabin. That took care of *Airport*.

After *Airport,* I acted occasionally on stage, most prominently with James Stewart in a revival of *Harvey.* Jimmy had played Elwood P. Dowd on Broadway in the '40s and in the 1950 film adaptation. In both versions he had been criticized for being too young for the role; now he had aged enough to make the part his own, and he scored a triumph. He seemed to project no more than he would have for the camera, yet every gesture went right across the stage and captivated the audience. I admired that.

We were in Ann Arbor, Michigan, preparing to give a preview performance for the University of Michigan students when, surprisingly, Jimmy confessed his anxiety: "I don't think these kids are going to know who I am. I'm a little worried about them seeing this old fellow and not accepting him." I scoffed, but I knew he was concerned.

The performance went off beautifully. When we took our curtain calls, they all stood up and cheered, and Jimmy came offstage from his solo call wiping a tear from his eye.

In 1972 I accepted an offer to play Mary Tyrone in Eugene O'Neill's *Long Day's Journey into Night.* It is a great but terribly arduous role, and I wasn't feeling well at the time. I've had attacks of asthma almost as long as I can remember, and early on I learned I was allergic to dust. The backstage area of any theatre is always layered with dust, no matter how diligent the cleaning, so the problem flares up when I am acting. But not until the run of *Time Remembered* did it cause me real distress.

During *Long Day's Journey* I was in such discomfort that I decided to quit once and for all. It seemed an appropriate moment: my career had begun in Washington, and it would end there. I liked the idea of a circle being completed. This time there was no public announcement of retirement. It was a promise I made to myself, and so far I've kept it.

I have never once had second thoughts about giving up the stage. Though I try to keep up with what's going on, I haven't yet seen a play that made me think, "Gee, I wish I had a chance at that role."

What's been happening on Broadway in recent years distresses me. Audiences seem to be going for plays with lots of brutality and what playwrights call "truth." Authors turn out graphic, nasty scenes that appeal to the instincts rather than to the imagination. I tend to avoid plays that I'm told are filled with brutality and obscenity. I'm not offended by swearing, but the repetition of four-letter words often seems a cheap shortcut to effective writing. A litany of such words isn't drama; it's a sign of a poverty of wit and invention. I resent those dramatists who feel they can reach us only through profanity.

A joke that recently made the rounds of Broadway sums up the situation pretty well. A bum approaches a well-dressed businessman for a five-dollar handout. The businessman wags a finger at the panhandler and says, " 'Neither a borrower nor a lender be.' William Shakespeare." The bum replies, " 'Fuck you.' David Mamet."

The real root of the theatre's troubles is economic. Everyone would be better off if production costs could be reduced to something within reason. A chorus member now gets seven hundred dollars a week, a thousand dollars if the show goes on the road. If a producer wants a chorus of twenty people, the standard in the past, that outlay alone will run to fourteen thousand dollars a week in New York. So don't ask why you have to pay fifty dollars for a ticket to see *Phantom of the Opera*.

It's true that there's a reason why actors' salaries are so high, and it's not only because of inflation. Few people outside the theatre realize that salaries in a show have to compensate for the periods when actors are unemployed, which may be most of the time, unless they happen to be very well established. Acting rarely brings a steady income and usually has to be supplemented by unemployment insurance or by side jobs as waiters or receptionists.

Still, something has to give. Lower salaries all around—for actors, musicians, stagehands, crew, *everyone*—would mean lower production costs, and that would result in cheaper ticket prices. That, in turn, would allow more plays to be produced, which would mean more employment for actors. Everyone would benefit, the theatre-going public most of all.

While serving on the board of Actors Equity in the '60s, I was dismayed by the excesses practiced, and I fought against them, but the cards were stacked against me. The threat of an actors' strike for a higher minimum wage arose during my term. Our actors' union had merged with Chorus Equity, whose members were much more militant than we. "Strike! Make the bastards pay!" That was their attitude.

Leland Hayward, who had been Charlie's agent and later the producer of such shows as *Mister Roberts, South Pacific,* and *The Sound of Music,* called me in distress. "Stop them, Helen," he pleaded. "If they strike, the Shuberts won't hold out. They'll meet the demands, and if that happens, it will be the end of the theatre as we know it."

The Shubert Organization was still pretty much a family affair at the time, originally run by three brothers, Sam, Lee, and John. They owned many theatres both in New York and across the country and they needed attractions to fill them. They were producers too, but their major concern was to book shows into their houses. They were very powerful and certainly could have weathered a strike, but as Leland had foreseen, they were too shortsighted to do so.

There was a strike, the Shuberts gave in, and other producers had to follow suit. The actors won easily. Salaries skyrocketed. Once the actors' minimum wage was raised, the craft unions

231

demanded higher base wages for their members too. Instead of eight-dollar tickets, we had a fifty-five-dollar top in 1989—and we now have seventeen theatres instead of thirty-three. Great dramatic productions with full casts have given way to one-man shows, taking the theatre back to where it started a few thousand years ago, before Aeschylus and other Greek dramatists hit on the idea of a second player or more.

The hottest ticket of the 1985 season was for Lily Tomlin's solo performance in *The Search for Signs of Intelligent Life in the Universe.* Lily created so many different characters that it didn't seem like a one-woman show. She is such a delight that audiences were treated to a complete stage experience. She won a Tony, and the production had not cost the investors much, so everybody was happy. But there aren't many Lily Tomlins.

Take another example. Zoe Caldwell is one of our finest actresses, a performer who brings out the best in actors playing with her. Cast members respond to her great ability by surpassing their own previous performance levels. And what has Zoe Caldwell done recently? *Lillian,* a one-woman show about the playwright Lillian Hellman.

By no means is it the actor alone who suffers from this trend. The playwright today faces a dilemma unlike that of any other era. Instead of giving vent to his imagination, he has to bow to the harsh economic realities of his trade. "I cannot have more than four people in the play," he says to himself. "Otherwise it may be impossible to produce at financial break-even. Three characters would be even better, and two would be ideal. And I'd better limit myself to one setting, since producers balk at plays with too many scene shifts. And the scenery mustn't be too elaborate—maybe just a tree, as in *Waiting for Godot.*"

It is criminal to impose such limitations on our playwrights. They cannot work that way, as I know very well from the experience of living with Charlie all those years. Their creativity, their inventiveness, should not be hampered like that. *Johnny on a*

Spot, a play Charlie wrote in 1941, was revived not long ago at the Brooklyn Academy of Music. It got good reviews, audiences loved it, and everything looked good for a Broadway transfer. But the play had a cast of twenty, which made the move prohibitively expensive. The prospects for profitability were too dim.

The Broadway I once knew has all but vanished, as have so many of the theatres that were home to me. Some have been converted into porn palaces, others simply razed. The demolition derby got under way with the Empire, a jewel box of a house rich in the lore of the American theatre—the Barrymores played there, as did Maude Adams, the Lunts, Kit Cornell, Ina Claire, Ethel Waters, Julie Harris, Shirley Booth, and I.

The Empire was torn down in 1953 and replaced by a nondescript office tower. One of the next to go was a theatre on Broadway and Forty-sixth Street, originally called the Fulton. It wasn't as grand as the Empire, but it was a beautiful theatre, a theatre where actors could be seen clearly from any angle and didn't require microphones to make themselves heard. This venue was very special to me, because it had been renamed the Helen Hayes to mark my fiftieth year in the theatre.

That was back in November 1955. It was quite a ceremony, with an opening address by Mayor Robert Wagner. At that time only two New York theatres had been named after actors—the Edwin Booth and the Ethel Barrymore—and I felt very honored. A year later another theatre was renamed the Lunt and Fontanne, which made me feel easier about the tribute.

Playing in *A Touch of the Poet* at the Hayes Theatre in 1958 made me feel somehow unreal, as though I'd become a walking legend. The theatre had its share of hits until the 1980s, when rumors about its possible demise began to circulate. For years the Broadway and Times Square area had been declining into a derelicts' wasteland. Although we theatre people sympathized with their plight, we had long complained about the panhandlers, addicts, and hustlers; they not only bothered us but, more important, they scared away people who wanted to come to see us perform.

For a long time nobody listened. Then Mayor Edward Koch came up with a harebrained scheme. His idea was to purge the area of pushers and hustlers by tearing most of it down and turning the land over to real-estate investors who wanted to build what sounded like the modern city in H. G. Wells's *Things to Come.* The section slated for disappearance included the Helen Hayes Theatre.

Mayor Koch invited me to his office for a meeting with several other city officials, two gentlemen from the Shubert Organization, and Mr. John Portman, who was proposing to build a big hotel on Broadway between Forty-fifth and Forty-sixth streets. That meant that not only the Hayes, but also two other beautiful theatres, the Morosco and the Bijou, would have to go. Ed Koch assured me that this was the first step to cleaning up Forty-second Street.

There was only one possible reason why I had been asked to attend this meeting of wheelers and dealers: I was going to be cajoled, and if necessary coerced, into approving the demolition of my theatre. Without my endorsement there might be protests from the theatre community. Though I was intimidated by all the high-finance brain power, I felt that I had to try to make a token protest at least.

It was a sad day for me, I told them. *What Every Woman Knows* had opened at the Bijou in 1926, and I remembered that first night as though it were yesterday. The Morosco was a dream of a theatre, and so was the one bearing my name. Why did they have to be reduced to rubble? How would erecting a hotel on Forty-sixth Street clean up Forty-second Street or Eighth Avenue?

Ed Koch assured me that there would be a snowball effect. The area was to be covered with walkways, elevated bridges, and lots of pedestrian malls, everything modern and clean and safe. When

234

construction began, the sleaze merchants would be forced out, and people would once again feel secure about shopping and amusing themselves along the Great White Way.

I didn't believe a word of it, but I knew nothing I could say would deter them, so I told them what they wanted to hear: I would not protest. Perhaps I was wrong, but I felt it would seem self-serving to participate in a fight to save a theatre bearing my name.

Though I gave in, a great many of my theatre friends did launch a battle against City Hall. They went to Forty-fifth and Forty-sixth streets and demonstrated, picketing outside the three theatres scheduled to be hit by the wrecker's ball. As a result, Colleen Dewhurst, Celeste Holm, Joe Papp, and many other stage friends now have police records. John Portman claimed he was building the Marriott Hotel to benefit theatregoers, and in one of her impassioned curbside speeches, Colleen asked where theatregoers would go to see a play if he continued to tear down theatres.

Today the Marriott Hotel is part of the Broadway scene, a monster of a hotel, all red and gilt and plastic, so vulgar it ought to be in Las Vegas. There are no malls, parks, or walkways anywhere near it, and the area still teems with pushers, panhandlers, and prostitutes. There is a theatre inside the hotel. New York City law requires that when a legitimate theatre is torn down, it must be replaced. To compensate for the loss of the Bijou, the Morosco, and the Hayes we now have the Marquis Theatre, a twenty-five-hundred-seat monstrosity. Performers hate it.

People commiserated after the Hayes was demolished, but I refused to get tied up in knots about it. "Look at it this way," I said. "It's gratifying that I outlived all that stone and mortar."

The Marriott people offered to name the new theatre for me, but I wanted no part of that. In 1984, however, it was nice to see a second theatre renamed the Helen Hayes. The house had begun life as the Little Theatre in 1912, built by Winthrop Ames, a producer I knew and respected. It was designed to present small, intimate plays that could not survive in big, commercial Broadway houses. In later years the Little was enlarged, but it still seats only five hundred, small enough for every member of the audience to be able to establish direct contact with the actors. I'm proud to have my name on it.

At the time the Little Theatre was renamed, Harvey Fierstein's *Torch Song Trilogy,* a play about a transvestite, had been running there for a year. I hadn't seen it, but I knew it had won all kinds of awards. Just after the change of name, Liz Smith wrote in her *Daily News* column about two smartly dressed matinee-goers standing on West Forty-fourth Street and gazing at the theatre. A large sign saying HELEN HAYES ran down the facade, and another around the marquee read TORCH SONG TRILOGY. One woman turned to the other and said, "You know, I hadn't planned on seeing this transvestite play, but if Helen Hayes is in it, it can't be all that bad."

Around the same time, the English actor Robert Morley took me to see *La Cage aux Folles,* Jerry Herman's musical about drag queens. Robert later ran into Carol Channing at a party and told her that he had just seen *La Cage* with me. Carol's eyes widened and she purred, "Gee, Helen is certainly doing a lot of homosexual plays these days!"

Well, why not? I've done every other kind.

≽·18·≼

Shortly after I left the theatre in 1972, I spent several weeks in Cuernavaca, and not long after my arrival, Eduardo Rendón and Meg Jessup, a friend of his, came for tea. Though Eduardo was the one who had picked out my house and restored it so skillfully, he now found things to criticize. For one thing, it was too far out of the mainstream. "Why be stuck out here in Never-never Land?" he asked. "Come downtown with us. Move to Netzahualcoyotl Street and be close to your friends."

One argument against that suggestion popped into my head immediately. My house was on Victoria Street, a name close to my heart for obvious reasons and one slightly easier to say than Netzahualcoyotl. But Eduardo replied that for Mexicans Netzahualcoyotl was a monarch as renowned as my beloved Victoria. He had been a fifth-century poet-prince, a gentle and saintly ruler held in great esteem. It was an appealing story, and it wouldn't hurt to take a look at the house Eduardo had in mind. He hadn't steered me wrong the first time, and he might be right again.

It was certainly a handsome, well-constructed house. One of the first things I look at when inspecting a house is its wood. The ceiling beams, carved doors, windows, and shutters of this building were superb. Many Mexican monasteries were razed in the 1920s during government persecution of the Catholic Church. Beams, columns, tiles, and even altarpieces were bought cheap or simply stolen. A few of those treasures had become parts of this house.

It was designed and built by Fendall Gregory, an Englishman who wanted to create a perfect Spanish Colonial residence. Many decorative details, including tiles and the fountain in the courtyard, dated from the late sixteenth or early seventeenth century, not long after the Spanish conquest of Mexico. On the outdoor terrace stood a profusion of sugar jars, more than seventy of them, which antedated the Mexican Revolution of 1910. It is almost impossible to find one of these treasures for sale today, and if you do, the price is exorbitant. The pièce de résistance was a superb mantel designed by Rodolfo Ayala, who apprenticed to Gregory and later went on to become one of Mexico's leading architects.

Had I been an architect myself, this might well have been the house I would design in my dreams. Still, I was reluctant to give up my Victoria Street home, which I also loved. Eduardo pointed out that it was really too small for my ménage. What if I married again? he asked. There wouldn't be room for a husband and all the guests I was inclined to entertain.

"Don't be silly," I said with a laugh. "I'm too old to remarry."

Which brings me to a brief digression. Eduardo had raised a question I've often been asked: Why didn't I remarry after Charlie's death? There were several offers, including one from a charming and persistent gentleman I had grown fond of. I was tempted, but I turned him down.

It has been said that people who have a happy first marriage tend to remarry swiftly after the death of a mate. My marriage had its moments of strain, as they all do, but it was a good, tight marriage through good times and bad.

238

The reason was more complicated than that. I couldn't imagine a companion as amusing and delightful as Charlie had been in his best days, and I felt it was unfair to expect anyone else to meet his standard. On the other hand, I remembered all too well the toll my career had taken on Charlie, and was unwilling to subject another husband to the same thing. Even if I gave up acting for marriage, he still would have to live in the shadow of a famous wife. That may sound self-important, but it's not; it's a reality I've had to live with.

Eduardo was right, however, that my house was too small. It had a master bedroom with bath and two guest rooms with a shared bath. One of the guest rooms was permanently occupied by Vera, my companion, and that left only one spare room— certainly not enough space for Jim and his wife and children when they came to visit. Someone had to camp out on a sofa on the patio.

So I moved downtown to Netzahualcoyotl Street, into a house with four bedrooms and baths, which means I can entertain now as much as I choose. Sometimes I feel the extra space makes me too hospitable, but it's always a delight to have Jim and his family around, or to play hostess to special friends.

Maurice Evans visited me once on St. Patrick's Day, which like all good daughters of Erin I celebrate no matter where I happen to be. I always give a party for St. Pat, even in Cuernavaca. All the guests wear something green, and the menu consists of corned beef, cabbage, and potatoes, followed by Irish coffee. Then there is always a short program, perhaps a student group called an *Estudiantina,* wearing medieval costumes and performing madrigals on authentic old instruments; or a guest telling about the San Patricio Battalion of the American army, which fought on Mexico's side during the 1848 invasion.

Maurice agreed to contribute to the entertainment after the St. Pat's dinner. He suggested that the two of us read a few poems by Synge, Yeats, and Shakespeare. Why Shakespeare? I asked. He wasn't Irish. Well, Evans answered, there were those who claimed there must have been some emerald blood in Shakespeare's veins. How else could he have been as swift, lyrical, and inventive with words as he was? Besides, he added with a wink, "Yeats, Synge, or Shakespeare—it'll all be English to your guests, won't it?"

Lillian Gish is another old friend who has spent several Christmases with me in Cuernavaca. We first met in New York back in the early 1930s, after Lillian left Hollywood because she didn't like the changes sound brought to moviemaking. She felt that the crude vocal reproduction of the early talkies distorted her voice, so she decided to give up filmmaking and return to the theatre, where she had worked before becoming D. W. Griffith's leading lady in silent films.

Around the time that Lillian came back to New York, Jed Harris was preparing a Broadway production of Chekhov's *Uncle Vanya*, and he chose Lillian for one of the two female leads. Jed was romantically involved with Ruth Gordon at the time, and Ruth met Lillian through him. I got to know Lillian through Ruth. This was somewhat ironic, as Ruth and Jed and I later became estranged, but Lillian and I are still close friends after fifty years.

We had only one bad patch. It happened a few years ago, when we were rehearsing for a TV production of *Arsenic and Old Lace.* We broke for lunch one afternoon well after 2 P.M., and Lillian and I headed for Longchamps, one of a chain of restaurants that offered good food and soft, flattering lighting. The latter, needless to say, was very popular with ladies of a certain vintage.

As we waited for lunch, Lillian started talking about her latest obsession: rejuvenating treatments offered by a Rumanian doctor she knew. His elixir of youth was administered in injections of certain animal substances—lamb embryos, or something like

240

that. This Dr. Feelyoung's cure-all had been rejected by the American Medical Association and the Food and Drug Administration on the grounds that it was pure quackery.

Ignoring that verdict, Lillian had gone to Rumania every year for the doctor's injections. Like too many stage and film people, she had fallen into a desperate struggle to retain her youth, and she believed the treatments worked. Why was the American medical establishment against the good doctor? It was just jealousy, she thought.

I listened quietly for a while, but finally I got fed up. There was a lot wrong with our system of medicine, I said as calmly as possible, and I was well aware of its shortcomings. But at least we were way ahead of other countries in protecting the naive against the flummery of mountebanks.

So far our voices had been modulated to match the soft lighting around us. But now Lillian became shrill. "Let me tell you what I think of American medicine," she burst out. "My banker, who is in charge of all my affairs, has a letter stating that if I get too sick to make my wishes known, I am to be taken to Europe immediately."

"To what country?" I asked.

"It doesn't matter," said Lillian. "Anywhere except America!"

That really irritated me. "Lillian," I exclaimed, "you're a bubblehead!"

Suddenly we were shouting, two gray-haired ladies yelling at each other while a group of waiters stood around nervously, probably fearful that we would soon start slinging china. What a tidbit that would make for the gossip columnists—Longchamps Brawl: Hayes vs. Gish.

But it wasn't only Lillian's strange fixation and the harm it might do her that bothered me. Her attitude toward American medicine offended me for a personal reason: I was deeply involved in working on behalf of a Nyack hospital that had been

241

named for me. This may sound self-serving, but the truth is that I was gratified that the use of my name could help win support for a hospital that provided good care and sponsored important research. I suppose Lillian's condemnation of all U.S. medicine struck me as an affront to *my* hospital and its dedicated staff, though of course she hadn't meant it that way.

We soon came to our senses. That was the only argument Lillian and I have ever had, and since then we have tacitly understood that medicine is a subject we have to avoid.

Lillian is full of surprises. Once, when she was visiting in Nyack, we took a long walk along an Indian trail on the cliffs above the Hudson. My three dogs were scampering beside us. We came to a point where the trail unexpectedly narrowed, and the dogs suddenly cowered at my feet. There was a washout a few steps ahead. I stood there frightened, the dogs practically clinging to me, as Lillian grabbed a tree limb and swung across the wash-out to safe ground on the other side.

"What are you doing, Lillian?" I gasped. "You'll kill yourself!"

"Nonsense!" she said airily. "In the old days we used to do things like this in the movies. There weren't any stunt people then." She swung back and forth like Tarzan.

In *Way Down East*, a D. W. Griffith masterpiece made in 1920, Lillian had had to float down a river on an ice floe. The scene was shot in Mamaroneck, New York, in the dead of winter, and Lillian spent so many hours filming the sequence—in which she is rescued by Richard Barthelmess, playing the hero—that she came down with a serious case of chilblains.

Way Down East was a great success, and Griffith wanted to give Lillian a special present out of gratitude for her unstinting loyalty and courage. Her birthstone is the opal, and in Australia Griffith found a gem known as "the Great Opal," which he purchased and had mounted in a cross designed by Tiffany. Maybe he would have scouted for another great opal if he could have seen her performing the same kind of feat more than fifty years later.

The heroines Lillian played for Griffith were invariably spiritual and slightly otherworldly, and there are times when Lillian herself seems a trifle vague, so closely in tune with her own drummer that she misses the beat of what is going on around her. This trait can be startling, as it was at one event we both attended a few years ago. I asked Lillian to join me at the cardinal's annual Christmas party in New York, a tradition initiated by Terrence Cardinal Cook and carried on by John Cardinal O'Connor. I'd been invited for more than twenty years, and I'd taken Lillian along once before. This time I was asked to bring her again—Cardinal O'Connor was a great fan of hers.

Lillian arrived all dolled up. All her clothes date from forty years back, but the dresses are still elegant, and she's proud that they still fit. The luncheon was held at the Waldorf-Astoria Hotel, and she sat beside His Eminence, who looked magnificent in his scarlet cape, biretta, sash, and gold cross. He was very courtly as they chatted, obviously so pleased to be next to Lillian that you could almost hear him saying to himself, "Imagine, here I am sitting beside Lillian Gish!"

If this were a scene in a movie, it would be called "The Cardinal and the Star." As the cardinal made a fuss over her, the star, too, was very animated. Then all at once she stared straight ahead, apparently puzzled. "Helen," she asked me in a loud stage whisper, "what church is he from?"

As I grow older, I get forgetful too, but I haven't reached that point yet. And neither had Lillian when it came to work. She's sharp as a tack then, as I discovered when we appeared on TV together in *Arsenic and Old Lace.* It was a challenging production, shot live on a multilevel set that would have tested Edmund Hillary's climbing ability.

Arsenic was one of several television and movie projects I took on in the mid-1970s. My role as Mrs. Quonsett in *Airport* launched a second career for me that got under way with three films for the Disney studios. The first was *Herbie Rides Again*, in which I played a little old lady battling big real-estate interests, aided by a '63 Volkswagen named Herbie, the real star of the picture. Then came *One of Our Dinosaurs Is Missing*, with Peter Ustinov, and finally *Candleshoe*. The titles alone should give you an idea of what these Disney films were like. But they were pleasant to do, and they did well at the box office.

Candleshoe was shot on location in Warwickshire, England. Working in that beautiful countryside was a joy, and so was the cast, which included David Niven, Leo McKern, and young Jodie Foster, who since then has drawn attention in two Martin Scorsese films, *Taxi Driver* and *Alice Doesn't Live Here Anymore*, and in an Oscar-winning performance in *The Accused*.

Jodie was in her early teens when we worked together in *Candleshoe*. When she wasn't needed on the set, she'd be out riding her bicycle. Then she'd arrive for a sequence at the last moment, overheated, her hair damp with perspiration. The makeup people would dry her off, dab something here or there, and Jodie would step before the camera, all business. She was already a seasoned professional, but she was still eager to learn.

When she wasn't taking off on her bike, Jodie would hang around the set, watching how things were done, learning her craft from every angle. She listened to the director with open pores— something I'd always done—and little escaped her gimlet-eyed curiosity. Now that she has finished college and is again concentrating on acting, I'm sure Jodie will become one of our most valuable players.

My first experiences with television date back to what is now rightly remembered as "the golden age" of that medium, the '50s and early '60s, when drama was live and viewers were eager. In those years the shows had the spontaneity and animation of "live" productions, unlike the canned tapes broadcast nowadays. And there were so many wonderful dramatic programs—"Omnibus," "Playhouse 90," "Hallmark Hall of Fame," "Studio One." These presented both new works and established gems. At one point in 1959 I was playing on Broadway in *Touch of the Poet* and doing another O'Neill play, *Ah, Wilderness!*, for TV. Every week you could turn on the television and find a new playwright, a promising actor, a favorite play that hadn't been staged anywhere else.

At first there was a certain snobbish resistance to television, as there had been to movies in the early days. But soon most of the great stage stars—the Lunts, Lillian Gish, Maurice Evans, Judith Anderson, Charles Laughton, Mary Martin, Ethel Merman, among many others—came to appreciate the potential of the new medium. The networks were producing so many quality programs that none of us dreamed they would soon be replaced by game shows, sitcoms, and police melodramas. Nowadays practically all quality television drama is found either in the late movies or in the British-made series imported by the public broadcasting stations.

Ross Hunter, who brought me back to the movies for *Airport*, also got me back to television. He had become a good friend and often visited me in Cuernavaca, along with Jacques Mapes, his associate. On one occasion Ross described his next TV project, "A Family Upside Down," about a family that learns to overcome the generation gap through mutual respect and love.

I liked the script, but what really persuaded me to appear in "A Family Upside Down" was the opportunity to work with Fred Astaire. Fred and I went back more than sixty years in the theatre. We knew each other casually, though we had never performed together. When he gave up dancing, Fred undertook a few dramatic roles, and I thought he was excellent in them.

245

When Fred made a screen test back in the late 1920s, a studio evaluator wrote of his performance, "Can't act, can't sing, dances a little." Fred disproved the first part of that penetrating assessment in "Family Upside Down," which won him an Emmy for best actor.

Shortly after that, Alan Shayne, an independent TV producer, created a series called "The Snoop Sisters" for me and Mildred Natwick, a brilliant actress who was also a close friend of mine. The series didn't catch on, but we had fun doing it, and it led to Alan's acquiring the rights to several of Agatha Christie's Miss Marple mysteries. He had me in mind as the amateur sleuth.

I wasn't keen on the idea, as Miss Marple had been played in the movies by Margaret Rutherford, who had become identified with the role. Those pictures had a cult following, and I was as uneasy about replacing Rutherford as I had been about taking over for Laurette Taylor in *Menagerie.* Shayne argued that Rutherford wasn't at all the Jane Marple described by Christie. That was true, but neither was I. At least Rutherford had the advantage of being English.

I let myself be talked into doing a few shows, and I can't say I was happy with the results. One was "Murder with Mirrors," not a particularly good Christie, but we had a major international cast to bolster its appeal: Bette Davis, John Mills, and Leo McKern were among my costars. The production was shot in England, at an estate in Hertfordshire called Brocket Hall, where we all lived during the filming.

Until the last moment no one was sure Bette Davis would actually join us. She wanted the production to be filmed in America, but Alan Shayne refused to change his plans to accommodate her. She arrived in a foul mood just before we were ready to begin. We all knew that she had recently had a stroke, and we were concerned about her health. We also knew that she was feisty, always poised to do battle for what she believed was her due. We knew it, but we all wanted to get along with her.

Bette made that virtually impossible. She shunned me and everyone else who tried to help. She couldn't stand anyone she considered a rival, though no one was trying to compete with her. Her physical condition made her hypersensitive to any potential charges that she was no longer capable of playing the role or any other role. She refused to take a nap between scenes, because that might confirm what she feared people suspected: that she was too much the invalid to be the great star and consummate actress she had once been. Bette drove herself mercilessly; she was her own worst enemy, at least during this production.

"Murder with Mirrors" was a great success, at least as success is gauged by TV standards. Alan Shayne called to report the good news the morning after it aired: more than twenty million people had watched. I've never understood how those ratings are arrived at, but they're said to be scientific, so I congratulated Alan, and he thanked me.

When I hung up the phone, the good tidings still ringing in my ears, I found that I felt depressed. Twenty million people! The total audience I had reached in eighty years in the theatre— all those plays, all those beautiful lines, all that shared intimacy with live patrons—amounted to a tiny fraction of the number of people who had watched me the night before in a mediocre TV show. Many of the viewers were young enough never to have seen me in anything else. Was this the way I wanted to be remembered? And what about the older segment of the audience? Actors can build up a lot of goodwill over the years, and their fans support them even when they are disappointed now and again. But goodwill can be stretched only so far, and I wondered if I hadn't approached the breaking point with some of my recent TV and movie appearances.

When Alan Shayne offered me another Jane Marple part, I

turned it down. He didn't believe me. I'd said no in the past and then had had my mind changed by a little artful persuasion. But not this time. No more acting on stage, screen, or TV. It was time to say good-bye.

Although I don't look back warmly on this final stage of my career, at least I am not embarrassed by anything I was connected with. There were no horror pictures and no sleaze. Everything was geared to what they call "family audiences." I'm proud of that.

≫·19·≪

Early in my career I met a woman who had once been a celebrated courtesan, one of the queens of the Paris demimonde.
Yvonne Duprès was in her fifties at the time of our encounter,
and though the years had added an unwanted inch here and
there, she had the unlined skin, clear eyes, and luxuriant hair of
a woman less than half her age.

How did she do it? I asked. Resting and fasting were the
secrets, she said. One day each week she sequestered herself in
her boudoir and stayed in bed—no men, no food, no champagne,
just a cup of tisane and the latest weekly magazines. This one-day
breather was said to restore the spirit and stave off crow's-feet.

I wasn't all that worried about wrinkles, and fasting was impossible for me—chocolate is too great a temptation—but the idea
of lolling in bed all day seemed tempting. Well, I tried it after
I retired, but found that I was not ideally suited to the role of
Lady Indolence. As I fluffed up the pillows and tried to keep the
sheets from bunching around me, I kept remembering something
Joan Crawford had once told me. Every morning she bounded
out of bed, changed the linens, and tidied up her room. A lot of

bending was involved, and the exercise tuned her up for a day at the studio. Maybe I'm more like Joan than Yvonne.

Every night before bedtime I arrange my clothes for the next day, hang them up to get rid of the wrinkles, and pick out accessories. The following morning I dress and go downstairs for breakfast—fruit juice, cereal, and coffee. When Lillian Gish is visiting, she always comes to breakfast in a peignoir. She makes a very pretty picture with her hair flowing down her back. But deshabille doesn't suit me; I can't function that way. I have to be fully clothed, because once the day begins, it gets beyond me, out of control.

Often I'm off to a charity luncheon or a meeting of some sort. Over the years I've done a lot of charity work and have received too much attention for it. Sometimes when I'm asked what I've been doing since retirement, I'm tempted to answer, "I accept honors." That may sound egotistical, but the truth is that almost every honor or award—and I've collected quite a few, including the Presidential Medal of Freedom—has embarrassed me. Why single me out just for doing what was asked of me? I didn't go out and serve, but was always recruited for some service or other.

This is not false modesty. I saw people working in polio research who never let up, who spent every waking hour for the cause. I am awestruck by people who see that something needs to be done and fight to make it happen, people like Dorothy Kirsten, who got a special hospital built for Alzheimer's victims. That kind of spirit is so admirable, but I have never had it; I'm not a leader and never have been the inspiration behind anything.

"Helen is catnip for academe," Anita Loos once said. Maybe so. But I feel like an imposter marching across a campus in cap and gown among worthy academics and getting an honorary degree. Still, if putting in an appearance and being photographed accepting some honor serves to focus attention on an institution or charity, that's fine with me. It is certainly an easy way to do good.

Any volunteer work we do seems picayune compared with the profound charity of someone like Mother Teresa of Calcutta. A true saint. There is no question in my mind that one day she will be canonized. A few years ago I went to hear her speak at Georgetown University in Washington, D.C. I showed up unannounced and was waylaid in the auditorium by a university staffer. "Miss Hayes, what are you doing here?" he asked. "You must meet Mother Teresa," he went on before I could answer. "She's right next door."

I reluctantly went along, wondering what to say to this woman I so revered. We entered a small room where some ten people were gathered around Mother Teresa, who was playing with a little girl about a year and a half old. What a beautiful sight! Mother Teresa is not pretty; in fact, she has a face that might be expected to frighten a child, but that small girl clearly adored her.

When the child was taken away, someone poked me in the shoulder to indicate that this was the moment for the introduction. By then I knew what to say, but Mother Teresa stole my opening line. "You do so much good!" she said as we shook hands. I doubt she knew anything about me, but probably applied that greeting to anyone she met, accustomed as she was to meeting people who supposedly did some good. Unable to think of an appropriate reply, I merely bowed my head, which I hope conveyed my deep respect for this saintly woman. I had been upstaged, but it took a saint to do it.

Another person I've come to admire is Father William Wasson, a priest I met when I came to Mexico after Charlie's death. At the time I was anxious to return to the Catholic Church. I had been denied the sacraments because of my marriage to a divorced man, which seemed unduly harsh to me. But

251

eventually I came to realize that the Church had laws guiding millions of people, and it was foolish to believe that I should be exempted from its rules of Christian behavior. I don't know if I missed the Church while Charlie was alive, but I missed it terribly when he was gone.

Father Wasson preached at San Francisco, a lovely little church in the compound of the cathedral in Cuernavaca. I went to the morning mass that he conducted in English and was very impressed. I then made an appointment to discuss reconciliation. We met several times, and he gave me spiritual guidance about returning to the Church, though our conversations often branched off into other areas.

Soon we were talking about Father Wasson's favorite project, the *Pequeños Hermanos,* Little Brothers, a group of abandoned children, male and female, whom he felt the Church should protect. He was already taking care of about seventy children, many rescued from the Tampico floods, a terrible disaster. Many of the children orphaned or separated from their parents might well have died had Father Wasson not gone down there and brought a planeload of them back to Cuernavaca.

One day we talked so long that we discovered we had been locked inside the church. The sacristan had gone home. "I don't mind spending the night here if you don't," Father Wasson said. "We can sleep in the pews. You're not afraid of bats, are you?"

Well, who isn't afraid of bats? When he saw my look of panic, Father Wasson admitted that he was pulling my leg. There was a way out. Behind the altar were two narrow staircases. One led to two cages where Carlota and Maximilian used to sit to hear mass when they were in residence in Cuernavaca, their favorite holiday retreat. They and their coterie would sit high up on either side of the golden Spanish Colonial altar, looking down from the cages of gold and latticework that hid them from the people below.

The second staircase led to the priests' quarters. That was the route we took. On our way we stumbled over a priest in his bathrobe, his feet propped up, enjoying a late siesta. We tiptoed past him and both burst into laughter when we were out of earshot.

Anyway, I had already taken quite a shine to Father Wasson, and this giddy adventure made us kind of soul mates. God works in mysterious ways, so maybe He stoops to farce—locked doors and snoozing priests—to get things done.

I volunteered to help Father Wasson with the *Pequeños*. He wanted to meet with Cardinal Cushing in Boston to discuss starting a school and orphanage for his children. I was able to arrange it, but the meeting proved difficult. "No, no," Cardinal Cushing objected. "Your plans are unrealistic. You must have an order behind you, and you don't belong to an order, do you?" Father Wasson admitted that he didn't. "But Your Eminence . . ." he tried to interject, but the cardinal wasn't about to have his harangue interrupted. It was just awful! I can't begin to say how dreadful I felt.

Finally, the tongue-lashing complete, the cardinal told Father Wasson that he would like to help him nonetheless. "I'll tell you what I'll do," he said. "I'll give you my own check for ten thousand dollars if you find someone to match it." He looked straight at me, and I knew who that somebody was supposed to be. "You brought him here, so you have to pay the consequences"—that was more or less the message.

"Sure," I stammered. "I'll put up the other ten thousand dollars." Maybe that was another of God's farces, but I've never regretted being part of it. Father Wasson built his first high school with that twenty thousand dollars. The money bought the material; the building was done by the high-school students with their own gifted hands. He wanted the *Pequeños* to have some religion in their schooling, but that wasn't possible in public schools. Separation of church and state is strict in Mexico. There is no mention of God on the money, and no public official gets sworn in on a Bible. So Father Wasson could expect no help from the government, but with support from Cardinal Cushing, me, and many others, he persevered. Today he has around 1,250 students. Between four and five thousand girls and boys have benefited from his care and have gone out into the world to make good lives for themselves.

Two of his pupils are my goddaughters. Lupe, the older one, is the eldest of eleven children. When their mother died, Lupe tried to keep them all together. She and her brothers and sisters begged at markets for damaged fruit and vegetables, for any food that couldn't be sold. They continued to live in the dirt-floor hovel where their mother had died giving birth to her fifteenth child—four had been stillborn or died in infancy. Their father, a schoolteacher, had a wife and twelve other children, so he couldn't help Lupe very much.

After trying for a year to look after her brood alone, Lupe took them to Father Wasson. Her father never forgave her, for he felt that accepting welfare was demeaning to him, even though he'd done little to support the children. He never went to visit them once they were under Father Wasson's care.

There are many histories like Lupe's among the *Pequeños*. Father Wasson accepts only orphans or children without a mother. Usually they remain with him until they finish high school, then spend a year working with the *Pequeños*, passing on what they have received before going on to make their own lives. They're trying to grow food on land that's been given to them and are self-sufficient in many ways, but it still takes a million dollars a year to keep them going.

I make frequent appearances in the States for the *Pequeños*, trying to help Father Wasson in any way I can. Recently I provided an introduction for a proposed television series about the *Pequeños*. I hope it will be screened, but with television you never know.

One of the rewards of retirement is the opportunity to travel. When I was working, my trips were limited mainly to big U.S. cities, the usual stops on cross-country stage tours. When I had time off in the summer, I'd hurry off to Italy, France, or England; now and then there would be a winter holiday in Florida or the Caribbean. Those State Department tours to the Orient and the Near East were all a rush, a blur of fancy receptions and guided tours.

In the past fifteen years or so I've been around the world at a more leisurely pace. I've been awed by the Parthenon and dazzled by the Taj Mahal; I've seen Alaska and sailed up and down the Mississippi on a steamboat. Whenever possible I travel by boat; planes and trains remind me too much of the old touring days. Water transport, whether by paddle boat or ocean liner, is far more appealing: the languid pace is ideal for a holiday.

One continent I'd regretted never having seen was Australia. It wasn't on the itinerary of my world tour, and fatigue had forced me to skip it on the State Department tour. At age eighty- seven I decided I had to see Australia before I died, so off I went, accompanied by an old friend, Richard Coe, drama critic emeritus of the *Washington Post*.

Among the ports of call on our cruise was Hobart, the capital of the island state of Tasmania, a charming place where boats sail up a marvelous long bay right into the heart of the city. The guidebook mentioned many points of interest, but what captured our attention most was a picture of an old theatre. Whenever I go, I always find a theatre to visit.

The one in Hobart surpassed our expectations. It was built in 1831, later burned down, and eventually was lovingly restored with the help of old photographs, drawings, and architectural plans. Tasmania is a younger and much smaller place than America, but it sure cares a lot more about its theatrical past!

As Dick Coe and I sat with the theatre manager in that intimate house, I wondered how the acoustics were. "Why not test them yourself?" the manager asked. I sprang from my seat, climbed onto the stage, and recited the first thing that popped into my head, some lines from *Twelfth Night*:

> *Make me a willow cabin at your gate*
> *And call upon my soul within the house;*
> *with loyal cantons of contemned love*
> *And sing them loud even in the dead of night . . .*

I was deeply moved, but I wasn't sure why. Perhaps it was the melancholy music of Viola's speech. But I had spoken those lines many times before without bringing myself to the brink of tears. Maybe it was that it seemed like one more farewell performance, and in Tasmania of all places. The aura of that entrancing, acoustically perfect little theatre surely contributed to the emotion I felt that afternoon.

As Dick and I were leaving, the manager gave us a booklet relating the theatre's history, illustrated with pictures of artists who had performed there in the past. Thumbing through it, I discovered a photograph of one of my ancestors, a great-great-aunt, Catherine Hayes of Ireland, about whom I had heard from both Graddy Hayes and my mother. How uncanny that she had appeared in this Hobart theatre! Had her ghost hovered over me as I stood on the stage, inducing that elusive emotion?

Catherine Hayes was a soprano known as "the Erin Swan." In her brilliant early years she had inspired her country's most celebrated poets to write songs for her. Later, after conquering the British Isles, she traveled to America, touring the West Coast and entertaining the Forty-Niners of the California Gold Rush. In 1866 she crossed the Pacific, working her way down to Hobart, where her performance earned her four hundred and fifty dollars, a fortune in those days.

Graddy and my mother felt that I'd inherited a talent for the stage from my great-great-aunt Catherine, but that had always seemed farfetched. My ancestor never had much reality for me until that afternoon in the Hobart theatre. Then, for just a moment, we really did seem to brush shoulders across two centuries.

When I'm at home, whether in Nyack or Cuernavaca, I try to fit in some kind of regular exercise. For years I used to walk three miles every day in Nyack, up to Hook Mountain and back. Nowadays I can't manage that distance, but I still enjoy a hike, even in the rain. In fact, I love walking in the rain. People think I'm balmy.

For a while I tried yoga, and I mastered some of the positions, but try as I might, I never could stand on my head. For some reason, that's supposed to be very important, so I gave up yoga. All those exercises started to bore me, and I refuse to be bored. Life is too short for that.

Swimming and walking are my favorite forms of exercise, but several years ago I found myself getting winded after just a few laps in the pool. Then my son Jim's wife, a professional golfer, told me about aqua-aerobics. These are exercises performed in water, which takes some of the weight and strain from your body. A couple of neighbors and I—all of us octogenarians—walk back and forth across the pool, lifting our legs waist-high. We can do sixty laps that way, and we don't gasp for breath, as we did from swimming.

Watching one's diet can be a tedious frustration, but luckily I don't have to worry about weight. I've gone on chocolate binges all my life, and the craving can strike at inopportune moments. Once, touring with a show, I arrived in Cleveland on a Sunday night. The company manager, one of whose duties was to look after me, met me at the train and escorted me to a hotel. "Is everything all right?" he asked when we got to my room.

"Yes, fine," I said, glancing around. "But I've got an intense craving for chocolate."

He offered to call room service, but I explained that what I wanted was a whole box of chocolate candies. It was quite late, but we set out in search of a drugstore that might sell Whitman Samplers. When we finally found what we were looking for, I devoured the top layer of a box before we got back to the hotel.

It may sound terribly self-indulgent, but there you are. Some people consider an addiction to chocolate very unhealthy, but it hasn't done me any harm. I have no sympathy for food fanatics who try to deprive us of little pleasures. Let them watch their own diets without imposing their strictures on others.

The actress Gloria Swanson was a diet fanatic, an ardent health-food advocate long before our current preoccupation with cholesterol, carbohydrates, fats, and imitation sweeteners. So was her husband, William Dufty, a writer who did a book called *Sugar Blues.* They proselytized whenever they got the chance, Gloria even more so than Dufty.

One winter, when they were in Cuernavaca, Gloria phoned me to say they would come by for a visit. She arrived all done up in tropical whites—turban, tunic, pants, shoes, handbag—sporting logos and monograms by Gucci or Pucci. She wore two big monogrammed gold bracelets, a *G* on one arm and an *S* on the other. Her oversized round sunglasses were out of proportion to her thin face and small stature, but she did look very glamorous, and she exuded energy. Dufty was a slight man, all skin and bones. Surviving on squirrel food as they did, they had not a spare ounce of flesh on them.

Gloria threw the hostesses of Cuernavaca into total confusion. They all wanted to entertain her and gave lavish luncheons and parties. But Gloria made them terribly nervous by refusing to eat anything. She carried a little plastic bag of raw vegetables with her wherever she went and would touch nothing else.

One night we all went to a dinner party given by Ray Coté, my next-door neighbor. A couple of young relatives were staying with me, so they were invited too. My cousin and her husband came from a small town in Florida, and they were all agog at meeting a great movie star. But they were shocked by Gloria's table manners. The main course was chicken, which she couldn't bear to eat, so she nibbled crudités from her plastic bag.

"Gloria Swanson said something to me that no one should ever say to anyone," the young man told us when we returned home.

"What was that?" I asked.

"I can't tell you," he replied. "I just can't repeat it."

Naturally, that whetted my curiosity. What in the world could it be that no one should *ever* say to anyone? Only later did I find out, and then I understood his reaction.

He was a good-looking young man, and our host, thinking that Gloria would appreciate the gesture, had seated him beside her. My cousin-in-law was overwhelmed by his proximity to the star. When a plate of chicken was placed before him, Gloria leaned over and whispered, "You know what you're eating, don't you? I would just as soon eat a cup of warm pus. That's what's in every chicken, and that's what you're eating."

That's the trouble with health freaks: they become obsessed and bully everyone to follow their regimen. Zealots just can't simply do what they want and keep quiet about it; they have to spread their message.

How Gloria had changed, I thought. When Charlie and I first got to know her, she was quite a clown, keeping us laughing at her antics. She was pretty tough and uninhibited too. But as she grew older, she got so concerned about fitness that she became unbearable.

Years ago, Gloria had appeared in a revival of *Twentieth Cen-*

tury, a play of Charlie's and Ben Hecht's that ranked not far behind *The Front Page* as an American classic. Charlie was grateful to Gloria for her splendid performance.

There are several high spots in my memories of her. In 1925, when she returned from France with her latest husband, the marquis de la Falaise de la Coudray, a party was given for them in the ballroom of the Ritz Hotel in Manhattan. Leading to the ballroom was a double stairway that joined into a broad, carpeted flight of stairs before it touched bottom. When the marquis and marquise arrived, they paused on the landing and gazed down like royalty on us humble theatre folk lined up below to greet them. The band played "La Marseillaise."

That marriage lasted no time at all. The marquis just faded away, like Gloria's other husbands. She was probably one of the first women to collect husbands, like Zsa Zsa Gabor and Elizabeth Taylor. Her first spouse was Wallace Beery. Somewhere along the way the financier Joseph Kennedy, father of the president, had a fling with moviemaking and with Gloria.

Before she developed notions of grandeur, Gloria's husbands were nice, ordinary men. But the French marquis was followed by Michael Farnum, an Englishman known around café society as a polo-playing playboy. He wanted to be an actor, a movie star no less, so Gloria put up her own money and, unbeknownst to us, took a company to Antibes to make a film in that lovely Mediterranean resort.

Around that time Charlie and I, having spent a couple of years working in Hollywood, wanted to get far away from the movies, so we took a holiday in Antibes, staying at the Hotel du Cap, a grand place. We unpacked, put on our bathing suits, and headed for the beach. And what did we see there but cameras, lights, and reflectors, an entire crew milling around. It was like a nightmare.

We soon spotted Gloria and Michael Farnum, shooting their

film. He wasn't much of an actor and apparently didn't like to work. When we went for a swim, Charlie and I would overhear Farnum telling Gloria, "I don't feel like it today" or "I'm not in the mood to work." Then he'd do a disappearing act, going off on some binge. In the meantime, Gloria's money was leaking away.

Gloria was unusually forbearing and didn't complain much. I suppose she was resigned to Farnum's irresponsible behavior—until she decided to get rid of him. Yet another divorce.

Gertrude Lawrence happened to be on vacation in Antibes at the same time, and she and I were recruited to appear in Gloria's film. It amused us to be extras in the background of a few scenes. I don't know whether the movie was ever finished or released.

We were pretty lighthearted in those days, and the people we knew were colorful and entertaining. Maybe mingling in that frivolous world didn't do me much good, but I got a kick out of it for a time. Nowadays everyone seems so serious, overanxious to make good in a very competitive society.

Jim and his wife are both strict about their diet, but they don't go around preaching as Gloria did. They asked me to try all those sprouts and grasses, that organic stuff they get from the health-food stores, but it wasn't for me. One Christmas, craving a traditional meal, I made a declaration of independence: "Look, I've been eating the wrong things for eighty-seven years. Maybe you should try it too. You should be as well off at eighty-seven as I am." Boastful perhaps, but I was trying to make a point: being too concerned about what you eat isn't good for you. Constant fear and stress are as bad as too much cholesterol.

I know only too well what stress can do to you. In my early days I used to get tied up in knots and didn't sleep well. My mother would call an osteopath, who would come to our room to straighten out my kinks. At times it was agony to go on stage and

261

perform night after night. My sometimes strained relationship with my mother probably made me nervous too. It's a wonder I didn't land on a psychiatrist's couch or undergo some kind of therapy.

That happened to one actress I greatly admired, Katharine Cornell, who pursued a difficult career as both producer and actress. I think she was weighed down by her very important position in the theatre. She fell into an acutely nervous state and went to her doctor, trying to get a grip on herself.

One day I went to see her at her house on Beekman Place in Manhattan, and there was the great Katharine Cornell sitting at a table stacked with cigar boxes. She had a little hammer and some tacks, which she was hammering into the boxes, forming designs with the tack heads. Her doctor had prescribed manual therapy, but Kit didn't know what to do with her hands. I suppose she had never done any needlepoint, knitting, or crocheting, so her therapy was to hammer little tacks into cigar boxes. I couldn't help being touched by the sight.

Kit Cornell was a very serious, romantic actress. With her tall, graceful figure, shining black hair, and creamy skin, she looked like a woman in a Renaissance painting. From a well-to-do family in Buffalo, where her father was a doctor, she was not dependent on her career for money. Yet she was dedicated, as was her husband, Guthrie McClintic, who was also a producer.

Oddly enough, Guthrie assumed there was rivalry between Kit and me, an absurd feeling we didn't share. The two of us were poles apart—yet a sense of competition always persisted in Kit's little entourage. Certainly nobody in my circle felt that way; we all admired her unstintingly. Kit had a surprising streak of humor and a delightful, deep-throated laugh that made her good company.

Her husband was more ambitious than she was, and determined to maintain her stardom. Perhaps he felt a bit like a

Svengali to her Trilby, as though she was his creation. I became quite sure of that when I read his book about her, *Me and Kit.* Talk about top billing!

Eventually the theatre became too tiring for her, and her health began to fail. But it was Guthrie who died first. News of his death reached us in Monterrey, Mexico, where we were playing on a State Department tour. Billy Miles, our company manager, had been Kit's manager for a spell, and when he got word Guthrie had died, he said he had to go back to New York immediately to help Kit out. "Kit will never walk on a stage again," he added sadly. "I know it."

"Oh, that's impossible!" I protested.

"No, she will not walk on a stage again," Billy repeated.

He was right. Kit bowed out, and she didn't seem to miss the theatre.

She once came to see me in a play in Boston, where she was getting some tests or treatment at the Massachusetts General Hospital. I was on tour in the APA-Phoenix Company production of *The Show-Off,* one of my last plays.

Kit came backstage to my dressing room. "Did you know they were standing up *ovating* you?" she asked. She was so generous, always ready to hand out praise. But Kit herself received plenty of ovations in her day.

In the past ten years or so I've become very involved in support for the elderly. I've gone to Washington several times to talk to Congress about bills affecting people of my age group, and I frequently speak to groups of senior citizens. Once I addressed executives of the Kentucky Fried Chicken chain, urging them to hire elderly persons as counter clerks. Certainly older people could hand out cartons of chicken and make change as swiftly as teenagers, and probably with more kindness. Surely other fast-food chains like McDonald's and Burger King could follow suit.

And oldsters could handle plenty of other jobs as well, if they were given the chance.

My main interest is in changing attitudes toward the elderly. People ought to be told well in advance what may happen to them as they age; if they don't like what they hear, then they should agitate for improved conditions. Sixty-five was once the mandatory retirement age. That never made much sense, but no one seemed to care, since there weren't many people in that category. But now twenty percent of our population is sixty-five or older, and that percentage will rise dramatically by the year 2000.

That this large group will be a powerful force in our civilization is a fact that should be recognized. Our senior citizens cannot be warehoused and forgotten. Part of the problem is that people are still taught that they should be put out to pasture at sixty-five. It's just not so.

Many people are still productive at an older age; they continue to enjoy life. A case in point is George Abbott, the director-playwright-actor, still active at over a hundred years of age. In 1986 I attended a party to celebrate his hundredth birthday. The guests included many noted theatre people, among them Jerome Robbins, who told a delightful story about George. When he was in his nineties, George married a charming woman about half a century younger than he. It's been a very happy match. They play nine holes of golf once a week, and George strides around the green as briskly as Lee Trevino. One morning, however, George stopped abruptly as they were walking down the last fairway. He closed his eyes and sank slowly to the ground.

His wife was terrified. She patted his cheeks and rubbed his wrists, but that didn't bring him around. She called for help, but no one was within shouting distance. Finally she said, "George, I don't know if you can hear me, but just lay there while I go and get help."

264

As she started to walk away, she heard George murmur, *"Lie* there."

That was typical of the George Abbott who had directed me in *Coquette* in 1928 and acted with me in *Skin of Our Teeth* in 1955. No calamity was ever so dire as to make him lose his grip on the proprieties of speech and behavior. I'm happy to say that whatever problem he experienced on the golf course that day vanished, and he was soon back at work on a new show, his 120th, directing "Frankie," a musical based on the Frankenstein story.

People who refuse to rest honorably on their laurels when they reach "retirement" age seem very admirable to me. This was eminently true of Eleanor Roosevelt. As an elderly widow, her hearing failing but her mind and spirit still strong, she carved out another career for herself, fighting for every great humanitarian cause in American life. Of all the people I've admired in my lifetime, Mrs. Roosevelt was always first in my heart. I think she should be a role model for all young women.

In the talks I give to people of my own age I always include a few pet phrases of advice. "Don't vegetate," I warn. "Don't sit back and relax." Often I feel just slightly dishonest as I say it, for sitting back and relaxing is exactly what I'd like to be doing then. But so far I've never given in to that temptation for very long. Something always comes along to get me out of bed or the easy chair.

My old friend Anita Loos once said that the bond between us was our insatiable curiosity. We were both so eager to know what went on in the world around us. Curiosity may have killed the cat, but it did all right by me.

"If you rest, you rust," I tell audiences who come to hear me speak. I hope I'm living proof that there's no reason to stop at sixty-five. My bones may creak a little now and then, but mercifully, rust hasn't set in yet.

George Bernard Shaw once wrote, in an unpublished letter: "I am of the opinion that my life belongs to the whole community and that as long as I live, it is my privilege to do for it whatever I can. . . . I want to be thoroughly used up when I die, for the harder I work, the more I live."

In much this same spirit, because I have looked upon the world with eyes of such greedy interest—eyes which, at eighty-nine, fortunately have never suffered from cataracts—I carry a card authorizing them to be given, upon my death, to an eye bank. I would like those eyes to go on giving joy to someone else.